Engaged Urban Pedagogy

ENGAGING COMMUNITIES IN CITY-MAKING

Series editors
Sarah Bell, Tadhg Caffrey, Barbara Lipietz and Pablo Sendra

This series contributes to the urgent need for creativity and rigour in producing and sharing knowledge at the interface of urban communities and universities to support more sustainable, just and resilient cities. It aims to amplify community voices in scholarly publishing about the built environment, and encourages different models of authorship to reflect research and pedagogy that is co-produced with urban communities. It includes work that engages with the theory and practice of community engagement in processes and structures of city-making. The series will reflect diverse urban communities in its authorship, topics and geographical range.

Engaging Communities in City-making aims to become a central hub for investigation into how disciplinarity, transdisciplinarity and interdisciplinarity can enable schools, teacher trainers and learners to address the challenges of the twenty-first century in knowledgeable and critically informed ways. A focus on social justice is a key driver. The series explores questions about the powers of knowledge, relationships between the distribution of knowledge and knowledge resources in society, and matters of social justice and democratisation. It is committed to the proposition that the answers to questions about knowledge require new thinking and innovation, that they are open questions with answers that are not already known and which are likely to entail significant social and institutional change to make the powers of knowledge and of knowing equally available to all.

Engaged Urban Pedagogy

Participatory practices in planning and place-making

Edited by
Lucy Natarajan and Michael Short

First published in 2023 by
UCL Press
University College London
Gower Street
London WC1E 6BT

Available to download free: www.uclpress.co.uk

Collection © Editors, 2023
Text © Contributors, 2023
Images © Contributors and copyright holders named in captions, 2023

The authors have asserted their rights under the Copyright, Designs and Patents Act 1988 to be identified as the authors of this work.

A CIP catalogue record for this book is available from The British Library.

Any third-party material in this book is not covered by the book's Creative Commons licence. Details of the copyright ownership and permitted use of third-party material is given in the image (or extract) credit lines. If you would like to reuse any third-party material not covered by the book's Creative Commons licence, you will need to obtain permission directly from the copyright owner.

This book is published under a Creative Commons Attribution-Non-Commercial 4.0 International licence (CC BY-NC 4.0), https://creativecommons.org/licenses/by-nc/4.0/. This licence allows you to share and adapt the work for non-commercial use providing attribution is made to the author and publisher (but not in any way that suggests that they endorse you or your use of the work) and any changes are indicated. Attribution should include the following information:

Natarajan, L., Short, M. (eds). 2023. *Engaged Urban Pedagogy: Participatory practices in planning and place-making*. London: UCL Press. https://doi.org/10.14324/111.9781800081239

Further details about Creative Commons licences are available at https://creativecommons.org/licenses/

ISBN: 978-1-80008-125-3 (Hbk.)
ISBN: 978-1-80008-124-6 (Pbk.)
ISBN: 978-1-80008-123-9 (PDF)
ISBN: 978-1-80008-126-0 (epub)
DOI: https://doi.org/10.14324/111.9781800081239

Contents

List of figures   vii
List of tables   viii
List of contributors   ix
Preface   xvii
Acknowledgements   xviii

1   Towards an engaged urban pedagogy   1
     Lucy Natarajan and Michael Short

Section I: Reviewing curricula   23

2   Race and space: a pedagogic intervention   27
     Yasminah Beebeejaun and Catalina Ortiz

3   Queering the built environment curriculum   44
     Celine Lessard, Renée Etokakpan, Juliana Martins, Corin Menuge, Jordan Rowe, Ramandeep Shergill and Michael Short

4   Co-designing educational assessments with students and external partners   61
     Gemma Moore and Maria Xypaki

5   Engaged pedagogy, informality and collaborative governance in South Africa   85
     Stuart Paul Denoon-Stevens, Lauren Andres, Martin Lewis, Lorena Melgaço, Verna Nel and Elsona van Huyssteen

Section II: Providing teaching — 103

6   Planning imaginations and the pedagogic value of external guest speakers — 109
    Lucy Natarajan and Mike Raco

7   Co-Producing planning? Neighbourhood planning as the context for participative pedagogy — 125
    Elena Besussi and Sue Brownill

8   Podcasting and collaborative learning practices in place-making studies — 144
    Silvia Gullino, Simeon Shtebunaev and Elodie Wakerley

9   Adapting the Civic Design Method to digital learning and collaboration with communities — 162
    Pablo Sendra and Domenico Di Siena

Section III: Embedding practices — 181

10 Co-production and the pedagogy of exchange: lessons from community research training in Birmingham — 185
    Sara Hassan and Liam O'Farrell

11 Role play activities: a methodology for transformative participation — 207
    Teresa Strachan

12 City-to-city learning as impulse for engaged urban pedagogy — 226
    Raphael Sedlitzky and Fernando Santomauro

13 Building together and co-building the city: do it yourself! — 241
    Dominique Lancrenon, Stephan Hauser, Patrick Le Bellec and Melia Delplanque

Conclusions

14 Critical pedagogy with urban participation — 258
    Lucy Natarajan and Michael Short

Index — 270

List of figures

1.1	Activities around a nexus of built environment higher education. Source: Author	3
1.2	Lammasu public art (left); queering public space (right). Source: Author	13
4.1	The domains of engaged learning within an MSc module. Source: Author	75
4.2	Summary of the action research process as applied in the coursework. Source: Authors	78
8.1	Workflow with timeline and main phases of the project. Source: Author	151
9.1	Circular process canvas in use May 2020. Source: Author	173
9.2	Civic realm canvas in use May 2020. Source: Author	175
9.3	Collective intelligence canvas in use May 2020. Source: Author	177
10.1	Area map of the USE-IT! transect. Source: Author	189
11.1	Diamond-ranking activity (based on Woolner *et al.*, 2010). Source: Author	216
11.2	'Canny' planners; the Healthy High Street game. Source: Author	217
12.1	Common challenge as entry point for actors in city-to-city learning (Sedlitzky and Santomauro, 2022).	230
13.1	Example activities of the Dunkerquois participatory circular project. Source: Author	248
13.2	Example of furniture created by En Rue. Source: Author	249
13.3	The abandoned garden city where the event took place. Source: Author	252
13.4	Map of the north region of France, with the metropolitan area of Dunkirk in dark grey, and the city of Teteghem in red. Source: Author	254
13.5	Map of the metropolitan area of Dunkirk, with the city of Teteghem highlighted in red. Made by S. Hauser on QGIS and based on OpenStreetMap.	254
14.1	Model for engaged urban pedagogy.	259

List of tables

4.1	Findings from workshop activity 1	71
4.2	Findings from workshop activity 2	72
4.3	Principles for co-designing educational assessment with community partners	73
4.4	Co-designing assessments with community partners – principles and practice	81
7.1	Phases of localism (adapted from Tait and Inch, 2016)	129
7.2	The neighbourhood planning initiatives	132
8.1	Relevant features emerged to guide the design and development of teacher-generated podcasts in Drivers of Change	158
11.1	Impact on young people's personal outlook (Hromek and Roffey, 2009)	219
11.2	Impact on young people's social and wider world outlook (Hromek and Roffey, 2009)	221
11.3	Creating a young person's sense of agency and a desire to take action	222

List of contributors

Editors

Lucy Natarajan is Associate Professor of Urban Planning at the Bartlett School of Planning, UCL. All her work centres on the interface between government and the public. She actively promotes wider engagement in urban decision-making, and her research and teaching span the gamut of strategic issues of planning – such as spatial plans, environmental/sustainability agendas, and urban infrastructures – where the involvement of the public is sorely undervalued. Lucy is co-editor of the *Built Environment* journal, and Secretary General of Territoire Europe, an association focusing on sustainable practices and participatory urbanism.

Michael Short is Associate Professor (Teaching) of City Planning at the Bartlett School of Planning, UCL. He undertakes practice-based projects, teaching and research in three main areas: how design issues are negotiated through the planning process and how they are implemented on site; the conservation and protection of buildings and areas of the recent past, and the challenges that this presents for practice; and the debates about increased building height and density in environments where the historic environment and character of place are relevant. Furthermore, Michael is interested in queer pedagogies and the experiences of LGBTQ+ staff and students in higher education.

Authors

Lauren Andres is Professor of Planning and Urban Transformations at the Bartlett School of Planning, UCL. Her expertise sits within the understanding of the intersectionality between people, space and temporalities in the process of urban making and living. Lauren's research contribution spans from developing alternative models to understanding cities with key account of locality and context, to re-thinking systematically the connection between cities, planning, health and sustainability with a specific focus on the most vulnerable communities.

Yasminah Beebeejaun is Professor of Urban Politics and Planning at the Bartlett School of Planning, UCL. Her work is concerned with feminist and anti-racist approaches to planning theory, practice and education. Yasminah's articles have been published in many journals including *Environment and Planning C*, *Journal of Planning Education and Research*, *Planning Theory*, *Planning Theory and Practice* and *Transactions of the Institute of British Geographers*. She is co-editor of the *Journal of Race, Ethnicity and the City*.

Patrick Le Bellec has led the Department for Culture in the city of Dunkirk and has been leading the En Rue collective since 2017. En Rue brings together local residents, artists, architects, sociologists and the street educators who work in the neighbourhoods of Dunkirk. He runs public space development projects and artistic interventions, as well as co-production as opportunities for sharing collective experiences, learning and creating. With En Rue Patrick partners with the Fab Lab social project, the Eco Chalet association and the Experice team. He is also a member of Territoire Europe and the association Bâtisseurs d'Economie Solidaire that rehabilitates an industrial wasteland in Coudekerque-Branche.

Elena Besussi is Lecturer (Teaching) and Director of the Undergraduate Programmes in Urban Studies and Urban Planning, Design and Management at the Bartlett School of Planning, UCL. Her research focuses on issues of justice, power and democratic scrutiny in urban planning, urban governance and land development in the context of capitalist urbanisation. Elena's teaching engages with issues of professional and distributed expertise through collaborative and community-based pedagogical methods.

Sue Brownill is Professor of Urban Policy and Governance at the School of the Built Environment, Oxford Brookes University. Sue's research interests focus on how planning and regeneration can both involve people and promote more socially sustainable and equitable places. She has carried out a range of research projects into public participation in planning and regeneration, with a recent focus on neighbourhood planning. She is currently leading an Arts and Humanities research Council (AHRC) research project on the hidden histories of community-led planning. Sue combines her academic interests with involvement with community and housing groups, including the Oxfordshire Community Land Trust. Before moving to Oxford she worked with community organisations in London's Docklands.

Melia Delplanque is President of Territoire Europe, a DPLG architect and urbanist with know-how in welding, carpentry, permaculture and 'ensemble faire' or co-production. She has been president of Les Saprophytes since 2007, president of the Association of Bergues in Transition (known as La Revanche de Wenceslas), working with a local group SEL de Bergues (Système d'Échange Local for place-based exchange). Melia is also am administrator at Acteurs Pour l'Economie

Solidaire, a network for the 'solidarity economy', and a contributor to the collegial council of la Fédération des accompagnateurs à l'autoproduction et à l'entraide dans le bâtiment that provides guidance to those working in self-build and promotes mutual aid in the construction industry.

Stuart Paul Denoon-Stevens is a senior lecturer at Nottingham Trent University and research associate at University of the Free State (South Africa). His research expertise lies in understanding the interface between the practical development of the built environment and the conflict and compatibility between this and the normative foundations and theory that underpin planning and governance. Stuart's research spans a plethora of topics, including development control in the Global South, housing and spatial planning in mining towns, and the interface between planning practice and academia.

Renée Etokakpan is a programme administrator at Groundwork London, a charity that has been at the forefront of social and environmental regeneration for more than 25 years. She leads on securing corporate partners for a youth development programme that aids more than 1,700 young people across London. Renee graduated from UCL with a first-class BSc in project management for construction and the Bartlett Faculty Medal.

Silvia Gullino is an architect and planner. She is Associate Professor in City Making at Birmingham City University. She is the Course Leader of the BSc in Property Development and Planning. Her research on placemaking aims to create diverse, healthy and active citizens. In the past 15 years, she has developed a portfolio of collaborative interdisciplinary research projects culminating in two main research areas: digital placemaking and active citizenship; and urban well-being agendas for liveable cities. More recently, she has researched how technologies can empower citizens to envision, design and shape the resiliency of future cities through local, bottom- up and innovative initiatives. She was recognised for the annual UK The Planner Women of Influence award (2021). She is a Built Environment Expert at the Design Council (2021) and Senior Advisor on Public Space for the international NGO City Space Architecture (2021).

Sara Hassan is a research fellow at City-REDI who has a strong multidisciplinary background in urban planning and social sciences. She is experienced in conducting qualitative research with both policymakers and vulnerable groups. Throughout her studies and career, the key thread has been understanding the role of place in social and economic inequalities. Sara is particularly interested in innovative policy evaluation models, policy reform issues, policy analysis and how it impacts on poor and vulnerable communities, community engagement and urban planning. She also researches in the area of local economic development, migration and sustainable urban transport.

Stephan Hauser obtained his PhD at the TU Delft Faculty of Architecture in the Chair of History of Architecture and Urban Planning. Coming from a legal background, his research focused on the impact of oil companies on the development of port cities and on the creation and application of regulations linked to spatial planning, as well as the protection of health and the environment. Stephan's publications focus mostly on the port cities of Dunkirk in France and Rotterdam in the Netherlands as two extreme examples of the oil industry's influences. He is now a postdoctoral researcher at Helsinki Institute of Sustainability Science looking for ways to forge sustainability science for societal change.

Elsona van Huyssteen holds a position as Principle Urban and Regional Planner at the Council for Science and Industrial Research, South Africa, and has a keen research and practice interest in processes to galvanise transdisciplinary collaboration and strengthen developmental impact and leadership. She believes in the capabilities and contribution of purpose-driven teams, leaders and collaborations to shape our collective future and address complex local and regional development (and regulatory) challenges. She currently acts as team leader for the Municipal Capability and Partnership Programme, a collaborative initiative between local government and industry partners to strengthen service delivery and livelihoods in rapidly changing mining regions in South Africa.

Dominique Lancrenon is an architect and urbanist, and one of the authors of the 'European Charter of Participatory Democracy via Spatial Planning'. She has carried out numerous studies with the Territoires Sites & Cités team, which she directed from 1989 to 2018. As key delegate of Territoire Europe, Dominique develops participative platforms for neighbourhoods and cities, and promotes exchanges on engagement experiences across countries in Europe. Her research focuses on the access to knowledge shared between urban residents, businesses and associations, as well as the resulting project dynamics. She has been co-president of the Société Française des Urbanistes, since 2020 and Présidente d'honneur of the ECTP-CEU since 2013.

Celine Lessard (she/her) is an urbanism professional and freelance queer-events producer. Her master's thesis focused on how policies for high streets affect queer spaces in London, and she has built on this work to produce research for the Greater London Authority on the barriers that community and cultural groups face in obtaining premises. Celine's professional experience includes project management, education and field research, and she has most recently worked as Policy Officer for Culture Strategy at the Greater London Authority.

Martin P. Lewis is Chief Executive Officer of the South African Council for Planners (SACPLAN). He is registered as a professional planner with SACPLAN, and a chartered planner with the Royal Town Planning Institute (RTPI). Martin has more than 30 years' experience in planning, which includes local government and academia. He has served as Head of Department, Town and Regional Planning, at the University of Johannesburg. Martin's main research interest is in planning education and transformation of the planning profession. Other areas of research include land use management, spatial planning, and property development.

Juliana Martins is Associate Professor (Teaching) in Urban Design at the Bartlett School of Planning, UCL. She has a background in architecture, a master's in housing and urbanism from the Architectural Association School of Architecture, and a PhD in planning studies from UCL. Before joining academia, Juliana worked as an architect, urban designer and policy adviser, in both the public and private sectors. She is Director of Education for the Bartlett School of Planning and teaches mainly in the field of urban design. Her research interests include the relationship between economic activities and the spatial configuration of the city, in particular the spatiality of work and urban design and planning education.

Lorena Melgaço is Associate Senior Lecturer at the Department of Human Geography at Lund University. She is an urban scholar navigating the multilevel entwinement of digital technologies and the production of space, especially in the postcolony. Lorena's research interests include the micropolitics of socio-spatial and technological peripheralisation; the intersections of technological dependency, capitalist production of space and the socio-environmental crisis in planning; and the challenges of planning education and practice from a socio-spatial justice perspective.

Corin Menuge is a 2020 graduate of the MSc Urban Development Planning course at the Development Planning Unit of the Bartlett School of Planning, UCL. During his studies, he explored possibilities to revisit existing theories and frameworks in urban development from a queer perspective. Corin currently works in the UK social housing sector and hopes to continue discovering ways to reimagine theory and practice for the benefit of all.

Gemma Moore is Associate Professor at the Institute for Environmental Design and Engineering at the Bartlett School of Planning, UCL. Gemma has been with the department since 2002, undertaking research and teaching in the field of sustainability, participation, community engagement, health and environmental quality. She leads the MSc module Health and Wellbeing in Cities: Theory and Practice for the Bartlett Institute of Environmental Design, and Engineering's MSc Health, Sustainability and Wellbeing in Buildings. Within the module she has built in a model of engaged teaching, involving community and policy partners within the assessment.

Verna Nel qualified as a town and regional planner at Wits University and obtained her MSc and PhD through UNISA. After three decades of working primarily in municipalities, she moved to the Urban and Regional Planning Department of the University of the Free State. Verna has diverse research interests that include spatial and urban resilience, local economic development and spatial governance. She has presented her work at international conferences and has published her research in leading journals and books.

Liam O'Farrell is a researcher who has worked on urban development and inclusion on multidisciplinary projects across Europe, including in the United Kingdom, the Republic of Ireland, Iceland, Switzerland and France. He has a particular interest in learning from international best practice and how findings can be translated into different cultural contexts. Liam has published on spatial justice and devolution and is currently working on a project to gather evidence on the local social, political and economic effects of freeports in Europe, using the case studies of Geneva, Monaco and Luxembourg.

Catalina Ortiz is a Colombian urbanist. She uses decolonial and critical urban theory through knowledge co-production methodologies to study the politics of space production in Latin America and South-east Asia to foster more just cities and the recognition of multiple urban knowledges. She currently works as Associate Professor and Co-Programme Leader of the MSc Building and Urban Design in Development at UCL.

Mike Raco is Professor of Urban Governance and Development in the Bartlett School of Planning, UCL. He has published and taught on the topics of urban governance, sustainability, social diversity and urban planning in multiple contexts. His latest book *London* (with Frances Brill) is published by Abacus Press.

Jordan Rowe (he/him) is a writer, curator and researcher with an interest in urban cultures, heritage and identities. As an independent cultural worker, Jordan has curated shows at the Bauhaus Dessau (2022), Stanley Arts (2022) and Zentrum für Kunst und Urbanistik (2021), alongside collaborations with the Whitechapel Gallery, De La Warr Pavilion and Greater London Authority, among others. He has previously served as Urbanist in Residence at the Museum of London, research fellow at Theatrum Mundi, manager of UCL's Urban Laboratory, and lead researcher compiling an institutional race equality implementation plan for UCL.

Fernando Santomauro has been working with local governments since 2002. Since 2018 he has worked at United Cities and Local Governments World Secretariat. Fernando was Municipal Secretary of International Relations of Guarulhos (2009–16) and an international relations officer at Belo Horizonte (2007) and São Paulo (2002–5). With a master's degree in social history from the Pontifical Catholic University of São Paulo and a PhD in international relations from the San Tiago Dantas Programme (2011–15), he has also been a visiting researcher in history of international relations at Sciences Po, Paris (2005–6) and Montclair State University, the United States (2013–14), as well as a postdoctoral researcher at University de Brasília (2017).

Raphael Sedlitzky is an urban practitioner that has been working with different international institutions on sustainable urban development. His key focus is on decentralised cooperation, city networks and urban sustainability transformations. Furthermore, he is a PhD candidate at the University of Vienna. In his research, Raphael takes a comparative perspective to analyse the challenges and enabling factors for urban sustainability transformations.

Pablo Sendra is an architect and urban designer. He is Associate Professor at the Bartlett School of Planning, UCL. He combines his academic career with professional work through his own urban design practice, Lugadero Ltd, which focuses on facilitating co-design processes with communities. At UCL, he is Director of the MSc Urban Design and City Planning Programme and Coordinator of the Civic Design CPD. Pablo has carried out action-research projects in collaboration with activists and communities. His work with communities can be accessed via the Community-Led Regeneration platform. Pablo is co-author of *Designing Disorder* (with Richard Sennett, 2020), which has been translated into seven languages; co-author of *Community-Led Regeneration* (with Daniel Fitzpatrick, 2020); and co-editor of *Civic Practices* (with Maria Joao Pita and CivicWise, 2017). He is part of the City Collective for the journal *City*.

Ram Shergill is an interdisciplinary researcher specialising in bio-integrated design, photography and creative direction. Internationally recognised for his contribution to the fashion industry, Ram has advanced his practice through science and wearable technology. Working in the field of bioastronautics, he is designing novel photobioreactor extensions to the body via biochemical engineering and architectural design. Speculatively designed portable life support systems are innovated working with microalgae, benefiting habitation in harsher environments on Earth and for potential life support beyond low earth orbit. Ram has been a speaker at various conferences internationally, including at the University of Oxford and the Massachusetts Institute of Technology, where he has delivered talks on science, art, technology and the ecological environment. He is a lecturer at the University of the Arts London and has previously lectured at the Arts University Bournemouth. In 2016, Ram was awarded the Arts Culture and Theatre Award for his contribution to the industry. His art and design work has been shown in exhibitions internationally including Sotheby's, the Wallace Collection, Somerset House and the Museum of Contemporary Arts. Ram's portraits are housed in the permanent collection of the National Portrait Gallery.

Domenico Di Siena designs and develops processes and tools to help local authorities, organisations, companies and universities collaborate with the citizens for the common good. He works as an urban and regional policy consultant for international organisations such as the United Nations Development Programme and the Inter-American Development Bank. Domenico is the instigator and co-founder of several spaces, networks and communities known for their capacity for innovation and knowledge exchange. Notable among them are the Volumes Lab spaces in Paris, Factoría Cívica in Valencia, the Ciudades Comunes platform, the international network CivicWise and the Civic Innovation School, which focuses on processes of collective intelligence and civic innovation. Domenico is the world's largest producer of content and research related to civic design practice. Many of these contributions are available for free at urbanohumano.com. He is the author of the *Civic Design Method Whitepaper,* in which he lays out his vision of civic design practice and presents three practical working tools: the collective intelligence canvas, the circular process and the civic scope matrix.

Simeon Shtebunaev is an interdisciplinary doctoral researcher at Birmingham City University, researching how young people engage in the planning of future 'smart' cities. He was a principal investigator on the AHRC-funded project 'Are you game for climate action?', developing the boardgame *Climania* with young people and focusing on the role of the built environment in climate change. Simeon was selected as the *RIBAJ* Rising Star 2021 and the RTPI West Midlands Young Planner of the Year 2021.

Teresa Strachan has a practice background in several planning sectors. It was her work in the third sector, with Planning Aid England, that inspired later research and student projects with young people while working as Senior Lecturer at Newcastle University. This role focused on the provision of academic support for students as they prepared for the workplace. Now retired, Teresa's writing continues to contribute to the discussion concerning the potential for youth engagement in planning and the skills that this practice requires of planning professionals.

Elodie Wakerley is Education Developer at Birmingham City University, where she specialises in academic staff development and student engagement initiatives. Elodie has a long-standing interest in student academic partnership and collaborative curriculum design. She has previously published work on integrating student perspectives into academic development and supporting technology enhanced learning for student engagement.

Maria Xypaki is an educationalist specialising in social justice pedagogies. She has been working for universities in the United Kingdom since 2012. Her scholarship focuses on education for sustainable development, critical service learning and critical urban pedagogies. She has raised more than £600,000 from higher education public bodies for knowledge exchange activities, staff-student partnerships, innovation and research projects. Maria is an alumna of the Bartlett School of Planning, and she is currently conducting her research at the Institute of Education.

Preface

During 2019, while co-teaching our university students about the management challenges that built environment professionals face today, we started to have a conversation about how to promote learning for students who come from a wide variety of backgrounds. We were also reflecting on our different intellectual starting points – given Michael's central interest in the quality of design outcomes in place-making and Lucy's core focus on the democratic potential within processes of planning for urban development – and how we were both driven by a focus on stakeholder engagement. Although we might not have described it as such at the time, together we were pursuing a more critical, participatory and equitable form of pedagogy for urbanism.

The genesis of those discussions led to further explorations during the start of the COVID-19 pandemic, culminating in research exchanges at the UK-Ireland Planning Research Conference 2020, hosted by the Bartlett School of Planning. We were worried about how participatory activities in teaching, research and urban development practices might fare if we were all socially isolated for long periods. We were able to reach out to others who we knew already shared our concern for 'widening participation' in our fields – we were hoping to at least talk it through. Others joined the debates, and there were even more questions around who might be involved in this 'nexus' of urban learning and to what end.

What struck us throughout was the recognition that built environment higher education is bound with urban development in very specific ways. There were such fruitful discussions about where the worlds of teaching, research and practice meet, and we agreed to look to publish examples and reflect on them. It didn't take long to agree that a work of this type should be open access and we were extremely fortunate to gain the support for this book from UCL Press. Along the way we have been heartened by the encouragement of others for the ideas behind *Engaged Urban Pedagogy*, and we very much see this as the starting point for ongoing exchanges.

Acknowledgements

We owe an enormous debt of gratitude to all the students whose learning experiences have helped shape this book; to each of the contributors for their dedication to the project; to the organisers and others involved in the Bartlett School of Planning research conference 2019 for the insights and exchanges; to Pat Gordon-Smith and UCL Press for their guidance; and to the anonymous reviewer whose helpful comments have undoubtedly helped made this work stronger.

1
Towards an engaged urban pedagogy
Lucy Natarajan and Michael Short

Why engaged urban pedagogy?

We have been inspired by the many different types of participatory activity found in urban planning and place-making teaching, and the consistency in their underlying values. Through our individual experiences, as well as shared teaching at UCL, we have become increasingly convinced that this indicates a distinctive educational praxis related to the built environment, where the approach to teaching and expectations of learning are shaped by ideas about co-produced places in participatory planning theory. Those ideas resonate with two complementary spheres of thinking – critical pedagogy and participatory urban development – and so we proposed a conceptual framing of 'engaged urban pedagogy' within higher education institutions, underpinned by principles of learning, inclusion and empowerment.

    The ambition of this book is to explore the interplay of critical pedagogy and participatory urban development through instances of so-called 'real world' engagement with higher education made possible by people within, and beyond, the university. Universities are not cloistered or ivory towers, they are full of participatory practices. It is clear that students are regularly in direct contact with non-academics, and commonly encounter urban professionals and local communities as part of undergraduate and postgraduate degree programmes. Such participatory activities have persisted in the face of the present COVID-19 pandemic, with all its social distancing requirements and consequent teaching adaptations. In our own work, we regularly 'blend' digital, three-dimensional, on-screen and in-person experiences to create opportunities for student learning, and these include interactions with non-academics. But this is just a small part of the story; these interactions have implications that go way beyond the institutional realms of education.

As we argue in this chapter, built environment education has much wider significance, particularly for educationalists and those interested in the social sciences. Our focus is on planning and place-making, which are the knowledge-based activities of determining and designing urban development and – according to participatory planning norms – these ought to include diverse actors and have collective societal goals. In any case, for built environment fields, the nature of engagement with the production of knowledge, and wider participation in teaching and learning, merit close attention. Moreover, given the socially constructed nature of 'places' and enormous political salience of urban development, they provide much wider insights about education, development and society.

Rather than hoping for some lofty best practice of engaged urban pedagogy, we seek to showcase the current range of activities in urban planning and place-making and consider lessons on critical pedagogy in these disciplines. Each chapter focuses on one activity where there is a discursive connection, or other form of link-up, that goes beyond the institutional bounds of universities. These activities help students in higher education to engage with research and practice agendas and, whether face to face, through traditional media or digital platforms, always involve communicative exchanges between people. They demonstrate three distinct types of activity: reviewing university curricula or evaluating education; providing teaching or contributing to delivery of education at universities; and embedding higher learning or educational practices in the built environment. As we set out here, and demonstrate throughout the book, these *review, provision* and *embedding* activities offer moments where learning and learners are transformed. Together the three complementary areas of pedagogy appear to 'loop' for an ongoing iterative process of higher education in the built environment (see Figure 1.1).

In the rest of this chapter, we present the concepts behind the proposal for engaged urban pedagogy and explain the participatory 'intellectual roots' within educational and urban research. We first consider active learning and the challenge of constructivist approaches to higher education. Then we turn to reflect on the synergy between foundational works in critical pedagogy and participatory planning. This sets the scene for subsequent chapters. Chapter authors share insights from Europe, South Africa and Latin America, and their contributions shine a light on the complexities of universities and the learning of a diverse

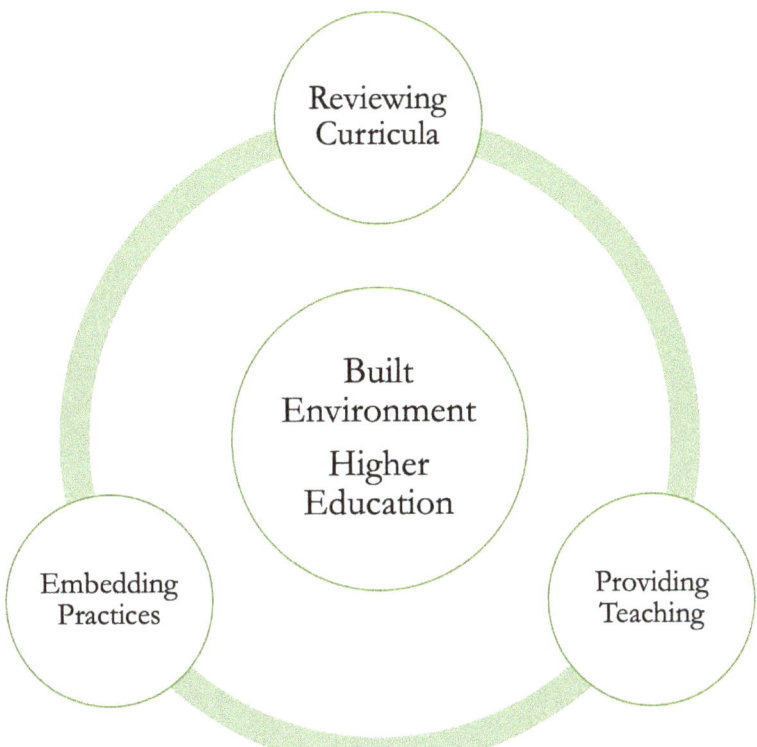

Figure 1.1 Activities around a nexus of built environment higher education.
Source: Author

student body. They show the range of higher education connections with the wider world and span the three participatory action areas of engaged urban pedagogy. Accordingly, they are presented in three sections, which cover: *reviewing* design and delivery of higher education; *providing teaching* and modes of delivery; and *embedding* higher learning practices in planning and place-making. In a short forward to each section, we consider the lessons from each of the four chapters included there and reflect on implications for the proposed engaged urban pedagogy. In the final chapter, Chapter 14, we draw these together and, conscious of the inevitable limits of any single inquiry, we highlight tensions in participatory thinking and practice, and offer critical questions for future engaged urban pedagogy research.

The construction of education

Ideals of higher education have moved away from imparting facts and towards honing skills for higher order thinking, with reflexivity of learners at the heart of the project. We briefly position the relevance of the constructivist turn in built environment education, with reference to concepts from key research on active forms of learning. The call of critical pedagogy, to embrace the student's role in their own learning echoes in the work on active learning. As expounded by Bonwell and Eison (1991), active learning connects most closely to the pragmatist thinking of Dewey (1924) with a focus on 'effectiveness' of educational strategies that has been well explored in relation to democracy through the expansion of collective planetary consciousness of the student as citizen (Roji, 2018) and inhabitant of planet earth (Marouli at al., 2018). In recognition of the power of the agency of the student in their own education, this was a pushback against passive learning primarily via attentiveness as a spectator to teaching. In other words, the more strategies are re-orientated around activation of thought, the more that student learning could come from within:

> Students are involved in more than listening. Less emphasis is placed on transmitting information and more on developing students' skills. Students are involved in higher-order thinking (analysis, synthesis, evaluation). Students are engaged in activities (e.g., reading, discussing, writing). Greater emphasis is placed on students' exploration of their own attitudes and values. (Marouli at al., 2018:19).

In particular, this was a challenge to any vestigial ideas of 'the lecture' as an informational transaction (i.e., left over from the original practice of provision of reading for the illiterate).

Despite initial concerns about resistance from faculty (Bonwell and Eison, 1991) and more recent woes such as class sizes (Wright *et al.*, 2019) and facilities (Bolden III *et al.*, 2019), the provision of active learning opportunities continues to grow. There are clear benefits in enhanced student reflexivity, and the critique of passive absorption of lecture or other materials is extremely robust. Nonetheless, it is important to understand the nature of new norms adopted by learners, and the standards asked of higher education should encourage further review of present student experience. Indeed, this is seen in studies of would-be consumers of a supposed 'higher education product' (Bunce and Bennett,

2021), faculty-student boundaries in teaching provision (Patrick, 2020), and post-educational aspirations (Trede and Jackson, 2012).

Within our own fields – planning and place-making – the role of active learning is key. As Bonwell and Eison sensed, it might be 'more appropriate for some disciplines than others' (p. 22). In our own teaching areas, there are live phenomena that must be explored *as* (rather than in) the field (Pattacini, 2018; Cohen, 2010; Cantor *et al.*, 2014) and lend themselves to inherently active tasks. For instance, those found in creating and sharing visual knowledge via GIS (Carlson 2007), designs, maps and others group work (Schweitzer *et al.*, 2008), among other things. This is evidenced by the rise of associated techniques in spatial planning – for example, Frank *et al.*, (2014: 75) found 'extensive use of an online, interactive, virtual learning environment'. There is also an alignment of active learning with the communities of learning as a praxis for planning (Cantor *et al.*, 2014; Kallus, in Frank and da Rosa Pires, 2021) and place-making (Altay, 2014; Salama 2010, 2016).

More fundamentally, and yet to be explored, there are synergies between the more recent constructivist framings of education and post-cartesian epistemologies of urban contexts, which underpin current thinking on participatory planning and place-making and frame place as a constructed phenomenon with layers of social and political meaning. Moreover, diverse individuals and communities who interact locally, regionally and internationally through urban processes, also have their own sets of knowledge formed through diverse experiential forms of place.

A key question then is how students approach understandings of planning and place-making. The term 'place' refers to the different elements that make up the unique character of somewhere, which includes physical elements but also how people experience the environment and their 'memory traces' upon it (Lynch, 1984). Arguably then, places represent urban processes, their practices and their socio-political meanings as well as imprints of the people(s) who have lived in those spaces over time. As such, students might understand place as a complex set of interconnecting tangible and intangible characteristics that coalesce in the built environment at different times and in different ways. Further, the experience of place is fundamental as a way of knowing for the student and connects them to others since, as Tuan argues, place conveys what it is to be human (1997).

Since our agenda is around teaching students to create societally valuable places that are inevitably full of diverse and contested meanings, the associated engaged urban pedagogy must recognise the inherent complexity in the ways that learners understand, read, interpret and therefore seek to create place. The positionality of learners in this urban development knowledge arena is therefore critical, and the place subjectivities of an individual or group of students will be a factor in learning that cannot be bracketed out or denied within education. In particular, the place attachment (Manzo and Devine Wright, 2021) of people and communities, those bonds to urban spaces that are inhabited over time, may be tacitly known or subtly expressed, yet again we cannot shy away from their central role in place-making. These dimensions of place speak to identity not only in association with lived experience of the urban environment, but in respect to an individual or communities. Therefore, they must be seen set against a background of intersecting issues and challenges of race, gender, sexuality and class. As bell hooks puts it, education requires students to engage with a 'radical space for possibility' (hooks, 1994: 12), and this book is an attempt to demonstrate, through a variety of examples, how those who participate in teaching and learning seek education that relates to the fullness of place and its complexity.

Given the multiple knowledges of a diverse range of actors that might be drawn on in planning and place-making, we ask how these might be reflected in the classroom. The move to experiential learning in recent decades in our own field must engage with these complexities and the construction of place-related knowledges. We present a range of chapters in this book that reflect on moments where experience and place are brought to bear in built environment education, as such approaches align well with experiential learning that 'incorporates experiences, reflections, and a learner-centred focus' (Foster *et al.*, 2021: 2). While a diverse range of ideas and methods are covered by the concept, at their heart is the constructivist ideal of active learning, that knowledge comes from within the learner, and that rather than passively receiving or 'banking' (Freire, 1970) knowledge, learners actively construct meaning from the interaction of their prior knowledge and current experience (Hanson, 2015). However, in view of the social construction and politics of place, the perspective of the knowledge of the other is more deeply imbricated.

Urban development activities surround socially constructed phenomena, and education in this field must explicitly contend with the diversity and multiplicity not only of knowledge but also of its users and uses. Diverse experiences and direct knowledges of urban 'users' have been explored in closely related architectural design courses (Altay, 2014; Öztürk and Türkkan, 2006). However, for planning, the focus is urban futures and public choices about change to development, and the resulting impacts must be accounted for. Inevitably, there are 'winners' and 'losers' even where those choices are popular or lead to progress in, for example, sustainability. Therefore, knowledge claims (Rydin, 2007) and socio-spatial learning processes (Natarajan, 2017) will always be deeply political no matter who the users are.

Students must grapple with matters around the production of urban development knowledge, including stakeholder learning practices and the politics of lay and professional expertise. Local understandings of the value of place are co-constructed and can inform public decisions, and social learning where local communities address shared problems, may be a form of democracy (Wildemeersch and Vandelabeele, 2007). However, these place-based ways to knowledge are not a panacea for urban choices, as they themselves are deeply political. Planning and place-making will involve diverse forms of expertise, such as local insight, technical skills and procedural knowledge, and they provide socio-legal governance of land use and urban assets. The associated decisions about the location, form, function and management of developments can have local and much wider impacts. Therefore, the ways that planning and place-making connect to learning within stakeholder communities, both professional and lay groups involved in decision-making, is a particularly important matter. Pedagogic practices in higher education are surely part of that urban development dynamic.

In light of the epistemological and political complexities of urban development knowledges, it is important to question who the built environment learner is and what teaching in higher education entails. Earlier research on critical pedagogy has already unsettled general assumptions about students, teachers and the boundaries of educational spaces. We drill down further into built environment higher education and expand the investigation of current practices that promote active learning specifically in the fields of planning and place-making. This is an exploration not only of student reflexivity but also of the diversity of learners, the nature of experience and how those matter in pedagogic terms.

Exploring practices of, and in, education

Engaged forms of education have emerged alongside a wider re-orientation within urban development fields, which have turned towards co-production (Rooij and Frank, 2016). Historical top-down expert-dominated urban development practices are generally understood to have failed, and the goal of participatory governance has risen. While full and meaningful participation in environmental decision-making remains elusive, there are still 'openings' (Brownill and Inch, 2019) for citizen empowerment, and stakeholder engagement remains a normative expectation. In this section, we set out the aspirations for learning in relation to urban development and knowledges in urban planning and place-making. This sets the scene for discussion of how participatory planning concerns echo within critical pedagogy, which promotes the agency of students and active learning.

Specific knowledges and capacities for learning are implicit within the activities of urban development, and they point towards matters of importance in built environment education. Today's cities visibly display levels of sophistication in architecture, engineering and construction; less apparent, but no less important, is the craft of determining where and how to develop. Decision-making is the critical function of planning, but the knowledges required are much more than can be gained from 'survey-analysis-plan' and any participatory planning would take sociological and cultural considerations into account. European planners' recent description of their work as concertation (Bouche-Florin, 2019) is apt and indicates multiple actors thinking and acting together in an evolving environment. The strong interest in participatory planning and place-making typically has a focus on community participation in professional spheres and an awareness of 'locus of control' (Frank, 2006). Planning also calls on 'civics' (Geddes, LeGates and Stout, 2021; Batty and Marshall, 2017), for place-making, which involves social learning and action within the public realm (Makakavhule and Hill, 2021; Wildemeersch and Vandelabeele, 2007) and has fuelled expectations of expert collaborations embracing diverse rationalities (Colman, 1993; Healey, 1997). For instance, planners need to develop intellectual skills around strategies for forecasting (e.g., developing logic around the data that is needed), and designers should understand how stakeholders evaluate spaces (e.g., through analysis of discourses within stakeholder negotiations). All this suggests built environment education comprises *practices of* socially sensitised learning about urban development, and *practices for* co-produced learning within urban governance.

Planning and place-making require learning about the scope of spatial and cultural factors, diverse material needs and ways of knowing that are suited to the task. In particular, the diversity of urban stakeholders demands attention. Research has moved on from remote forms of ethnography, such as looking down from towers onto the city to review behaviours (Whyte, 1956), or recounting others' fantasies, such as those of suburban commuters (Gregg, 2012; Vaughan, 2015). Methods more suited to seeing street level and diversity of human behaviours, such as site reconnaissance, participant observation or field interviewing, are now fairly common (Dandekar, 2019: 26). When thinking about wider urban impacts, the stakeholders may be beyond a set of fixed place-based groups (Natarajan, 2017; 2019). Therefore, to build an understanding of any society in all its fullness, techniques are needed that can both appreciate and connect diverse situated viewpoints, and the modes of enquiry will matter as much as the questions being asked (Young and Ewing, 2020). This sphere of learning is part of a fundamental political struggle around knowledge *for* planning and place-making.

Urban decision-making has historically been an extremely exclusive sphere, and this has been politically and epistemologically detrimental. The reliance on the authority of ruling powers and knowledges of a close coterie of experts has left little space for contestation, let alone civics (e.g., Healey, 1997). In research terms, it prevents questioning of the value assumptions behind development choices (e.g., linguistic binaries such as governed/governing, researcher/researched (John 2006)) and other implicit hierarchies of the dominant cultural norms (Walters, 1980). In practice, the result is a series of poorly informed interventions that privilege those already in power, the well-off social groups and the established institutions of governance – research and teaching practices are implicated. Historically, the position of educators, given their significant power within cultural networks, has rightly attracted scrutiny (Jackson Lears, 1985). While the 'programming' of education *for* a normative vision of co-productive governance is of interest, for instance promoting the power of communication and negotiation skills (Briassoulis, 1999), there are the 'complex dynamics influencing planning education' including the growth of territorial integration policies of the European Union (Frank *et al.*, 2014), and the power geographies of those who teach and those who are taught within global education networks (Sanyal, 1989). More directly, universities have agency in urban development as powerful actors and investors in regional innovation systems (Benneworth *et al.*, 2017; see also Chapter 10).

A key backdrop for engaging with present urban development is the geological era, referred to as the Anthropocene, where human activity is shaping planetary ecosystems. While planning and place-making orientate towards co-production, they are also the means to constructing environments and must contend with questions of future sustainability (Rees, 2017) and coping with climate change effects (McLean, 2015), including extreme weather events and changes to vital natural ecologies. Such issues focus thinking on the scale of response that is needed, and forms of learning that can connect global and local concerns (Ostrom, 2010; Geels, 2016). Research now takes a global lens in respect of knowledge sharing and forms of learning necessary for climate transitions and environmental justice (Agger, 2021; Castán Broto and Westman, 2019) and for adaptive governance that could manage and plan future urban development (Schmitt and Wiechman, 2018; Scott and Moloney, 2022; Sullivan *et al.*, 2019). Thus, the aims of collaborative governance include reshaping knowledge and rethinking global power structures.

The turn to collaborative governance is clearly relevant to education *for* urban development, which would focus on, while recognising how it is bound up in, knowledges and their cultural referents. Researchers continue to grapple with the many challenges of embracing the agency of diverse actors in planning (Legacy, 2017), and there has been a good deal of scepticism and suggestions of naivety about participatory practices in the face of the forces of global capital. However, the underlying goal of improving knowledge practices continues to hold promise and to be seen as important to the legitimacy of public institutions. The idealised democratic form of governance would be open to conflicting experiences and views and support stakeholder inclusion within environmental decision-making. This is a normative expectation at every scale of governance, from the civic association's climate declaration (Howarth *et al.*, 2021), to the international forums for sustainable urban development (Patnaik, 2021). The knowledge complex may offer space for connecting institutional planning and place-making with other forms of expertise, based on a fundamental premise that socially just and sustainable development requires conscious engagement of a diverse set of actors particularly that of lay communities (Natarajan, 2019). This framing suggests that the intellectual and communicative capacities would be a key means to empower and emancipate urban development stakeholders from the clutches and effects of top-down practices. In turn, this implicates education; and so we turn to liberation pedagogies.

Liberation pedagogies

The field of critical pedagogy is an approach to teaching that appreciates the power of learning and focuses attention on the wider societal impacts of education. As discussed in this section, foundational critiques of school education have highlighted how the ways of thinking and organisational processes of the day were failing to deliver for wider society. Learning spaces were seen as exclusionary and teaching was delivered in a way that privileged powerful sections of society. Freire's foundational work *Pedagogy of the Oppressed* (1970, originally 1968 in Portuguese), is well noted for critiquing education and seeking to transform structures (Dale and Hyslon-Margison, 2010). Critical pedagogies were then a means to liberating individuals and empowering them to change society (Freire, 1985). In that sense, engagement meant expanding students' critical faculties with respect to their positionality as an individual within the world they inhabit.

At its heart, this reworking of education promoted a more holistic intellectual development, as well as engagement of students and educators with the social realities surrounding education and their involvement in that sphere (Freire, 2014). This type of education was interested in the agency of students and a form of active learning rooted in an appreciation of lived experiences of disadvantage in society. It meant encouraging questioning of contexts of learning, as well as wider structures of power, including classroom practices that culturally reinforced social injustices and were a matter of lived experience for students. These issues were taken up in relation to race and gender by bell hooks (hooks, 1994; 2010), with new insights that drew even closer attention to subjective perspectives of educators and students. Bell hooks expanded on how people's backgrounds and identities shaped the knowledges at hand in the classroom and those subjectivities that were preconditions for an individual's engagement with education, and the affective side of foreclosing on critical thinking. Notwithstanding the occlusion of prevailing cultural norms, students were being alienated from their own learning when insights from lived experience were ignored. For bell hooks, that alienation further drove her own engagement with higher education: 'I came to theory because I was hurting – the pain within me was so intense that I could not go on living. I came to theory desperate, wanting to comprehend – to grasp what was happening within and around me. Most importantly, I wanted to make the hurt go away. I saw in theory then a location for healing.' (hooks, 1994: 59).

The concerns of critical pedagogy echo those of participatory planning, which would promote openness in institutions and inclusiveness in learning processes. Both rest on engaging the agency and diversity of stakeholders, although critical pedagogy mainly considered the role of individual students and educators. Both have democracy and social justice in mind, and for liberatory forms of pedagogy the search was rooted in the fundamental value of higher learning and on-going reflexivity to human beings. The goal is to push forward higher education by facilitating students' learning, building on an individual's personal engagement with subject matter and higher order thinking capacity. The additionality of critical or 'engaged' pedagogy was in pro-active encouragement of thinking about the societal effects of education and explicitly opening up opportunities for students to connect the educational material to their own lives.

The 'socially constructed' views of the world found in liberation pedagogies, were helping deconstruct the claims to truth of modernist grand narratives, and the logics and evidence employed in producing them were also coming under scrutiny. Critical pedagogy required academic freedoms, open-mindedness and critical thinking from both educators and students in an effort to navigate the multiple subjectivities of those involved in learning. This extended intellectual work into what might be seen as a more participatory mode, as it involved sharing different types of knowledge in the classroom or expanding enquiry about the teaching space.

To broadly characterise the practices of critical pedagogies, they centred on the precondition of open-mindedness. Rather than insisting on any particular starting epistemology or political standpoint for either students or educators, teachers would acknowledge the diverse potential interpretations of the world and students would be encouraged to ask, 'what counts as knowledge, what is significant, and why'. Education was not a particular set of knowledge that could be banked (Freire) as an asset, but critical engagement with one's own positionality in society. It involved reviewing not just educational materials, but institutions and practices of learning, such as the important question about how people approached the subject and what factors shaped their 'route' into it. Teachers may be expected to spend time studying such matters to hone their pedagogy, but for critical pedagogy debating the choices around knowledge was the tool for learning, inclusion and empowerment. One of the key challenges is the ways that the educators are bound up in the problematics of the day, and just as important is the individual student's own experience of the world and its power structures.

Broadly speaking, the critical turn pedagogy is part of a wider trend of 'engagement' in learning about the world, and it has great synergy with participatory planning and place-making. Critical pedagogy studies make the case that, under certain conditions, there can be educational purpose in direct engagement with the world as it is experienced, replete with complexities, nuances and uncertainties. Importantly, the goal is not to dismiss intellectuals or create a new totalising experientialism, but to reinvigorate it by embracing the fluidity of meaning. The plurality of knowledges is seen to be a means to review and critically engage with theories. Hooks put it this way: 'combining the analytical and the experiential is a richer way of knowing' (1994). Thus, engagement with complexity may be seen as a pillar of scholarship, which rests on acceptance of the socially constructed nature of knowledge.

There are clear synergies with participatory development concerns, which include the subjectivities of stakeholders, multiple ways of learning and political uses of knowledge. A more 'engaged' pedagogy would account for experiences of students as urban development stakeholders, as well as how higher education institutions are entangled in the hierarchical power structures of urban processes. These can be framed as areas of active learning that have a particular relevance within built environment education, but it is not clear how they open up thinking on epistemic choices about urban development (Winkler, 2013). Here, it is important to note that those in higher education are unlikely to represent 'the oppressed', certainly not the entirety of the diverse stakeholder communities in urban development.

In participatory urban development, sociocultural complexities are key for learning about built environments. Likewise, critical pedagogy scholars rejected 'totalising' modernist accounts of the world, including narratives about historical progress in urban development. They take particular interest in the uncertainties of socially constructed reality and the provisional nature of meaning. Meaning for students must be negotiated

Figure 1.2 Lammasu public art (left); Queering public space (right).
Source: Author[1]

in relation to, for example, a person's identity or the particular socio-economic, cultural or political context. The salience of such matters to planning and place-making is demonstrated, for instance, by 'Rhodes must fall' and other international student campaigns and direct action around the removal of statues of historical figures, whose physical and metaphorical elevation is viscerally contested (Chaudhuri, 2016). Built environment education likewise would embrace the fluidity of meaning and subjective experience, but again we note the importance of diverse stakeholders for participatory urban development.

The role of the university is important both as an education institution and as a stakeholder in urban development with great power and visibility. Debates continue about the purposes and policies of higher education in view of a creeping instrumentalism associated with industrial capitalism that claims learning for applied skill/labour production (Payne 1999). Kromydas (2017) offers a thoughtful synthesis of the systems broadly linked to European pedagogic traditions and suggests that 'higher education cannot be solely conceptualised by the human capital approach and similar quantitative interpretations, as it has cultural, psychological, idiosyncratic and social implications' (Kromydas, 2017:8). This raises three considerations regarding the built environment-higher education nexus. First, universities are materially entangled within built environments, practically in their real estate and in terms of local learning, including through their student body. Their campuses and estates are part of the built and natural environment and give rise to activities, such as local commuter flows, uses of green infrastructures and outreach through provision of local facilities/investment/community training (or otherwise), all of which directly shape local places. Second, universities today are major institutional players in global urban development processes, interacting with governance networks in cities and regions. They are involved in the socio-economic, cultural and political workings, and it is reasonable to assume that their educational offer would shape the activities of a sizeable international alumni body. Third, academics may generate new approaches to urban subject matter. Planning scholars study policy and practices, their rationalities and societal effects, among other things. Through their research, they can grow and share knowledge of phenomena, including via education, publications and other connections into planning and place-making. Thus, both the urban and universities are entangled in 'the urban', which is an important area for research (Kronydas, 2017) as well as for reflexivity within a critical education.

Awareness of the role of universities in urban processes heightens interest in how higher education might be put 'to service' for wider society; for instance, boosting economic performance or investing sustainably. A 'third mission' has arisen from ideas of a corporate responsibility imperative, which has been linked to staff and student expectations of (Coelho and Menezes, 2021; Auerbach *et al.*, 2022). There are diverse frameworks around research and teaching modes currently in play, and how they might contribute to this mission (Heffernan, 2001; Winkler 2013; Zimmerelli and Bridges, 2016). Students may, for instance, be involved in community service, apprenticeships or service learning, the last of which is more akin to engaged pedagogy and distinguished by qualities of 'integrated learning, high-quality service, collaboration, student voice, civic responsibility, reflection, and evaluation' (Faulconer, 2021: 100).

In short, there is already an array of 'others' implicated in critical pedagogy, given the diverse urban stakeholders. Students' engagement with their powers, experiences and mental models will be relevant to critical pedagogy in planning and place-making. An *urban focused* pedagogy would surely then expect that each individual student would actively learn in a way that not only relates to their own positionality but also develops their critical thinking on a range of subjectivities in relation to urban development. Whether they emerge from university as a professional practitioner, researcher or activist, or take another path entirely, by enhancing their critical capacities, *they will be* growing power in relation to the built environment. Might this empowerment not also demand the appreciation of diverse perspectives?

To recap, whereas critical pedagogy looks at universal studentship and a general citizen education, our book has a different focal point. It is concerned with pedagogy in universities and higher education in the urban subjects of planning and place-making. In this context, the intellectual development of an individual must be related to the built environment. Students have very likely chosen a subject of study with greater freedom and intentionality than earlier years schooling. Choosing an urban subject, we would hope, indicates a student's position as interested in active learning and urban development knowledge. They enrol in a relatively lengthy and costly university education (whoever foots the bill). While there are a range of learning objectives, for engaged urban pedagogy it is assumed that they would be related to on-going endeavours using urban development knowledge, whether future civics, professional practice or further study in planning, urban design or another field. Indeed, some of the activities showcased in this book are part of programmes to qualify for professional practice in urban planning, while others are explicitly linked into on-going studies such as doctoral research and alternative forms of continuing professional development. Whatever learning goals a student may have, they certainly include expanding intellectual skills and developing a specific area of knowledge. We see this as a tacit agreement between student and educator, which underpins their active learning and our critical pedagogies. In the fields of planning and place-making, the learners are many and 'engagement' is politically and epistemologically complex, which aligns with the goals of liberation pedagogy. In response, we propose there might be engaged urban pedagogy – a distinctive approach to education that is infused with both active learning and participatory principles.

Experiences in universities today

Following this chapter, there are three sections that explore the notion of an engaged urban pedagogy, which can enhance students' capacities for critical appreciation of urban development. Over 12 chapters, we learn about diverse activities emerging in, and beyond, universities where there is a participatory approach within built environment higher education. The sections focus on one of three engaged urban pedagogy activity types: reviewing curricula; providing teaching; and embedding practices.

Each section contains a brief editorial introduction and four chapters. These provide reflections on the chapter authors' own activities, the voices of academics working with non-academics, as well as professionals within and beyond universities, people from civil society, and students in planning and place-making courses. We hear about the 'participatory' dimensions of learning, inclusion and empowerment in their activities, and how they relate to aspirations for change in higher education and the wider world of urban development.

The collection of chapters (Chapters 2–13) demonstrate a range of higher education on the built environment. As summarised in the editorial introductions, each section sheds light on how engaged urban pedagogy might catalyse change through that area of activity. Whether reviewing curricula, delivering teaching or embedding education, they all take a critical approach to teaching and show how higher education is connected to wider urban processes.

The first section of the book, on reviewing curricula, centres on how education can be redesigned. The four chapters explain ways that curricula, and the very means of assessment, are being reviewed. The activities are part of a continual process of reviewing and refreshing curricula, which is a standard expectation within universities. However, the work discussed here is explicitly participatory, and it includes new collaborations with diverse actors across higher education students and staff, and from built environment international contexts. Furthermore, the work generates new and more open forms of revision, including the production of a manifesto, open access syllabus and direct co-assessment with students.

Chapters on reviewing curricula reveal how academics are working to change the higher education 'offer' in their disciplines. They focus on concerns about diverse experiences, including monetary poverty, racial justice, queerness and student perspectives. The key pedagogic issue is how staff and students might better engage with urban challenges such as housing, health, culture and economic development. The work has a clear sense of direction in terms of empowering students to learn for themselves, and to help transform urban practices alongside other stakeholders. Overall, the section suggests the participation of different actors in reviewing built environment curricula can powerfully reshape ways of thinking about urban problematics.

Again, the second section of the book, on providing teaching, has four chapters, and these focus on the techniques employed for participatory critical pedagogy. They discuss the ways of 'delivering education' in universities and the crucial rationalities or purposes in respect of students' higher learning and potential for re-shaping the urban world. Two of these techniques are longstanding: guest talks that are usually given by invited urban practitioners and include discussions with students; and organising student field work involving them with local community activities and urban development processes. The others benefit from new technologies with the involvement of non-academics: using podcasts within course materials and assignments; and online sharing for digital co-design.

In the third section, on embedding practices, the four chapters present lessons from extra-mural spaces of learning. While engaged urban pedagogy creates change in the world indirectly through university students' endeavours, the activities discussed here plug those working and studying within higher education into urban learning processes. This happens within specific arenas: introducing urban planning to school children; community research capacity building; city-to-city learning; and artistic spaces for urban co-production. In the overview for each section, we draw out lessons on the value proposition of an engaged urban pedagogy and the capacities implicated in reviewing curricula, providing teaching and embedding practices.

Across the 12 chapters, we see an array of linkages between education and live urban processes, all created within spaces of academic–non-academic exchange. The authors include planners and urban designers, both staff and students involved in teaching and learning at universities, and their non-academic collaborators from civil society, government and professional organisations. What binds us all is a focus on built environment challenges and a search for social justice through better decisions in urban development. As such, the critical pedagogy under examination in this book is not only an opportunity for those in higher education institutions, but a means for fomenting reflexivity in live urban knowledge networks with ongoing research, learning and practices that can continue to shape the world.

In the concluding chapter, we argue that through wider connections and live partnerships there might be a distinctive form of teaching and learning that transforms higher education institutions. We acknowledge this is a provocation for the sector, and that change is never an unmixed blessing. Indeed, the activities shown here are chosen because they differ from traditional modes of higher education, such as passive listening to a lecturer or rote learning of facts. At the same time, they are all based in, and fundamentally rely on, the core academic functions of researching, publishing and reading. More practically, given the relational work involved in exchanges with non-academic actors such as are shown here, these activities are onerous in terms of time given over to meetings and discussions of temporal considerations. As illustration, protocols for research collaborations involving UCL staff and students with London community/activist groups are live and co-crafted ongoing as an open-source online resource (JustSpace, 2018). This can be an extra workload that, for those facing structural injustices, creates further inequality. However, we argue that engaged urban pedagogy ought not involve any 'extra task' for educators, and the expectation should be simply for teachers' critical engagement with their own materials in respect of the learners involved. Indeed, we are wary of the current pressures on resources for foundational scholarship that underpin teaching (Leathwood and Read, 2020) and the trends towards responsibilising students in major projects or 'life' projects" (Frank *et al.*, 2014: 6). Instead, our hope is that *Engaged Urban Pedagogy* may stimulate new ways of thinking about higher education based in helping students to engage with the distinctive built environment problematics of our times.

Note

1. Fluidity of meaning can encourage footfall around particular spaces, as well as creativity and interest in the symbolic power of built environment: on the left plinth (one of four) that hosts only temporary installations (Sumartojo, 2013) from 2018–20 Michael Rakowitz's date syrup can recreation of the Assyran Diety Lamassu of Nineveh provided a haunting manifestation of past urbanisms in central London (Moffitt, 2018); on the right, one of many diverse pedestrian-crossing green lights with symbols of people and love, which have replaced the uniform, lone man.

References

Agger, A. 2021. 'Democratic innovations in municipal planning: potentials and challenges of place-based platforms for deliberation between politicians and citizens', *Cities* 117: 103317.

Altay B. 2014. 'User-centered design through learner-centered instruction', *Teaching in Higher Education*, 19(2):138–55, https://doi.org/10.1080/13562517.2013.827646 (last accessed 29 November 2022).

Amati, M., R. Freestone and S. Robertson. 2017. '"Learning the city": Patrick Geddes, exhibitions, and communicating planning ideas', *Landscape and Urban Planning* 166: 97–105.

Auerbach, J., S. Muñoz, U. Affiah, G. Barrera de la Torre, S. Börner, H. Cho, R. Cofield, C. M. DiEnno, G. Graddy-Lovelace, S. Klassen and V. Limeberry. 2022. 'Displacement of the scholar? Participatory action research under COVID-19', *Frontiers in Sustainable Food Systems* 16.

Batty, M., and S. Marshall. 2017. 'Thinking organic, acting civic: the paradox of planning for cities in evolution', *Landscape and Urban Planning* 166: 4–14.

Benneworth, P., R. Pinheiro and J. Karlsen. 2017. 'Strategic agency and institutional change: investigating the role of universities in regional innovation systems (RISs)', *Regional Studies* 51(2): 235–48.

Bolden III, E. C., T. M. Oestreich, M. J. Kenney and B. T. Yuhnke Jr. 2019. 'Location, location, location: a comparison of student experience in a lecture hall to a small classroom using similar techniques', *Active Learning in Higher Education* 20(2): 139–52.

Briassoulis, H. 1999. 'Who plans whose sustainability? Alternative roles for planners', *Journal of Environmental Planning and Management* 42(6): 889–902.

Bunce, L., and M. Bennett. 2021. 'A degree of studying? Approaches to learning and academic performance among student "consumers"', *Active Learning in Higher Education* 22(3): 203–14.

Campanyà, C., D. Fonseca, D. Amo, N. Martí and E. Peña. 2021. 'Mixed analysis of the flipped classroom in the concrete and steel structures subject in the context of COVID-19 crisis outbreak: a pilot study', *Sustainability* 13(11): 5826.

Cantor, A., V. DeLauer, D. Martin and J. Rogan. 2015. 'Training interdisciplinary "wicked problem" solvers: applying lessons from HERO in community-based research experiences for undergraduates', *Journal of Geography in Higher Education* 39(3): 407–19.

Carlson, T. 2007. 'A field-based learning experience for introductory level GIS students', *Journal of Geography* 106(5): 193–8.

Castán Broto, V., and L. Westman. 2019. *Urban Sustainability and Justice: Just sustainabilities and environmental planning*. London: Bloomsbury Publishing.

Cerra, J. F., B. W. Muller and R. F. Young. 2017. 'A transformative Outlook on the twenty-first century city: Patrick Geddes' Outlook Tower revisited', *Landscape and Urban Planning* 166: 90–6.

Chaudhuri, A. 2016. 'The real meaning of Rhodes Must Fall', *Guardian*, https://www.theguardian.com/uk-news/2016/mar/16/the-real-meaning-of-rhodes-must-fall (last accessed 29 November 2022).

Coelho, M., and I. Menezes. 2021. 'University social responsibility, service learning, and students' personal, professional, and civic education', *Frontiers in Psychology* 12: 436.

Cohen, N. 2010. 'Designing the sustainable foodshed: a cross-disciplinary undergraduate environmental studies course', *Innovative Higher Education* 35(1): 51–60.

Dale, J., and E. J. Hyslon-Margison. 2010. *Paulo Freire: teaching for freedom and transformation, the philosophical influences on the work of Paulo Freire*. London: Springer.

Dandekar, H. C. (ed.). 2019. *The Planner's Use of Information*. London: Routledge.

Esteban, M., T. Akiyama, C. Chen, I. Ikeda and T. Mino (eds). 2016. *Sustainability Science: field methods and exercises*. Cham: Springer International Publishing.

Foster, M. K., V. Fairbanks Taylor and J. L. Walker. 2021. *Experiential Exercise in the Classroom*. Northampton: Edward Elgar Publishing.

Frank, A. I. 2006. 'Three decades of thought on planning education', *Journal of Planning Literature* 21(1): 15–67.

Frank, A. I., I. Mironowicz, J. Lourenço, T. Franchini, P. Ache, M. Finka, B. Scholl and A. Grams. 2014. 'Educating planners in Europe: a review of 21st century study programmes', *Progress in Planning* 91: 0–94.

Freire, P. 1970. *Pedagogy of the Oppressed*. New York: Herder and Herder.

Freire, P. 1985. *The Politics of Education: culture, power, and liberation*. South Hadley MA: Bergin and Garvey.

Freire, P. 2014. *Pedagogy of Hope: reliving pedagogy of the oppressed*. London: Bloomsbury.

Geddes Institute for Urban Research (no date). *Patrick Geddes, 'Think globally act locally': The Outlook Tower*, https://www.dundee.ac.uk/geddesinstitute/outlooktower/ (last accessed 29 November 2022).

Geddes, P., R. LeGates and F. Stout. 2021. *Cities in Evolution*. London: Routledge.

Geels, F. W., F. Berkhout and D. P. Van Vuuren. 2016. 'Bridging analytical approaches for low-carbon transitions', *Nature Climate Change* 6(6): 576–83.

Gregg, M. 2012. 'The return of organisation man: commuter narratives and suburban critique', *Cultural Studies Review* 18(2): 242–61.

Hanson, J. M. 2015. 'Business education and the constructivist teaching debate'. In *Proceedings of 32nd International Business Research Conference* 23–25 November 2015, Rendezvous Hotel, Melbourne.

Hayden, D. 1997. *The Power of Place: landscapes as urban history*. Cambridge MA and London: MIT Press.

Healey, P. 1997. 'Traditions of planning thought'. In P. Healey (ed.), *Collaborative Planning*. Palgrave, London, 7–30.

Heffernan, K. 2001. 'Service-learning in higher education', *Journal of Contemporary Water Research and Education* 119(1): 2.

Heinen, D. 2020. 'Growth management for low-carbon development patterns–leverages in state planning enabling legislation', *Urban Research and Practice* 1–23: 72–93.

hooks, b. 1994. *Teaching to Transgress: engaged pedagogy as two-way learning*. New York: Routledge.

hooks, b. 2010. *Teaching Critical Thinking: practical wisdom*. Abingdon: Taylor and Francis.

Howarth, C., M. Lane and S. Fankhauser. 2021. 'What next for local government climate emergency declarations? The gap between rhetoric and action', *Climatic Change* 167(3): 1–22.

Jackson Lears, T. J. 1985. 'The concept of cultural hegemony: problems and possibilities', *The American Historical Review* 90(3): 567–93, https://doi.org/10.2307/1860957 (last accessed 29 November 2022).

John, P. 2006. 'Methodologies and research methods in urban political science'. In *The Comparative Study of Local Government and Politics: overview and synthesis (World of Political Science: development of the discipline)*. Opladen: Barbara Budrich Publishers

JustSpace. 2018. *Just Space: research protocol*, https://justspace.org.uk/history/research-protocol/ (last accessed 29 November 2022).

Kromydas, T. 2017. 'Rethinking higher education and its relationship with social inequalities: past knowledge, present state and future potential', *Palgrave Communications* 3(1): 1–12.

Leathwood, C., and B. Read. 2020. 'Short-term, short-changed? A temporal perspective on the implications of academic casualisation for teaching in higher education', *Teaching in Higher Education* 1–16.

Legacy, C. 2017. 'Is there a crisis of participatory planning?', *Planning Theory* 16(4): 425–42.

Lynch, K. 1984. *Good City Form*. Cambridge MA and London: MIT Press.

Makakavhule, K., and D. Hill. 2021. 'The role of planners in public open space production in contemporary African cities: a reinjection of the social agenda in planning practice', *Journal of Urban Design*, https://doi.org/10.1080/13574809.2021.2014308 (last accessed 29 November 2022).

Manzo, L., and P. Devine-Wright. 2013. *Place Attachment: advances in theory, methods and applications*. Abingdon: Routledge.

Marouli, C., A. Misseyanni, P. Papadopoulou and M. D. Lytras. 2018. 'A new vision for higher education: lessons from education for the environment and sustainability'. In *Active Learning Strategies in Higher Education*. Bingley: Emerald Publishing Limited.

McLean, J. E. 2015. 'The contingency of change in the Anthropocene: more-than-real renegotiation of power relations in climate change institutional transformation in Australia', *Environment and Planning D: Society and Space* 34(4): 508–27.

Moffitt, E. 2018. 'Michael Rakowitz: the invisible enemy', *Frieze*, https://www.frieze.com/article/michael-rakowitz-invisible-enemy (last accessed 29 November 2022).

Natarajan, L. 2017. 'Socio-spatial learning: a case study of community knowledge in participatory spatial planning', *Progress in Planning* 111: 1–23.

Ostrom, E. 2010. 'Polycentric systems for coping with collective action and global environmental change', *Global Environmental Change* 20(4): 550–7.

Öztürk, M. N., and E. E. Türkkan. 2006. 'The Design Studio as Teaching/Learning Medium: a process-based approach', *International Journal of Art & Design Education* 25(1): 96–104.

Patnaik, H. A. 2021. 'Gender and participation in community based adaptation: evidence from the decentralized climate funds project in Senegal', *World Development* 142: 105448.

Patrick, L. E. 2020. 'Faculty and student perceptions of active learning'. In *Active Learning in College Science*. Cham: Springer, 889–907.

Pattacini, L. 2018. 'Experiential Learning: the field study trip, a student-centred curriculum', *Compass: Journal of Learning and Teaching* 11(2): 2.

Payne D. 1999. 'Composition, interdisciplinary collaboration, and the postindustrial concern', *JAC* 19(4): 607–32.

Rademaekers, J. K. 2015. 'Is WAC/WID ready for the transdisciplinary research university?', *Across the Disciplines* 12(2): 1–14.

Rees, W. E. 2017. 'Planning in the Anthropocene'. In V. W. Michael Gunder and Ali Madanipour (eds), *The Routledge Handbook of Planning Theory*. London: Routledge, 53–66.

Rodwin, L., and B. Sanyal (eds). 2000. *The Profession of City Planning: changes, images, and challenges 1950–2000*. New Brunswick NJ: Transaction Publishers.

Roij, A. B. 2018. 'The Pedagogical Legacy of Dorothy Lee and Paulo Freire'. In *Active Learning Strategies in Higher Education*. Bingley: Emerald Publishing Limited.

Rooij, R., and A. Frank. 2016. 'Educating spatial planners for the age of co-creation: the need to risk community, science and practice involvement in planning programmes and curricula', *Planning Practice and Research* 31(5): 473–85.

Rydin, Y. 2007. 'Re-examining the role of knowledge within planning theory', *Planning Theory* 6(1): 52–68.

Salama, A. M. 2015. *Spatial Design Education: new directions for pedagogy in architecture and beyond* (1st edn). London: Routledge, https://doi.org/10.4324/9781315610276 (last accessed 29 November 2022).

Salama, A. M. 2010. 'Delivering theory courses in architecture: inquiry based, active, and experiential learning integrated', *ArchNet-IJAR: International Journal of Architectural Research* 4(2–3): 278–95.

Sanyal, B. 1989. 'Poor countries' students in rich countries' universities: possibilities of planning education in the 21st century', *Journal of Planning Education and Research* 8(3): 139–55.

Schmitt, P., and T. Wiechmann. 2018. 'Unpacking spatial planning as the governance of place: extracting potentials for future advancements in planning research', *disP – The Planning Review* 54(4): 21–33.

Schweitzer, L. A., E. J. Howard and I. Doran. 2008). 'Planners learning and creating power: a community of practice approach', *Journal of Planning Education and Research* 28(1): 50–60.

Scott, H., and S. Moloney. 2022. 'Completing the climate change adaptation planning cycle: monitoring and evaluation by local government in Australia', *Journal of Environmental Planning and Management* 65(4): 650–74.

Sharma, M. 2022. 'Understanding the impact of social learning forms on environmentally sustainable consumption behavior among school children', *International Journal of Educational Management* (ahead of print).

Sullivan, A., D. D. White and M. Hanemann. 2019. 'Designing collaborative governance: insights from the drought contingency planning process for the lower Colorado River basin', *Environmental Science and Policy* 91: 39–49.

Sumartojo, S. 2013. 'The Fourth Plinth: creating and contesting national identity in Trafalgar Square, 2005–2010', *Cultural Geographies* 20(1): 67–81.

Trede, F., and D. Jackson. 2021. 'Educating the deliberate professional and enhancing professional agency through peer reflection of work-integrated learning', *Active Learning in Higher Education* 22(3): 171–87.

Tuan, Y. 1997. 'Sense of place; what does it mean to be human?', *American Journal of Theology and Philosophy* 18(1): 47–58.

Vaughan, L. 2015. *Suburban Urbanities*. London: UCL Press.

Walters, R. G. 1980. 'Signs of the times: Clifford Geertz and historians', *Social Research* 47(3): 537–56.

Whyte, W. H. 1956. *The Organization Man*. New York: Simon and Shuster.

Wildemeersch, D., and J. Vandenabeele. 2007. 'Relocating social learning as a democratic practice'. In *Democratic Practices as Learning Opportunities*. Leiden: Brill, 19–32.

Winkler, T. 2013. 'At the coalface: community–university engagements and planning education', *Journal of Planning Education and Research* 33(2): 215–27.

Young, R. A., and R. Ewing. 2020. '3 Types of Research'. In R. Ewing and K. Park (eds), *Basic Quantitative Research Methods for Urban Planners*. London: Routledge, 46–60.

Section I
Reviewing curricula

In this first section, the focus is on the engaged urban pedagogy activity of 'reviewing curricula', where teaching and learning in universities is evaluated in ways that can be considered 'participatory'. The participatory perspective here relates to ideals of inclusivity and how they manifest within built environment higher education. They speak to the need to include the diversity of people and knowledges both within the practices of education and in current urban processes. The authors reflect on their own activities around the re-design of curricula and assessments, and share details of how their approaches to reviewing have changed. In their work, they draw connections to the urban realities of today and the need to promote equality within opportunities provided by urban development and education. They consider issues of experience that cut across socio-economic, racial, gender and sexuality, as well as the agency of students in their own education. Their work suggests that there is great potential for participatory reviewing to connect to these participatory agendas by opening up the sets of knowledge and skills that are brought to bear. In extending the study of active learning into reviewing, the positionality of the student is foregrounded and situated in relation to urban development challenges. The exchanges between teachers, students and non-academics, demonstrate the fluidity of learners and learning processes within evaluations of built environment higher education.

There are four chapters in this section. The first two chapters present recent work at UCL focusing on race, gender and sexuality, which are historically bound up with social injustice in urban development practices. They set out the importance of the multiple intersecting categories and the need to make these more visible within the curricula. The activities are participatory in that they explicitly bring in a range of actors beyond faculty; question whose evaluations have been shaping university and urban practices; and seek to expand the set of people and knowledges that are given consideration.

In Chapter 2, Beebeejaun and Ortiz set out their own work in moving built environment curricula towards greater inclusion of issues of racial justice in both pedagogy and practice. The initiative *Race and Space* emerged from the involvement of an interdisciplinary group of students and staff, including academics and academic services professionals. The collaboration sought to tackle the invisibility of race in urban planning education, which is a matter of great concern as that form of marginalisation is not only invidious but serves to intensify continuing problems of racism in the practices of urban development. Race has great relevance given the international nature of urban development cultures, as well as staff and students' own ethnic diversity and lived experiences of built environment higher education. The *Race and Space* collaboration articulated the importance of speaking openly and confidently about race, particularly vis-à-vis students' positionality in the urban world and the structural effects of institutional silence on racism and the ethical dimensions of professional skills. They reflect on educational spaces where the absence of thinking on race and ethnic diversity has been perpetuated over time. Acknowledgement of past harms and racism is framed as part of the transformative action, and discussions with students and staff matter to create opportunities for change. Critical thinking about urban practices might also be shored up with skills in urban ethnography. However, in hearing about racial diversity and existing sensibilities, the authors stress it is important to avoid extractive learning practices, whereby communities are 'learned from' but do not themselves benefit.

Following on from this, in Chapter 3, Lessard *et al.* explore ways in which spatial processes can construct and impact on experiences in relation to gender and sexual identities. This collaborative project, *Queering the Curriculum*, includes university actors, again bringing in diverse staff and students as a means to address issues of breadth of engagement in places and in learning. Drawing inspiration from the *Race and Space* agenda outlined in the previous chapter, the authors seek to illuminate the underlying forces behind commonly accepted ways of knowing, teaching and learning through a queer lens. Challenging established power structures, the authors draw on queer pedagogies to highlight the imperative to disrupt hierarchies and established ways of thinking. They reveal how the norms and expectations impact on students and place experience, and reflect on how those within the institutions of higher education can redress the situation. The chapter concludes with a call to action; investigating, amplifying and representing queer lives in curricula will not only be more representative of the student and staff bodies but, more fundamentally, it will encourage critical learning and reflection.

In other words, queering the curriculum is a strong mechanism of, and for, transformation.

These forms of critical pedagogy operate at a strategic level in universities. In relation to race, the modern history of colonisation of industrial development that defines major 'global cities' prefigured the rapid urbanisation and underlies present sustainability and climate concerns. Remembering bell hooks' lessons on engaged learning, this underscores the importance of evaluating the cultures in higher education with learners' identities in mind and their positionality in the present globalised context of urban development. Queering the curriculum practices, where representation diversity of experience and continual reflexivity on those practices, provide a beacon of active learning in the institution. By espousing and extending the *Race and Space* agenda, the LGBTQ+ collaboration also provides a live demonstration of the value of solidarity with agendas of 'others' in urban development.

In Chapter 4, Moore and Xypaki present their work on co-designed educational assessments, where students and non-academics share in the evaluations of teaching and learning. They stress the context dependency of learning and the need for value beyond the higher education institution. As such, the transfer of skills between communities and students is in itself a key outcome.

Again, this work provides insights on participation in reviewing, but it delves deeper into the role of the individual student. Moore and Xypaki's work helps position the inclusion of students' perspectives as a critical element in co-producing evaluations of higher education. The lessons point to the learning value of an active learning approach for the wider world and the challenges of self review where there are diverse learners.

The fourth chapter provides lessons from a study of the landscape of planning education in South Africa, undertaken by a collaboration between universities in England and South Africa, which Denoon-Stevens *et al.* have undertaken. The mission of reviewing the education system draws on their research into planning. There are multiple layers to their enquiry around the need for more inclusive urban governance. They consider the exigencies of informal urban development and poverty, as well as sustainability concerns, politics of institutions of governance and the work of professional planners.

Denoon-Stevens *et al.* highlight a disconnect between the planning systems and the realities of urban experience, particularly for people living in informal settlements who are not well involved in urban governance. In considering the social dimensions of cities, as well as issues of sustainability, and the fast-paced nature of change in urban development, it becomes clear that priorities must change. The places where development attention is focused are not those of the greatest need and the nature of urban challenges in those places do not lend themselves to the sets of knowledge in use in planning. So, the search is on for education that can promote practices that are more compatible with excluded residents' lived experiences. This would require that students have critical understandings of the nature of social divisions and specific urban governance contexts, and the capacities needed for understanding marginalised places and engaging with previously marginalised social groups. For this reason, the authors call for an education that can nurture skills of citizen engagement and understandings of social divisions in cities. This means that the ask of higher education suggested here is one of indirect advocacy, via awareness of urban systems and capacities for professional interactions, which is directed at changing processes of planning and empowering the student as a future planner.

2
Race and space: a pedagogic intervention

Yasminah Beebeejaun and Catalina Ortiz

> Engaged pedagogy necessarily values student expression. (hooks, 1994: 20)
>
> The argument was always that European colonialism was and continues to be a shaping force of modern history and pedagogy, and that this is overlooked – particularly in Britain – in our education system out of discomfort with the truth that it harbours and the reality that it reveals. (Bhambra *et al.*, 2018: 23)
>
> Racism, specifically, is the state-sanctioned or extralegal production and exploitation of groups differentiated vulnerability to premature death. (Gilmore, 2007: 247)

In 2018, the authors met with several colleagues at the Bartlett Faculty of the Built Environment and the Institute of Education at UCL to discuss how to take forward equality and diversity concerns within teaching programmes. Our team is a collaboration between seven people: four members of academic staff, two doctoral students and one member of professional services staff. The process that unfolded over a series of meetings and collaborative writing ended with the production of a freely available document that the team wanted to resonate not just with staff and students at UCL, but with wider audiences. Our group included academic staff in the Bartlett School of Architecture, the Bartlett School of Planning, and the Development Planning Unit, which all have significant research experience on race and ethnicity, alongside a member of professional services staff and two doctoral students, one in Architecture and the other in the Institute of Education. Our discussions were convened by Vice-Dean for Equality Diversity and Inclusion, Kamna Patel, but the process of developing and writing the resource was collaborative and non-hierarchical. The title came from our wider discussions – *'Race' and Space: what is 'race' doing in a nice field like the built environment?* – and was intended to be thought-provoking and challenge the normative niceties of a field that actively sidelines discussion around race.

Despite the increasing profile of issues of race and exclusion, in our discussion the team agreed that race remained largely absent from the classroom in built environment disciplines in the United Kingdom. Although it formed part of our own research and pedagogic practice, the team also understood that some educators felt reticent to discuss the issues in the classroom. However, collectively we were aware of instances where students thought important topics of race had been mishandled by teachers or that other students had made stereotypical statements about race and ethnic identity that went unchallenged. The team understood that some may be reluctant to engage with the topic, but we also considered teaching to be a space where we have a professional responsibility to engage with equality both as an important pedagogic topic but in thinking about interpersonal interactions in the classroom. The team wanted to support pedagogic practices that addressed race but also contributed to empowerment and the capacity to challenge others in the classroom. We wanted our initiative to explore how to get a better understanding and ability to imagine how to dismantle the racial disparities embedded in the institutional settings and the built environment where they operate (Ortiz, 2020).

Race is too important an issue to remain sidelined within urban pedagogy. The 2014 UCL student organised event *Why isn't my professor Black?* forms part of a wider landscape concerned with how to decolonise universities and spans political and pedagogic practices. Despite race being a central dimension to the production of the built environment, it has all too often been consigned to the margins of education and research in the British context (see Gale and Thomas, 2020, for a discussion) despite a wealth of work in postcolonial and settler-colonial contexts (see, e.g., Njoh, 2009; Porter, 2010; Winkler, 2018). The nexus between the British imperial project, coloniality and racial capitalism has been overlooked in the ways we conceive urban pedagogy to date in British planning education (see Beebeejaun, 2021).

In this chapter, the authors set out some of the challenges and possibilities for urban pedagogy that engages with race, identity and practices of exclusion drawing on our reflections from developing our *Race and Space* syllabus. Teaching and working in London, at the heart of former colonial metropoles, we are keenly aware of the tensions of seeking to challenge Eurocentric knowledge within a British university (Bhambra *et al.*, 2018; Gopal, 2021). The lack of engagement with race within our respective disciplines of architecture, development studies, urban education, and urban planning rooted within an imperial history reflect the decolonial challenge. The authors start by sketching out some of the limitations within the discipline's approach to race and space in professional and aligned education settings. We then turn to our open-access syllabus, *Race and Space*, that emerged from our collaborative work. Finally, we turn to the wider implications and directions for engaged urban pedagogy. We argue that turning attention to these challenges is not only necessary to open up and challenge the Eurocentric histories of the built environment professions but a necessary step to future practice.

Race and space

Our frustrations with the lack of material in the British context led to our decisions to collectively author *Race and Space*. The aim of this curriculum is to provide an accessible set of resources mainly for students and teachers interested in questioning racial disparities in the myriad disciplines linked to the built environment. The team wanted to not only identify the many barriers and challenges, the absences and neglect of race and racism, but to also consider alternative futures and possibilities given the nature of our disciplines, ones concerned with the everyday material experience of urban denizens, as well as creating inclusive urban futures. To do this, we knew we could not restrict our materials to academic articles and books, we needed to go much further into thinking about how race and space are intimately intertwined and how that experience is lived.

For many of our intended audience being racialised is a familiar lived experience, but the team also wanted to reach out to all students. By asking people to reflect and engage with their own experiences or challenge their preconceptions, we hoped to create a space for personal reflection as a starting point (see also Knapp, 2021). We decided to divide our curriculum into six sections with their respective trigger questions to navigate incrementally each part:

- Encounters with race: what racial encounters have you had?
- Racialised landscapes: where are you located?
- Race becomes place: does 'race' affect where you feel you belong?
- The colouring of space: can you see 'race' in cultural symbols around you?
- Speculative futures: what is the future you can imagine?
- Call to action: what are you going to do?

The curriculum emerged as a short book that offered a series of self-guided commentaries along with an extensive list of further resources within academic texts, films, artworks and other forms of writing. While our work is offered as a self-guided resource, we drew on our experiences of those difficult discussions about race in the classroom and beyond. The team conceived the curriculum as an open resource. We wanted to ask readers to reflect not only on the absence of race within their discipline, but to observe how race is constructed in London, both in the city and in the university.

Questioning the values within planning and our own positionality was an important starting point for developing our curriculum. However, there are challenges in asking people to do so and it is fraught with complexities. Thus, in our opening section 'encounters with race' we asked readers to reflect on their own experiences. We were mindful that a majority of UCL students are international, and we have many students from mainland China. While these form a diverse group, it is likely that many of them have experienced being an ethnic majority but that their experience of being in London, despite its diversity, may throw questions of ethnicity into sharper relief. Through each section, we wanted to be alert to different representations and their power to give meaning in ways that open up rather than instruct.

Our resources included academic articles and books but went beyond that to fiction and films (see Lung-Aman *et al.*, 2015). Resources were selected by members of the group who wrote short summaries for the syllabus. These were materials that members of the group had found meaningful in some way and that offered important representations and insights into racialised and intersectional experiences. There were limits on what could be included but we turned to a series of novels and films that speak to the particularities of being racialised. The team called them primary sources as this material engaged with popular culture and everyday narratives that allow an entry point de-linked from academic language.

Planning, race, pedagogy

Race is central to the production of the built environment (Bhandar, 2018) but within the United Kingdom there remains a small field of scholarship examining British planning in relation to race, racial minorities and the racialised production of space (see Beebeejaun, 2021; Beebeejaun *et al.*, 2021, CRE/RTPI, 1983; Gale and Thomas, 2020; Thomas, 2004 for a discussion). Very little has been written about the teaching of race, racial inequality and racism in urban planning education in the British context. This reflects the ongoing marginalisation of race and ethnicity within urban planning. Up until the 1980s much of the discussion around race was framed around migration and the challenges of 'accommodating' racially different people despite their status as British citizens and members of the Commonwealth (see Patel, 2021). The Royal Town Planning Institute (RTPI), planning's professional accreditation institute, was involved in one of the first significant interventions in 1983 along with the Commission for Racial Equality (CRE) (which merged to form the Equalities and Human Rights Commission in 2007). The report *Planning for a Multiracial Britain*, jointly commissioned by the RTPI and the CRE, found that there was limited understanding of race and racism in the professional activity of planning. Moreover, the absence of an understanding of 'race' contributed to a planners' believing that the discipline's purported public interest role meant that racism was not an issue that planning had to contend with. The lack of critical reflection is surprising given that the Scarman Report had been published in November 1981 and remains one of the most significant government inquiries into the inequalities faced by people of colour in Britain. The Scarman Report followed the Brixton Riots, which were spurred by the inequality and racism that Black communities were facing in everyday life, and looked at racist policing practices but fell short of acknowledging institutional racism. The RTPI/CRE report found that 'the planning system could become an arena for sometimes crude and sometimes unwitting discriminatory attitudes and practice' (Thomas, 2008: 1). Despite initiatives in several local authorities, a follow-up survey commissioned by the RTPI showed little progress in engaging with racial justice within professional practice just 10 years later (see Thomas and Krishnarayan, 1994).

Understanding how racism is institutionalised remains contested in Britain. The Metropolitan Police Force was charged with institutional racism in the 1999 Macpherson Inquiry for its handling of the criminal investigation into the racist murder of the Black British teenager Stephen Lawrence in 1993. However, many public services grabbed hold of the term 'unwitting racism' to suggest that the racism lacked agency or intent, instead of engaging with the embedded structures of racism. The planning scholars Richard Gale and Huw Thomas recently reflected that there is little evidence that the discipline has progressed the understanding of race over the past 40 years. Our work and reflections concur with this assessment. We now turn to how the framing of the discipline around race has sidestepped questions of power and the continuing absence of engagement with structural racism as part of spatial practices undermines efforts to address equality.

The continuing neglect of the topic in British urban planning is surprising given the extensive field of work that has examined the ongoing coloniality of planning and the impact on settler-colonial societies (see, e.g., Roy 2006; Porter 2000, 2006). Despite these important interventions, the absence of clear connections to race and space in our own British and wider European context create significant challenges for an urban pedagogy fit to engage with some of the most important political and social issues in contemporary cities. In this context, decolonisation aims at undoing the colonial matrix of power 'understood as the oppressive and imperial bent of modern European ideals projected to, and enacted in, the non-European world' (Mignolo, 2009: 39). At the same time effective urban pedagogy emphasises inclusion and engagement, underpinning ideas of ethical professionals able to tackle a multitude of challenges spanning from social justice to tackling climate change (see Frank and da Rosa Pires, 2021; Peel and Frank, 2005).

These challenges are significant and beyond the scope of any one profession. However, urban pedagogic practice must be alert to the embedded assumptions about race identity and the complex racial history of the United Kingdom. The RTPI has recently centred efforts on increasing diversity, yet all too often these concerns displace attention away from racism and do not dismantle structural inequalities. Sara Ahmed's (2007: 605) discussion in the context of the university problematises this shift, noting that 'We could describe diversity as a politics of feeling good which allows people to relax and feel less threatened as if we have already "solved it"'. While addressing the diversity of the profession itself and more inclusive engagement and participation are important goals, they conceal a longstanding complacency with the normative historiography of planning. Planning's imperial history often remains unspoken in British debates and accounts. The retreat from engaging with racism and structural inequality and the embrace of diversity conceals the necessity of a fuller engagement with the imperial and colonial history that enabled the British planning discipline to prosper (see also Beebeejaun, 2021). This silence is complicit. It is long overdue for planning practice and education to engage explicitly with the struggles and debates around racial justice in pedagogy and practice.

The aspirations of planning education are important and, where they have turned to race, it is now centred on aspirations to diversify the people that comprise the profession. These are important aims given that evidence on the racial and ethnic composition of the UK planning profession remains gloomy, although there have been significant increases in gender equality (in numbers) over the past few decades. However, only 7 per cent of RTPI members are from BAME groups, against a national average of 14 per cent (2011 Census), although the institute estimate that only 3 per cent are chartered (professional accredited to practice) (RTPI, 2019).

Questions of representation are important and the desire to increase the proportion of ethnic minority planners is welcome. However, there is a contradiction between the ongoing assertion that planners are neutral and able to sit out highly controversial events that reinforce racial inequality and a purported assertion that the discipline strives to be racially inclusive. This is exemplified by a recent comment on 'How the RTPI is tackling inequality' in April 2021 following the publication of the widely discredited government-commissioned Sewell Report, which asserted that institutional racism did not exist in the United Kingdom. The RTPI set out the government's assertion that the report was mispresented. However, it offered no substantive criticism, although a series of individuals and organisations – including the British Medical Association – condemned the report. Baroness Lawrence, prominent anti-racism campaigner and politician, and mother of Stephen Lawrence, said that the Sewell Report gave 'the green light to racists'. The chief executive of the RTPI instead said, 'While the Royal Town Planning Institute (RTPI) chose not to get drawn into the specifics of the argument, I felt it was, nonetheless, important to state that we, as an Institute, recognise that inequality still exists in the UK and there is much work to be done' (RTPI, 2021).

These types of statement raise a series of challenges for the pedagogic environment into which students enter. Recognising inequality is a starting point but, despite decades since the Macpherson Inquiry, institutions still seem to struggle to address racism. If students come from minority groups they may find a broad aspiration towards diversity but little substance in how this may be addressed and a reticence to engage with racism. Educators must then question the inclusivity and anti-racist commitment of our discipline. Questions are raised about both how racism is understood by planners and the sincerity of any anti-racist initiatives.[1] Aspirations towards a more diverse profession may be important, but there remains little evidence in terms of race and ethnicity within those that make up the profession and within the academic faculty of built environment programmes.

Urban planning pedagogy will not get far if planners seek to abstract race and inequality and present them as ahistorical 'facts' that the discipline can distance itself from. It will also struggle if the accrediting professional body remains blind to the contribution that planning can offer racial inequality. As Ortiz (2020) puts it, 'We all need to unlearn white privilege. It becomes an imperative that cannot longer wait to ask how that privilege has not only produced the absence of certain voices, bodies, views and sensibilities but the systemic oppression of racialised minorities in the field' (Ortiz, 2020: 57). It is in the specifics of the argument where we can understand the role of planning and planners in mediating forms of spatial inequality within its colonial history and in British planning. To suggest otherwise is to sustain the false narrative of planning's normative legacy, something that is fundamental to challenge in pedagogic and research interventions.

North American scholarship is an important referent given that planning schools and the professional accreditation board have looked to inclusion and diversity within programmes since the 1990s (Sweet and Etienne, 2011). However, scholars have identified an ongoing contradiction between these professional exhortations and both pedagogic practice and student experience within professional planning schools. Sweet and Etienne point out the lack of a clear definition of what it means to take diversity into account within curricula (2011: 34), warning that 'Women and people of colour being on the front lines of diversity pedagogy and curriculum has its drawback'. Diversity is all too often praised in the abstract, but when educators try to make specific engagements with questions of racism, sexism or discrimination either within the institution or the profession they experience hostility.

The planning scholars Garcia and colleagues have recently made an important series of interventions into student experiences of diversity. They explore the contradictions emergent in spaces that aspire to diversity and inclusion, but which create tensions and barriers for people of colour. Based on a survey of 451 students and 14 interviews, they conclude:

The survey and interviews with African American and Latinx students highlight the lack of diverse faculty and students, the Eurocentric curriculum, limited pedagogical styles, and a hostile classroom setting, all of which effectively erase African American and Latinx voices from the classroom. The subtle and everyday forms of racism described above create an environment that directly contradicts the claims planning programs make about their learning objectives. The inability of the faculty to facilitate meaningful conversation further exacerbates the problem. The classroom experience contributes to African American and Latinx students feeling alienated, tokenized, and dismissed in planning programs. These feelings lead some students to stop speaking and others to modify how they contribute. Alternatively, if students participate and share their opinions, they are left feeling responsible for calling out ignorance or experience eventual fatigue in addressing these comments. (Garcia, *et al.*, 2021: 116)

While universities have been implementing broader equality and diversity reforms, including responding to calls for diversified and decolonised curriculum, the broader learning experience, including the everyday learning experience of diverse students, has been relegated to the background in planning studies (see Garcia *et al.*, 2021; Denoon-Stevens *et al.*, 2020 for notable exceptions). The studies show that students from minority groups face challenges in planning education and do not find that the educative experience reflects their understanding of communities or their aspirations of social justice in more concrete ways.

It is important to exercise caution towards claims that the existing pedagogic framework tends towards inclusion or equality, given that the professional institute, which accredits academic programmes, has demonstrated a rather confused approach to race and planning and demonstrated limited leadership in tackling racism. These reflections emphasise the importance of not assuming that diversity or inclusion initiatives necessarily lead to a more critically aware classroom. Having more people of colour in the classroom and profession may reveal the embedded neglect or even hostility to understanding race and racism within the majority ethnic group.

Towards a more critical engaged pedagogy?

Engaged pedagogy asks us to consider learning, inclusion and empowerment. It draws from a series of sometimes disparate values, goals and aspirations. A critical engaged pedagogy needs to resonate with Brazilian thinker Paulo Freire's ideas to further the commitment to work towards a radical democracy by bringing 'students' worldview into the educational process' (1993: 77) under the premise that 'the pedagogic practice requires an understanding of the genesis of knowledge itself' (1996: 137). Engaged pedagogy, of course, has more radical roots and the work of radical scholars including bell hooks turn towards the liberatory force of education. Bell hooks was influenced by Freire's vision of liberatory learning, and she contrasts that to her own educative experiences. She writes that the classroom can be empowering only if it is a space where 'Progressive professors [work] to transform the curriculum so it does not reflect biases or reinforce systems of domination' (1994: 21). Given the importance and significance of the built environment professions to the place-making of cities and urban spaces, it is essential that educators understand power relations within and between communities, as well as inequalities generated through racial, gender, sexual and other forms of difference in ways that encompass the role of institutions and disciplines.

Engaged pedagogy brings with it risks and challenges in finding different ways of educating beyond the classroom. But planning is well placed to do this given the longevity of community planning and the centrality of participation. North American planning education has long prioritised forms of what it terms 'service-based learning' through projects that work directly with communities (Forsyth *et al.*, 2000; Angotti, *et al.*, 2011; Botchwey and Umemoto, 2021), framing a critical engaged pedagogy as something that educators must engage with if we are to hope to decolonise the field and as part and parcel of a broader struggle for epistemic justice that is:

> a struggle that demands equality between knowledges and contest the order of knowledge imposed by the West … They contest the Western-patriarchal economic ideology that turned women, Black people, Indigenous people, and people from Asia and Africa into inferior beings marked by the absence of reason, beauty, or a mind capable of technical and scientific discovery' (Verges, 2021: 13).

Decolonisation is both an aspiration and a set of practices that asks us to bring our own reflexivity as educators in our specific field to a dialogue with both our students and the institutional and disciplinary landscapes in which educators work. In some ways these may appear to mesh well with the wider aspirations of the built environment professions that have turned to the challenges of community engagement. Drawing from these debates, Ortiz and Millan (2022) have developed the concept of critical urban pedagogy understood as a 'situated pedagogy derived from everyday relations of place, body and materiality infused by memory and articulated by storytelling' (Ortiz and Millan, 2022: 822).

The relationship between planners and the wider communities that they ostensibly serve has remained under intense scrutiny since the critiques that crystallised in the 1960s (see, e.g., Arnstein, 1969). The outcomes of planning were argued to be failing communities and instead embedding further gendered and racial inequalities within urban renewal and development programmes (see Sandercock, 1998, 2003). These have spurred a series of theoretical and practice-based interventions around what could be loosely termed collaborative and participatory planning (Healey, 1997). Educational programmes must move beyond the nascent planner as expert and reflect on planning's relationship with communities. At the same time, British universities have increasingly marketised as part of a broader neoliberal shift in higher education. These multiple pressures on planning education emphasise a bewildering array of competencies:

> future planners are to be facilitators and coordinators of change – change agents who empower others, co-create and co-shape urban districts, neighbourhoods and spatial development trajectories. There is also a need for more integration and merging of different traditions into single innovative and visionary programmes and developments. (Frank and Rosa Pires, 2021: 3)

Such intentions, while laudable, highlight the tensions about the extent to which planners are able to decentre themselves away from claims of expertise that now are able to co-ordinate and choreograph the activities of others.

There is a recognition that planners must work with communities and also seek to understand them as part of a transformative practice for both groups. The planning literature on urban pedagogy remains largely hopeful for positive transformation, yet the articulations around pedagogy in urban studies remain sparse (Ortiz and Millan, 2022). Agyeman and Erikson (2012) set out the concept of cultural competency as a way to reconceptualise how planners and planning students should think about difference and diversity. Instead of the emphasis on the 'problems' presented in working with marginalised groups, '*proactively* [engage] with diversity and [promote] intercultural relations', whereby 'recognition of difference and different cultures may lead not to *equality* of treatment for all but to *different* treatment based on the particular difference and cultural needs' (2012: 5, emphasis in original). Developing cultural competency requires supported pedagogic learning/interventions. However, educators must be attentive to the different life experiences and identities of our students and these difficult conversations. Lung-Aman (2015: 338) and colleagues point to the specific neglect and discomfort of engaging with topics of race and the lack of critical reflection that students may have of their own positionality.

Asking students to reflect on their racialised identities and how they have been formulated and are reinforced in urban space is instructive. Training students to be race critical also requires that they develop skills in urban ethnography. They must learn to see the ways in which race has and continues to construct urban parks, playgrounds, neighbourhoods, cities, civic spaces and everyday social relations.

The 'white gaze' has defined what counts as the canon of the discipline making 'other' perspectives not apt or legitimate enough to be integral part of that 'canon'. As educators we ought to ask ourselves what is the responsibility of urban planning in the reproduction of racial inequalities and the symbolic and physical violence that it entails? (Ortiz, 2020). That is why it is imperative to begin changing our curricula and more substantively centring anti-racist praxis.

Reflections

This chapter has argued that curricula design is one crucial entry point to address the intended absence of discussions around racial justice in the classroom in built environment disciplines in the United Kingdom. Opening up other ways of understanding and knowing the city is critical to urban pedagogy. However, it cannot be done in abstract ways that do not consider lived differences and the racial inequalities that exist. The geographer McFarlane (2011) emphasises the importance of 'dialogic exchange' that is attentive to the power relations in forms between actors within the city. He notes that:

> The critical purchase of conceptualisations of urban learning lies not in a straightforward call to know *more* of cities, but to expose, evaluate and democratise the politics of learning cities by placing learning explicitly at the heart of urban planning debate. (30)

Here, McFarlane makes a critical point about the nature and purpose of learning. While attempts to engage communities are important and vital, educators must always be cautious about how these activities unfold on the ground. A major critique has been that these types of research or inquiry project can become extractive endeavours, taking community knowledge and then repurposing it to give legitimacy to planning. Thus, the call for urban learning must form part of a more reflexive and critical endeavour that places us and our students within these spaces. While McFarlane is commenting on these power gaps between communities and professionals, we extend this to thinking about the heterogeneity within the existing and future profession. Seeking to encourage those from marginalised groups to enter the planning discipline is reckless if educators fail to critically interrogate the spaces of whiteness and do not address anti-racism inside and outside the classroom.

It is no accident that our co-authors are all deeply concerned about race and pedagogy as well as actively researching and writing in the subject area. Our decisions to make this critical pedagogic intervention result not only from our broader research and praxis, but from our own frustrations at the striking absence of race from mainstream planning and urban development discourses in the United Kingdom. We thought it important to turn to the future goals and aspirations of the discipline and to centre the agency of the reader, ending with speculative futures and a call to action. Our curriculum ended with the importance of pedagogy, rethinking the canon and political activism as intersecting dimensions of the struggle for racial equality and challenge Eurocentric knowledge production. To challenge this perspective, Sweet (2018) suggests engaging in 'cultural humility' in planning education to reach beyond 'cultural competence' as it is:

> linked to colonial thinking and Western dominance, specifically in placing practitioners in the position of knower and Others in the position of known … The power dynamics such a competent/incompetent framework are socially constructed but have real-world consequences for the subjects of planning. A risk of cultural competence in planning is the preservation of the status quo and a lack of acknowledgement of the impacts of Western cultural imperialism. (n.p.)

The 'race' and space curriculum also requires its use to build on the notion of cultural humility. We see this effort as a first step to promote solidarity with the collectives doing anti-racist work and to foster new imaginations among all interested in challenging the *status quo* of planning education. Situating the problematic histories of planning need not be a location from which action becomes impossible but should be one of transformative work if we can acknowledge these pasts.

The planning theorist Porter cautions us not to become complacent in our perspective. She questions the wide-ranging literature whereby 'positive reflexivity and qualities of personal interaction as key to enacting transformative planning practice' rests on 'the adequacy of relying on the "goodwill" of planning practitioners'. Rather, Porter urges us to do something much riskier and more uncertain; namely, 'unlearning one's privilege'. By opening the door to our well-meant intentions we engage in something riskier but potentially transformative – to question the values inherent in our practice. This connects with what bell hooks refers to as 'self-interrogation' and what Sweet calls 'locating oneself', as it 'lays the groundwork for cultural humility and strengthens the potential for "radicality" – opening opportunities to create equal partnerships and decenter the power of the expert' (2018, n.p.). This was put in motion in the making of the 'race' and space curricula, where the team that co-created it included not only teaching staff but also representatives of students and academic services. This gesture also points towards challenging where the intellectual capacities lie in higher education. Universities constitute all its members and as such we also need to learn how to work together to explore the underlying presumptions within disciplinary practice.

Bell hooks reminds us that engaged pedagogy can only hope to work if both educators and students are open to learning. Our decision to provide this curriculum was not to suggest that this is the only way that 'race and space' can be taught, but to provide a useful resource for students and educators. There are challenges in addressing the history of the discipline and challenging current conceptions where race is left as an abstract topic or one deemed difficult to engage with. However, without doing the work of understanding and turning to the legacy and ongoing ways in which British planning has harmed ethnic and racial minorities, the discipline will struggle to meaningfully engage with the possibilities of a socially and racially just urban future. These conversations are potentially uncomfortable, but incomparable to the legacy of colonial thinking that underpins the British planning discipline and creates inhospitable environments for scholars and students of colour as well as those concerned with racial equity.

The role of city-making and urban knowledge production in the perpetuation of racial violence continue to form blind spots in several disciplines dealing with the built environment. Therefore, the commitment to challenge the white supremacy built into the curriculum requires urgent action. However, there is no single approach to tackling these deeply embedded issues. Rather, collaboration and openness to learning is a necessary precondition. With the resources compiled in the *'Race' and Space* booklet,[2] educators can find different ways to link their pedagogical strategies with the myriad primary and secondary sources offered. In sharing these reflections, our hope is that the syllabus provides one of the many resources necessary for a meaningful urban pedagogy.

Notes

1. It is worth noting that the two RTPI EDI initiatives recently announced are in partnership with two primarily white managed agencies.
2. *'Race' and Space: a new curriculum*, https://www.ucl.ac.uk/bartlett/about-us/our-values/equality-diversity-and-inclusion/race-and-space (last accessed 29 November 2022).

References

Ahmed, S. 2007. 'You end up doing the document rather than doing the doing: diversity, race equality and the politics of documentation', *Ethnic and Racial Studies* 30(4): 590–609.
Agyeman, J., and J. S. Erickson. 2012 'Culture, recognition, and the negotiation of difference: some thoughts on cultural competency in planning education', *Journal of Planning Education and Research* 32(3): 358–66.
Angotti, T., C. Doble and P. Horrigan (eds). 2011. *Service-Learning in Design and Planning: educating at the boundaries*. New York: New Village Press.
Arnstein, S. R. 1969. 'A ladder of citizen participation', *Journal of the American Institute of planners* 35(4): 216–24.
Beebeejaun, Y. 2021. 'Provincializing planning: reflections on spatial ordering and imperial power', *Planning Theory* 21(3), https://journals.sagepub.com/doi/10.1177/14730952211026697 (last accessed 29 November 2022).
Beebeejaun, Y., K. McClymont, A. Maddrell, B. Mathijssen and D. McNally. 2021. 'Death in the peripheries: planning for minority ethnic groups beyond "the City"', *Journal of Planning Education and Research*, https://journals.sagepub.com/doi/full/10.1177/0739456X211043275 (last accessed 29 November 2022).
Bhambra, G. K., D. Gebrial and K. Nişancıoğlu. (2018). *Decolonising the University*. London: Pluto Press.
Bhandar, B. 2018. *Colonial Lives of Property: law, land, and racial regimes of ownership*. Durham NC: Duke University Press.
Botchwey, N., and K. Umemoto. 2020. 'A guide to designing engaged learning courses in community planning', *Journal of Planning Education and Research* 40(3): 332–44.
Denoon-Stevens, S. P., L. Andres, P. Jones, L. Melgaço, R. Massey and V. Nel. 2020. 'Theory versus practice in planning education: the view from South Africa', *Planning Practice and Research* 509–25.
Forsyth, A., H. Lu and P. McGirr. 2000. 'Service learning in an urban context: implications for planning and design education', *Journal of Architectural and Planning Research* 17(3): 236–59.
Frank, A. I., and A. da Rosa Pires. 2021. 'Introduction: transformational change in planning education pedagogy?'. In *Teaching Urban and Regional Planning*. London: Edward Elgar Publishing.
Freire, P. 1993. *Pedagogy of the City*. New York: Continuum.

Freire, P. 1996. *Letters to Christina: reflections on my life and work*. New York: Routledge.
Gale, R., and H. Thomas. 2020. *Race, Faith and Planning in Britain: the British experience in context*. London: Routledge.
García, I., A. Jackson, S. A. Harwood, A. J. Greenlee, C. A. Lee and B. Chrisinger. 2021. '"Like a Fish Out of Water": the experience of African American and Latinx planning students', *Journal of the American Planning Association* 87(1): 108–22.
Gilmore, R. W. 2007. *Golden Gulag: prisons, surplus, crisis, and opposition in globalizing*, vol. 21. Berkeley CA: University of California Press.
Gopal, P. 2021. 'On decolonisation and the university', *Textual Practice* 35(6): 1–27.
Healey, P. 1997. *Collaborative Planning: shaping places in fragmented societies*. London: Macmillan.
hooks, b. 1994. *Teaching to Transgress: engaged pedagogy as two-way learning*. New York: Routledge.
Knapp, C. E. 2018. 'Integrating critical autobiography to foster anti-racism learning in the urban studies classroom: interpreting the "race and place" stories of undergraduate students', *Journal of Planning Education and Research* 42(3), https://doi.org/10.1177/0739456X18817822 (last accessed 29 November 2022).
Lung-Amam, W., S. A. Harwood, G. F. Sandoval and S. Sen. 2015. 'Teaching equity and advocacy planning in a multicultural "post-racial" world', *Journal of Planning Education and Research* 35(3): 337–42.
Njoh, A. J. 2009. 'Urban planning as a tool of power and social control in colonial Africa', *Planning Perspectives* 24(3): 301–17.
Mignolo, W. 2009. 'Epistemic disobedience, independent thought and decolonial freedom', *Theory, Culture and Society* 26(7–8): 159–81.
Ortiz, C. 2020. '"Race" and Space', *RIAS* 43, https://media.rias.org.uk/files/2020/10/29/12CC0906-68DF-6F9E-1EC1-B355A097F088.pdf (last accessed 29 November 2022).
Ortiz, C., and G. Millan. 2022. 'Critical urban pedagogy: convites as sites of southern urbanism, solidarity construction and urban learning', *International Journal of Urban and Regional Research* 46(5): 822–44.
Patel, I. 2021. *We're Here Because You Were There: immigration and the end of empire*. London: Verso Books.
Peel, D., and A. Frank. 2005. 'The internationalisation of planning education: issues, perceptions and priorities for action', *Town Planning Review* 79(1): 87–107.
Perera, N. 2008. 'The planners' city: the construction of a town planning perception of Colombo', *Environment and Planning A*, 40(1): 57–73.
Porter, L. 2010. *Unlearning the Colonial Cultures of Planning*. London: Ashgate Publishing, Ltd.
Porter, L. 2007. 'Producing forests: a colonial genealogy of environment planning in Victoria, Australia', *Journal of Planning Education and Research* 26(4): 466–77.
Porter, L. 2006. 'Planning in (post) colonial settings: challenges for theory and practice', *Planning Theory and Practice* 7(4): 383–96.
Roy, A. 2006. 'Praxis in the time of empire', *Planning Theory* 5(1): 7–29.
Royal Town Planning Institute. 2019. *The UK Planning Profession in 2019: statistics on the size and make-up of the planning profession in the UK*. London: RTPI.
Royal Town Planning Institute. 2021. https://www.rtpi.org.uk/blog/2021/april/change-oneyear-on-how-the-rtpi-is-tackling-inequality/ (last accessed 29 November 2022).
Royal Town Planning Institute and Commission for Racial Equality. 1983. *Planning for a Multiracial Britain*. London: CRE.
Sandercock, L. 1998. *Making the Invisible Visible: a multicultural planning history*. Berkeley CA: University of California Press.
Sandercock, L. 2003. *Cosmopolis II: mongrel cities of the 21st century*. London: A and C Black.
Sweet, E. L. 2018. 'Cultural Humility: an open door for planners to locate themselves and decolonize planning theory, education, and practice', *E-Journal of Public Affairs* 7(2): 1–17.
Sweet, E. L., and H. F. Etienne. 2011. 'Commentary: diversity in urban planning education and practice', *Journal of Planning Education and Research* 31(3): 332–9.
Thomas, H. 2004. *Race and Planning: the UK experience*. London: Routledge.
Thomas, H. 2008. 'Race equality and planning: a changing agenda', *Planning, Practice and Research* 23(1): 1–17.

Thomas, H., and V. Krishnarayan. 1994. '"Race", disadvantage, and policy processes in British planning', *Environment and Planning A* 26(12): 1891–910.

Vergès, F. 2021. *A Decolonial Feminism*. London: Pluto Press.

Winkler, T. 2018. 'Black texts on white paper: learning to see resistant texts as an approach towards decolonising planning', *Planning Theory* 17(4): 588–604.

Zewolde, S., A. Walls, T. Sengupta, C. Ortiz, Y. Beebeejaun, G. Burridge and K. Patel. 2020. '"Race" and Space: What is "race" doing in a nice field like the built environment?'. London: The Bartlett, UCL Faculty of the Built Environment.

3
Queering the built environment curriculum

Celine Lessard, Renée Etokakpan, Juliana Martins, Corin Menuge, Jordan Rowe, Ramandeep Shergill and Michael Short

> Working towards equality, diversity, and inclusion should challenge us and disrupt our current systems, attitudes, and behaviours. Without such disruption we risk tweaking the edges of inequality. (Patel, 2021: online)

It is undeniable that LGBTQ+ staff and students have come a long way towards equality, diversity and inclusion in UK higher education. Many institutions have set up equality, diversity and inclusion groups and developed initiatives and policies to address these issues (Buitendijk *et al.*, 2019). In particular, the queerness of staff and students is increasingly acknowledged and celebrated as a badge of diversity and progressiveness. Having said that, institutional language surrounding it sometimes veiled in terms of inclusion and equality to existing norms, and often silences the voices expressing non-normative queer[1] experiences in pedagogic approaches. As Vallerand states, 'the idea of queerness has yet to fully transform the way we practice and teach' (2018: 141).

This is particularly relevant in the built environment fields. These practices have the unintended consequence of diminishing queer voices in pedagogic approaches to teaching and learning in the exploration of our built environment subjects. But spatial processes can construct and impact gender and sexual identities. Involving and understanding diverse voices more meaningfully is crucial to improve human spaces for all. Within our institution – the Bartlett Faculty of the Built Environment, UCL – models of responding to the need for curricula review exist, and the work in respect of racial equity provides a powerful example. The groundbreaking *'Race' and Space* curriculum, authored and curated by a multidisciplinary group of Bartlett staff (see Chapter 2), challenged prevailing conceptions of the built environment field as 'race-neutral' and proposed an educational framework for identifying and engaging with links between 'race' and space through an 'interdisciplinary corpus of literature' (Zewolde *et al.*, 2020: 7). The curriculum ultimately seeks to challenge and destabilise the centrality and power of 'whiteness' in the contemporary world, focusing on the built environment field.

At the same time, the Bartlett as an institution is increasingly adopting, promoting, supporting and connecting with agendas of reflexivity with regard to its part in upholding and perpetuating systems of power and oppression cutting across all areas of society and within built environment disciplines, including planning and urban design. For example, holding town hall-style discussions on experiences of racism and racial marginalisation at the institution appears to reflect growing recognition of the importance of confronting inequality and oppression within it, while seeking ways to formulate new practices that are anti-oppressive. This context provides fertile ground for pedagogical projects that seek to illuminate the underlying forces – such as white supremacy, patriarchy and colonialism – behind commonly accepted ways of knowing, teaching and learning.

The project 'Queering the Curriculum' – a student-staff partnership undertaken by an interdisciplinary group of queer students and staff with diverse roles at the Bartlett – aims to contribute to this imperative agenda by interrogating built environment education regarding how the field obscures and upholds hegemonic norms that shape marginalisations, and to develop ways in which built environment curricula (at the Bartlett) can be reframed through a queer lens for the benefit of students and staff. Queering has a focus on concerns of gender and sexuality, which also relate to the body and self-expression, but are distinctive and deserve particular attention. A 'queer' approach has been described as one that questions normativities, orthodoxies and the assumed stability of categories (Browne, 2006), and which examines how overlapping systems of dominance based on concepts such as 'heterosexuality' or 'race' are co-constructed (Oswin, 2008). A queer curriculum, therefore, can further the agenda of developing built environment academics', students' and practitioners' capacity to recognise and challenge the operations of normative structures – and ultimately address the socio-spatial inequalities that result. Drawing from a comprehensive literature review, this chapter proposes three themes for reframing pedagogical practices for queering built environment education: awareness; representation; and action.

In this chapter, the word 'queer' as it refers to populations will be treated as referring to people who have non-normative sexual and/or romantic attractions and/or gender identities and/or presentation; that is, people for whom these aspects of identity deviate from those typically assumed by cis-heteropatriarchal expectations. Where introducing the work of other authors, the terms used by those authors to refer to the above populations will be used, for the sake of maintaining the integrity of analysis. It should also be noted that the language around genders and sexualities is constantly shifting, that not all individuals with similar experiences use similar language to describe themselves, that language is a source of significant contestation, and that terminology may become inaccurate, misleading and/or offensive over time. This work was created during a specific moment in time and reflects the scholarship and conversations occurring at that period. This clarification emphasises the point that there are important reasons to critically consider the language used in pedagogy and research, and to carefully and explore the meanings behind commonly used terms.

Queering the Curriculum project: an engaged student-staff partnership for change

The Queering the Curriculum project aimed to queer the curriculum at the Bartlett and was funded through the university's ChangeMakers scheme, which 'provides project funding and support to students and staff who want to work together to enhance the learning experience of students'.[2] The funding programme, which has run since 2014, is underpinned by a student-staff partnership (an approach more commonly known as 'students as partners') to encourage active collaboration in teaching and learning across disciplines. More traditionally, universities have tended to seek 'student voice' through feedback, comments on teaching and assessment, more formal surveys, and other more 'remote' forms of evaluation.

For these student-staff partnerships, students are seen as partners in teaching and learning, with 'values-based practices' (Mercer-Mapstone and Marie, 2019: 7) rooted in:

- *a way of thinking* that positions students as partners, experts and colleagues in – rather than evaluators of – teaching and learning;
- *a way of engaging* where teaching and learning is something that is *done with*, rather than *done to*, students; and
- *a way of working* that nourishes partnerships based on respect, reciprocity and shared responsibility.

The project started with discussions on a Queering the Curriculum manifesto to guide our approach, followed by a review of the literature on queer pedagogies and their relevance to the work of queering the curriculum, and the three themes of awareness, representation and action. The final stage, which is ongoing, is to develop a resource to help and support staff and students to adopt queer pedagogies and practices of, and in, built environment higher education.

A framework for queering the built environment curriculum

Queer pedagogies: challenging normative power structures

Queer pedagogies are related to the pedagogical acknowledgement of queer people. But their scope and aims are broader. Overall, the suite of approaches to queer pedagogies highlights the imperative to disrupt hierarchies and established ways of thinking, reveal how normative structures impact on students and people, and work to redress these norms.

Halberstam (2003; 363) distinguishes queer pedagogy from queer/sexuality studies, noting that the former aims to disrupt a false 'logic of coherence that creates a term like LGBT'. This work notes the often-problematic conflation of 'queer' with concepts such as 'LGBT', 'LGBTQ+', 'gay', among others, and emphasises the distinction between these identity categories and queer responses to hegemonic norms (see, e.g., Browne 2006; Bell and Binnie 2004).

According to this perspective, queer pedagogies challenge rather than shore up practices based on arbitrary categorisation (in this case of sexual identities). For Halberstam (2003), a central concern of queer pedagogy is the ability to choose methodologies that match projects rather than 'discipline-appropriate' methods (363), destabilising hierarchies and constraints in the academy.

Jones and Calafell (2012) delve into the idea of categorisation, arguing that within the academy, difference and diversity are most often celebrated according to neoliberal commercial prerogatives, while at the same time expressions of variance from middle-class white heterosexual norms are sanctioned – therefore reinforcing categorisation and the supremacy of the valued categories. The authors therefore frame research and teaching as a 'matrix of domination' (Jones and Calafell: 963) that 'inhibit[s] the academic freedom of cultural Others (959), implicitly connecting this 'matrix' to the inhibition of freedoms in wider life. In their view, queer pedagogy is not used to extend promises of emancipation to individuals experiencing heterosexism, but explored to account for how power and agency operate across multiple identities (971). In practice, Jones and Calafell (2012) propose a response based on coalitional activism, using the pedagogical tools of personal narrative sharing to develop educators' self-reflexivity and alternative educational strategies (972).

This perspective of queer approaches interrogating power and agency is echoed in Smith's position arguing for a queer pedagogy where students not only examine the oppression they experience as queer and gendered subjects,[3] but also work to recognise the ways in which they simultaneously benefit from the 'cultural logics of normalcy' that produce these oppressions (Smith, 2013: 469). Smith argues for striving towards a decolonial queer pedagogy – they connect the goal of working towards rights and recognition within existing societal structures, to the ongoing colonial structure of privileges being unevenly distributed by a powerful 'centre' (468). For Smith (2013), queer pedagogy instead leads students and practitioners to 'critically question the colonial institutions through which their rights are sought' (470).

Regarding the built environment, while queer theory has been widely applied in architecture, queer pedagogies have rarely been adopted in design education. A notable exception is Vallerand's (2018) work, which explores how all these perspectives can be incorporated into teaching in a specific field: interior design. They highlight the need to incorporate both queer experiences and theory into design pedagogy, noting how different facets of identity impact experiences of physical space(s) in diverse ways. They call for queer pedagogies to encourage questioning of assumptions, in this case to 'envision space as a collective and layered environment constantly being reperformed' (143), and to disrupt existing teaching practices such as 'studio culture' in design fields (145), as part of the destabilisation of accepted methods and views of success.

Vallerand (2018) cites different approaches to incorporating queer methods in the field of architecture; while the goals of increasing the visibility of queer people's contributions to the field, and designing to reduce harm and oppression to the 'end users' of space(s) relate to the question of how identity interacts with experience of space, the approach of disrupting traditional methods in architecture (144) aligns with a wider adoption of queer methodologies to analyse spatial phenomena in/or the built environment. Queer pedagogies should be viewed across identities in space, but also in terms of methods and ways of doing.

Awareness

Structural norms and their supposed 'violation' reveal the diversity of genders and sexualities, as well as their intersectionalities. Awareness of that diversity is a crucial first step towards realising a queer curriculum; the acknowledgement of our existence and our imprints on the built environment cannot be ignored. Explorations of the built environment thus need to examine, understand and account for the multiple spatial experiences and knowledges paying attention to this 'diversity' but also the conflicts and tensions that may arise. This awareness must be incorporated with two activities for built environment education.

The first is to 'create awareness about the place of sexual and gender diversity' (Nemi Neto, 2018: 589) in the organisation. This is true of 'educators themselves being aware of sexual orientation, gender and gender-identity issues' (Zacko-Smith and Pritchy Smith, 2010: 4), but also among students and professional services staff too. The second is to acknowledge the multiple experiences of space, and how these are affected, included or excluded by the built environment in its material and symbolic dimensions.

Benedicto (2014) proposes that queerness is a means of questioning notions of truth, thus suggesting an analytical framework where accepted 'truths' of the built environment can be destabilised. Maher and Perez Gayo (2020) deploy this framework when examining the phenomena surrounding a Netherlands fashion marketing billboard campaign for the 'Suit Supply' brand featuring homoerotic images of men. They argue that both the images and reactions to the campaign, as well as the campaign's situatedness within global geomarketing tactics, show the non neutrality of spatial environments and how they reflect and reinforce social divisions. The authors refer to the 'media-architecture complex' to analyse these processes, pointing out that both visual media and the surveillance processes of geomarketing transform 'spatial experiences of public space as well as the social relationships established within this context, and the identities generated within' (89).

As such, the Suitsupply campaign constitutes an example of how built environment processes can construct and manage gender and sexual identities – often reconstituting normativities of how gender and sexuality should be expressed. Based on this analysis, Maher and Perez Gayo (2020) argue for changes to design practices, calling for designers and the design field to reconsider their relationship to the commercialisation of public space and evaluate how their discipline 'contributes to these normative processes and the (re)production of hegemonic heterosexism' (99).

Moore and Castricum (2020) examine architecture with a similar lens, discussing its role in perpetuating – or confronting and dismantling – gender essentialism.[4] They note a historical resistance to breaking binaries in architectural and client practice and relations, most notably through the continued reliance on a binary-gendered bathroom typology. As the authors note, this situation not only fails to represent the complexity of lived experiences, but is associated with 'histories of erasure, murder, violence, and ridicule in public space' for trans and gender-diverse people (191). The authors call for queer methodologies to be embedded in architecture, which they define as those that resist authority and reinvent social norms in design and the use of space, incorporating intersectional, anti-capitalist and anti-colonial lenses.

Also discussing public toilets, Marshall and Campkin (2020) provide a potential example of these methodologies in practice. They explore the experiences of trans and gender-diverse people using public toilets in Britain, noting that these experiences often represent encounters with forces of cisheteronormativity[5] and arguing that 'affect, emotion and sense of self' are essential sources of knowledge for designers shaping the built environment and public space (228). Moore and Castricum (2020) extend their call to each part of the design process, arguing that each stage (from issuing briefs to procurement) must be 'queered' in order to destabilise norms and enable trans and gender-diverse people to feel like they belong in architectural space (192). Notably, they provide a strong critique of the notion that acknowledging sexual diversity constitutes a queer methodology in built environment fields – labelling this an 'appropriation' and contrasting it with the goal of resisting harmful norms (190).

Other authors have examined queer experiences of the built environment through an intersectional lens by adopting the queer approaches of questioning the meaning of the LGBTQ+ category and its relationship to wider norms. Ehrenfeucht (2013) explores how more privileged subsectors of the LGBTQ+ population can secure their representation in the built environment as standing for the whole population, while excluding others from space. Examining a street redesign in West Hollywood, California, they argue that while planning in the United States previously emphasised the separation of so-called 'desirable and undesirable' uses, diversity of uses has now ostensibly become valued, but only within an 'acceptable' diversity that increasingly controls non-conforming groups (64).

In the West Hollywood case, urban design interventions that included visual references to LGBT symbols made public spaces inhospitable to the homeless and to non-consuming groups, while an associated campaign to eliminate sex work negatively impacted on trans women sex workers and forced the closure of a trans-friendly restaurant. Importantly, Ehrenfeucht (2013) notes that despite these disproportionate impacts on marginalised groups in West Hollywood, the street design won prestigious awards in built environment fields, highlighting that norms within built environment practices – and their valorisation by formal institutions of our disciplines – can cause significant harm to those of marginalised sexual and especially gender identities in ways that are largely invisible to – or ignored by – built environment professionals.

As Moore and Castricum (2020) apply a queer perspective to conceptual analyses of physical space (e.g., describing buildings as potential archives of trauma), a central point to their argument is an examination of queer subjects' lived experiences in the built environment. They argue that the 'diversity of experiences and demands for building and space' (182) requires design responses that can address violence and erasure, and that recognising these aspects of queer lived experience highlights the urgency of queer approaches that seek to challenge and dismantle norms in the built environment. As Beebeejaun (2016) points out, rights in urban contexts have both spatial and material dimensions, which are contested along lines of gendered (and classed, racialised, etc.) dominations – in other words, rights are not abstract, but the negotiation of rights between urban dwellers has a direct impact on their daily experiences. Beebeejaun argues that there is an 'increasing mismatch' between the 'direct experiences of marginalised urban dwellers' and how their rights are framed in official ways of viewing the built environment, highlighting the complexity of gender and gendered experiences (2).

Representation

The second stage proposed for queering is one of *representation* in the materials, structures, regulations and policies of the university where we study and work. Most commonly this might be undertaken through the production and use – and even co-production – of queer-related materials for students by staff. As set out here, current research suggests that there is a rich tapestry of material that is emerging that can guide curriculum development, course material and voices which can be elevated in the classroom. But the discussion also encompasses how representation is expected to be enacted in relation to 'queering' of space (and the production of queer space), given the complex material and symbolic roles of the built environment, and multi-layered queer contributions and interventions.

Marshall and Campkin (2017) examine the material dimensions of the right to the city exploring the effects of accessing LGBTQ+ nightlife venues in London for these spaces' users. They argue for the value and social reach 'within but also far beyond venues' (9) and provide data on the significant mental health benefits of such spaces in creating feelings of belonging and freedom from hegemonic heteronormative (and cisheteronormative, racist, misogynistic, etc.) outside pressures; their social benefits for organising and distributing information;[6] and how witnessing venues' closure intensifies feelings of continued exclusion and erasure. This lends weight to Moore and Castricum's (2020) argument that architecture can be used to perpetuate the erasure of certain queer publics. Marshall and Campkin (2017) note that while the physical presence of LGBTQ+ nightlife venues is crucial, non-physical aspects such as the programming, visual symbolism or management of spaces are also key to enacting the potential positive impacts of LGBTQ+ spaces. The authors identify a strong link between those elements and patterns of structural oppression in London, noting that QTIPOC[7] groups, trans groups and women lack ownership of physical LGBTQ+ venues and frequently experience discrimination or exclusion by managers or other patrons at LGBTQ+ venues they attend.

Other authors have further highlighted the intersectional effects of queer space phenomena. Like Perez Gayo, Doan, and Higgins (2011) examine how capitalist urban transformation processes impact on queer people, in this case studying the impact on LGBTQ+ populations of normative redevelopment projects in Midtown Atlanta. They argue that in these processes, the conceptual erasure of LGBTQ+ people – manifested in the complete lack of acknowledgement of the queer history and presence in the area in regeneration and planning documents describing the area and in local historical narratives – has been accompanied by a physical erasure of LGBTQ+ people as the new developments force queer businesses to close due to rising rents or direct enforcement pressure on their activities. These phenomena, alongside the associated rising housing costs, have significantly harmed vulnerable LGBTQ+ populations, particularly the disabled, poor and elderly, by dispersing queer establishments to less transit-accessible areas – while increasing pressures on historically Black neighbourhoods as white LGBTQ+ populations move to them. This example shows the complex intersectional impacts of overlapping oppressions, similar to Benedicto's (2020) critique of Manila's cosmopolitan gay bars excluding both those perceived as feminine and the lower-income classes.

Andersson (2015) discusses racial contention in the processes that shape queer urban space, describing how white gay residents and business owners in New York's West Village applied regulatory pressure to a Black queer bar and to queer youth of colour in attempts to displace them from the area and defend their own visions of 'appropriate' queer space. Andersson highlights the different dimensions of space and the contestations between these, arguing that queer youth socialising and performing on the West Village's sidewalks are participating in the production of queer space, extending beyond the physical and social limitations of the white gay businesses in the area. Like Marshall and Campkin (2017), Ehrenfeucht (2013) and Andersson (2015) emphasise the importance of both materiality of the built environment and the social and symbolic processes, in impacting the experiences of queer people in built environment space. Projects of domination and oppression, as well as reclaiming rights, occur along material and cultural lines. Therefore, an understanding of the complex interaction of these spatial processes is key and will underpin any queer built environment practice that seeks to challenge power structures.

Zebracki and Leitner (2021) draw on queer perspectives in an analysis of monument construction by 'LGBT+' groups, arguing that monuments have the potential to destabilise norms within the contexts they are situated in, creating alternative memories to hegemonic heteronormativities (1). They contend that LGBT+ monuments can become implicated in processes of 'queering', challenging identity categories, representations, assumptions and norms regarding gender and sexuality. Notably, the authors address the complexity and multilayered nature of queer interventions in the built environment, noting that there are widely varying constraints and opportunities around how monuments are 'embodied through memorial practices, interpretations, responses, and usages or misusages', leading to different 'queer potentials' for destabilising norms' and different ways of negotiating formal and informal rights to space, depending on the contexts in which monuments are situated (8). As a result, monuments memorialising and/or visualising LGBT+ populations or histories can address the 'exclusionary processes that affect 'othered' ways of living and knowing' overall (2), thus creating the potential for alliance-building and solidarity both within and beyond LGBT+ populations.

Zebracki and Leitner (2021) raise the question of how queer monuments are implicated in the issue of whether pro-LGBT+ actions and policies are translated into material change for sexual and gender minority populations and all those who are 'othered' – foregrounding the complex relationship between the physical and metaphysical aspects, and implications, of 'queer' elements of the built environment such as London's LGBT+ night spaces (Campkin, 2022). Extending their argument that the physical violences often enacted upon recognisably LGBT+ monuments reflect societal cleavages over LGBT+ rights, the wider built environment itself can be considered as both site and tool of physical and symbolic violence.

Reed (1996) also considers the relationship between physical and metaphysical aspects of 'queer space' and addresses the example of monuments from a different angle. Reed contrasts the examples of *Homomonument* and *Gay Liberation*. *Homomonument* is a triangular-shaped monument in Amsterdam installed horizontally on the ground, visually referencing the pink triangles that designated supposed homosexuals under the Nazi fascist regime, and commemorating the designated gays and lesbians murdered under that regime. *Gay Liberation* is a monument located in New York, comprising two life-size statues of a gay male couple standing together, and two life-size statues of a lesbian couple sitting on a park bench together, commemorating the Stonewall uprising against police violence targeting queer venues. They argue that while *Gay Liberation* is 'conventionally monumental', *Homomonument* 'disappears as art in order to emerge as the embodiment of a community' (65), therefore representing an 'imminence' that Reed argues is what makes a space queer – indications of a process of '*taking place*, of claiming territory' (64, emphasis in original).

Reed critiques cultural geography for ignoring visual analysis and instead emphasising the importance of social structures and imaginations, arguing that an accumulated 'index of the impulses of many individuals, marks certain streets as queer space', while certain 'social forms of queer culture' such as pedestrian orientation and 'camp' transformation of 'what the dominant culture has abandoned' (1996: 66) are reflected in space. Here Reed reveals the interaction between physical and non-physical aspects of space, reflecting on how knowledges and understandings can lend interpretations of queerness to physical entities – for example, how the renovation of a historic building by 'gay' populations can reference the ways that camp performance revivifies supposedly outdated cultural signifiers.

Benedicto (2014) extends these approaches by examining how queerness can be situated with relation to hegemonic forces such as 'modernity' and 'neoliberalism', analysing Manila's postcolonial modernist transformation and arguing that queers were portrayed as 'agents' of the violent renovation process implementing a modernist fantasy urbanism. Discussing the figure and actions of Imelda Marcos, the powerful first lady and politician who led an authoritarian physical transformation of the Philippines' capital city, Benedicto interprets architecture and urban planning as a means of both fashioning and embodying ideals, aligning with Zebracki and Leitner's analysis of monuments.

However, Benedicto notes the physical violence of demolition and eviction that accompanied the attempted implementation of modernist ideals in Manila, arguing that the link between visions of beauty and queer spectacle in Marcos' 'modernizing' project forced queer formations outside this vision of 'gay modernity' to become 'spectral' (582). They note that the violent renovations paradoxically also ultimately created a queer 'underworld' that came to occupy the modernist spaces in their later decline. This process of developing an 'underworld' happened both in a physical sense, with queer groups gathering in the largely abandoned and crumbling modernist structures and spaces; and, as Benedicto argues, in a figurative sense, where *bakla*[8] and 'feminine' subjectivities and performances are relegated to these relics of the modernism dream while 'contemporary urban gay culture' of 'hypermasculine bodies' is integrated into the 'pink economy' in the new, middle-class gay bars aligning themselves with global gay consumption (591).

Space is an essential factor in the representation of queerness; the contributions of queer people, and our legacies, to spaces is now well recognised and deserves greater critical attention. The production of queer spaces, and the ways in which they are represented in our fields in teaching and learning, are of paramount importance in engaged pedagogies.

Action

Finally, queer pedagogies cannot be dissociated from action when it is actively disrupting norms, engaging a wider set of people and empowering marginalised voices in shaping the built environment, as well as in professional practice. Seal (2019) points to material experiences as key to the relevance and aims of queer pedagogy, arguing for a 'critical realist' approach: this would link methods of enquiry exploring individual meanings to teaching actively challenging structures of heteronormativity. According to Seal, queer pedagogies should contest, seek out and contribute to paradigm shifts – and should activate students to themselves become pedagogical practitioners by working towards this goal. Seal emphasises the concept of agency, acknowledging that non-normative sexuality can potentially challenge social constructions and highlight the fact that heteronormativity is not an unbreakable hegemony. Thus, in Seal's framework, both partial subjective perceptions and real causal mechanisms are crucial to the development of queer pedagogies.

Martino and Cumming-Potvin (2019) also point to ways that queer pedagogies can engage with specific structural challenges affecting queer and trans people, describing the need for teaching methods that represent queer, trans and gender-diverse subjects while avoiding essentialising or using categories to reduce or represent 'others'. They argue that pedagogies focused on LGBTQ+ visibility and the centring of different types of LGBTQ+ 'subjects' run the risk of reinforcing homonormativity, while pedagogies that 'direct the gaze of students to the "violence of normativity"' (146) can enable all students to engage with their own experiences of gendering and counter heteronormative frameworks. Martino and Cumming-Potvin propose using texts that are 'voice and experience-based' to lead students to reflect on the politics of representation (143).

While all queer people are impacted by and have an impact on the built environment, an underexplored area of research is the queer experiences of those who most directly physically produce the built environment (i.e., those working in the construction industry and trades). Frank (2001), in an exploration of the experiences of lesbians working in the building trades, shares the finding that nearly all tradeswomen have been 'dyke-baited' or antagonistically labelled as a lesbian, whether they are or not (2). Frank argues that this tactic is an 'expression of male hostility when men's power and privileges are threatened by women's transgression of traditional gender roles' (2), connecting this hostility to the 'encroachment' of women into a historically white, male-controlled industry (3).

Denissen and Saguy (2014) echo the argument that labelling female employees as lesbians is an attempt to neutralise the 'threat' of female workers in construction, arguing that 'the presence of women in male-dominated jobs threatens the perception of this work as inherently masculine' (382). The authors further the argument by examining the experiences of women of colour in the trades, noting that race and body size also played significant roles in the hostility that the women faced and the identity management strategies they adopted. Their interview data shows the ways in which lesbians and other women in construction enact and portray their sexual and gender identities in different ways, in response to the enforcement of norms around male and heterosexual dominance.

Chan (2013) also examines the 'performative' nature of gender relations, in particular exploring how varying masculinities affect queer acceptance in the construction industries (817). They apply a lens to deconstruct the typically accepted view of hegemonic masculinity in construction-related industries, and note how masculinities expressed in interviews with non-heterosexual participants affect minority groups such as women and disabled people in workplaces. Although they find that these masculinities are often deployed in attempts to exclude, they also note that heteronormative (and ableist, misogynist, among others) assumptions can be challenged through workplace interactions. Brown and Phua (2011) similarly argue for the centrality of identity to construction managers' work, pointing out that the socially constructed worlds of managers affect their social interactions and performance, and thus the 'success' of projects. They further note that identities are negotiated and contested through interacting with others in the classroom, in ways in which issues of 'power and impression management' come to the fore (88).

Brown and Phua refer to the performance of appropriate behaviours as a key means to achieve perceptions of competence and professionalism, which likely strongly impacts on queer people. This is in line with Barnard and Dainty's (2018) note that openly LGBT workers face high degrees of scrutiny in the workplace. While Barnard and Dainty examine a range of concrete impacts of LGBT workers in the construction industry, such as obstacles to advancement and harassment, they also argue that queer theory should be used to more deeply interrogate 'traditional notions of power' and hierarchy within the construction industry's workplace climate (146). The queer experiences of those who physically construct most of the built environment are essential to consider when addressing queer experiences in the built environment overall. In keeping with examinations of users of the built environment, the literature around the experiences of those constructing emphasises both symbolic and (concrete) aspects of those experiences, which must be incorporated into pedagogies that aim to meaningfully address the realities of queer people in the built environment field.

Towards queering as engaged urban pedagogy

The intention of this project is to use the queer lens to explicitly support the Bartlett's *'Race' and Space* agenda. Recognising that education is a platform for 'powerful institutional discourses that help to create and maintain prejudice' (Zacko-Smith and Pritchy Smith, 2010: 7) echoing Fraser and Lamble (2015: 74), students and staff seek to take risks with the power to transform pedagogy. As such, and recognising that the authors are a group of engaged academics, students, alumni and researchers at the Bartlett, we align ourselves with the decolonising the curriculum agenda to challenge the prevailing norms of white supremacy and cis-heteropatriarchy in built environment teaching, and to embed other forms of knowledge in pedagogy. Indeed, a queer approach in our curricula can not only do this but can also contribute to the liberatory intentions of the decolonising agenda.

We argue that for pedagogies to be engaged we must challenge and critique dominant ways of 'doing' teaching and learning in the university setting. This is rightly both complex and uncomfortable for those involved. It is also a process that is iterative and is, in some senses, therefore never fully complete; as curricula are reviewed, we become aware of new approaches and complexities that can be absorbed into the cycle of review, reflection and rewriting.

We conclude by saying that 'Queering the Curriculum' is, above all, a call to action. By investigating, amplifying and representing queer lives, curricula will not only improve by being more representative of the student and staff bodies, but in encouraging critical learning and reflection. Queerness offers opportunities to reflect on stories, experiences and approaches that are not only ignored but often intentionally silenced. This is our call to embrace queerness to challenge those silences, and to empower future built environment practitioners to enact queer approaches in processes of urban change.

Notes

1. 'Not only describes the cultural, social, and political needs, interests, experiences, and struggles of non-heterosexual desires and representations, but it also includes an array of identity formations' (Roy, 2020: online).
2. For details of this and other ChangeMakers projects, please see: https://www.ucl.ac.uk/changemakers/ (last accessed 30 November 2022).
3. Discussions of gender inequality in this work refer to all inequalities and disparities associated with norms of gender, gender performance and gender presentation, and are thus understood to encompass inequalities relating to trans and non-binary identities.
4. 'Gender essentialism is the belief that gender roles and stereotypes are the natural result of biological or neurological differences between males and females. Gender essentialists assume that AMABs [those for whom medical institutions assign a male gender identity at birth] are by nature men, that AFABs [those for whom medical institutions assign a female gender identity at birth] are by nature women, and that the societal roles assigned to both are acceptable based on those differences. Gender essentialism generally denies the natural existence of transgender, intersex, and non-binary people, and tends to be closely linked to misogyny, heteronormativity and cisnormativity.' (The Queer Dictionary, 2014).
5. Cis-heteropatriarchy: 'A system of power based on the supremacy and dominance of cisgender heterosexual men through the exploitation and oppression of womxn and the LGBTQIA+

community.' Stellenbosch University Transformation Office. n.d. *List of Definitions and Terminology*, http://www.sun.ac.za/english/management/wim-de-villiers/Documents/Transformation%20Terminilogy%20and%20definitions.pdf (last accessed 30 November 2022).
6. For example, HIV prevention information or sexual education materials.
7. Queer, Trans and Intersex People of Colour (9).
8. Benedicto notes that *bakla* is often translated as 'a variant of "drag" and "trans" femininity' (582), although this translation is problematic as *bakla* is 'not a monolithic identity or subculture, but a loose formation that is often tied to a folkloric belief in homosexuality as having "a male body with a female heart"' (588). According to Benedicto, *bakla/kabaklaan* is often associated with the beauty industry and relates to notions of exposing a true inner beauty found within, often while adopting the appearance or symbols of powerful (feminine) figures. While the concept might not be easily understandable or explainable to Western readership, Benedicto explains that their key concern is to examine the figure of the *bakla* in relation to urban modernism in Manila in order to analyse 'the gendered logic of urban modernization in the postcolony' (582).

References

Andersson, J. 2015. '"Wilding" in the West Village: queer space, racism and Jane Jacobs hagiography', *International Journal of Urban and Regional Research* 39(2): 265–83.
Barnard, S., and A. R. J. Dainty. 2018. 'Coming out and staying in industry: how sexual orientation and gender identity matters in construction employment', *Proceedings of the Institution of Civil Engineers – Municipal Engineer* 171(3): 141–8.
Beebeejaun, Y. (ed.). 2016. *The Participatory City*. Berlin: Jovis.
Buitendijk, S., S. Curry and Katrien Maes. 2019. *Equality, Diversity and Inclusion at Universities: the power of a systemic approach*. League of European Research Universities, September 2019.
Bell, D., and J. Binnie. 2004. 'Authenticating Queer Space: citizenship, urbanism and governance', *Urban Studies* 41(9): 1807–20.
Benedicto, B. 2014. *Under Bright Lights: gay Manila and the global*. Minneapolis MN: University of Minnesota Press.
Brown, A., and F. Phua, F. 2011. 'Subjectively construed identities and discourse: towards a research agenda for construction management', *Construction Management and Economics* 29(1): 83–95.
Browne, K. 2006. 'Challenging queer geographies', *Antipode* 38(5): 885–93.
Campkin, B. 2022. *Queer Premises: London's LGBT night spaces*. London: Bloomsbury Publishing.
Chan, P. W. 2013. 'Queer eye on a "straight" life: deconstructing masculinities in construction' *Construction Management and Economics* 31: 816–31.
Denissen A. M., and A. C. Saguy. 2014. 'Gendered homophobia and the contradictions of workplace discrimination for women in the building trades', *Gender and Society* 28(3): 381–403.
Doan P. L., and H. Higgins. 2011. 'The demise of queer space? Resurgent gentrification and the assimilation of LGBT neighborhoods', *Journal of Planning Education and Research* 31(1): 6–25.
Ehrenfeucht, R. 2013. 'Nonconformity and street design in West Hollywood, California', *Journal of Urban Design* 18(1): 59–77.
Frank, M. 2001. 'Hard hats and homophobia: lesbians in the building trades', *New Labor Forum*, 25–36.
Fraser, J., and S. Lamble. 2018. 'Queer desires and critical pedagogies in higher education: reflections on the transformative potential of non-normative learning desires in the classroom', *Journal of Feminist Scholarship* 7: 61–77.
Halberstam, J. 2003. 'Reflections on queer studies and queer pedagogy', *Journal of Homosexuality* 45(2–4): 361–4.
Jones, R., and B. Calafell. 2012. 'Contesting neoliberalism through critical pedagogy, intersectional reflexivity, and personal narrative: queer tales of academia', *Faculty Research and Creative Activity* 28: online.
Maher, G. A., and R. Perez Gayo. 2020. *A Glitch in the System: deconstructing JCDecaux| decoding Suitsupply*. London: Routledge.

Marshall, L., and B. Campkin. 2017. *LGBTQ+ Cultural Infrastructure in London: night venues, 2006 – present*. London: UCL Urban Laboratory.

Martino, W., and W. Cumming-Potvin. 2018. 'Transgender and gender expansive education research, policy and practice: reflecting on epistemological and ontological possibilities of bodily becoming', *Gender and Education*, 30(6): 687–94.

Mercer-Mapstone, L., and J. Marie. 2019. 'Practical Guide: scaling up student-staff partnerships in higher education', *Institute for Academic Development*. Edinburgh: University of Edinburgh.

Moore, T., and S. Castricum. 2020. *Queering Architecture: Simona Castricum and Timothy Moore in conversation*. London: Routledge.

Nemi Neto, J. 2018. 'Queer pedagogy: approaches to inclusive teaching', *Policy Futures in Education* 16(5): 589–604.

Oswin, N. 2008. 'Critical geographies and the uses of sexuality: deconstructing queer space', *Progress in Human Geography* 32(1): 89–103.

Patel, K. 2021. *Equality, Diversity, and Inclusion*, https://www.ucl.ac.uk/bartlett/about-us/our-values/equality-diversity-and-inclusion (last accessed 30 November 2022).

Reed, C. 1996. 'Imminent domain: queer space in the built environment', *Art Journal* 55(4): 64–70.

Roy, A. 2020. 'Non-normative sexuality studies', *Oxford Bibliographies*, https://www.oxfordbibliographies.com/view/document/obo-9780199756384/obo-9780199756384-0238.xml (last accessed 30 November 2022).

Seal, M. 2019. *The Interruption of Heteronormativity in Higher Education*. Cham: Palgrave Macmillan.

Smith, K. 2013. 'Decolonizing queer pedagogy', *Journal of Women and Social Work* 28(4): 468–70.

Stonewall. 2020. *The Truth About Trans*, https://www.stonewall.org.uk/the-truth-about-trans (last accessed 30 November 2022).

Vallerand, O. 2018 'Learning from … (or "the Need for Queer Pedagogies of Space")', *Interiors: design, architecture, culture* 9(2): 140–56.

Waite, S. 2018. 'Intersectionality: embodied bodies, bodies of knowledge'. In E. McNeil *et al.*, *Mapping Queer Space(s) of Praxis and Pedagogy*. Cham: Palgrave MacMillan.

Zacko-Smith, J. D., and G. Pritchy Smith. 2010. 'Recognizing and utilizing queer pedagogy: a call for teacher education to reconsider the knowledge base on sexual orientation for teacher education programs', *Multicultural Education* 18(1): 2–9.

Zebracki, M., and R. Leitner. 2021. 'Queer monuments: visibility, (counter)actions, legacy', *Journal of Homosexuality*, https://doi.org/10.1080/00918369.2021.1913917 (last accessed 30 November 2022).

Zewolde, S., A. Walls, T., Sengupta, C. Ortiz, Y. Beebeejaun, G. Burridge and K. Patel. 2020. *'Race' and Space: what is 'race' doing in a nice field like the built environment?* London: The Bartlett, UCL Faculty of the Built Environment.

4
Co-designing educational assessments with students and external partners

Gemma Moore and Maria Xypaki

Over the past 15 years there has been a gradual shift within universities to widening their main functions of teaching and research to include a 'Third Mission' (Compagnucci *et al.*, 2020) that includes their contribution to society (Urdari *et al.*, 2017). This Third Mission has broadened the traditional roles and remit of universities to include activities that involve engagement with various stakeholders outside the university (Bourke, 2013; Pinheiro *et al.*, 2015). University engagement with external partners aligns with a paradigm shift within a number of disciplines grouped under built environment education (i.e., planning, urban design, urban studies, geography, architecture and engineering) that are embracing the fact that diverse actors are implicated in the process of city-making to address global societal developments (Lamb and Vodicha, 2021). Built environment students require education systems that support the critical questioning of key concepts such as 'urban', 'community' and the interrelationships between place and space (Casey, 2013; Dovey, 2010).

Critical postmodern pedagogies (Andreotti, 2010) enable critical enquiry, and one way to achieve it is by placing community engagement at the centre of student learning to enable students to learn to respect local knowledges and contribute to transformed subjectivities (Yonder *et al.*, 2021). University-community relationships offer a range of other opportunities for built environment students; for instance, they can provide students with an opportunity to learn practical skills in situ, while community partners benefit from technical know-how (Brand and Rincon, 2007; Millican, 2007). Students engage with real people and authentic issues, and they engage with personal and professional dilemmas (Kallus, 2021).

There are various pedagogical approaches that involve the engagement of external partners into teaching, such as citizen science, community engaged learning and service-learning. Despite their differences, these pedagogies all introduce experiential learning that includes users (students and partners from the community) within the knowledge production process as part of formal teaching. These pedagogies focus on teaching and learning activities associated with live projects, community-based research and project-based learning but usually not those of assessment. The closest term to describe assessment where external partners are involved is 'authentic assessment', which refers to assessments designed to achieve learning outcomes that reflect the tasks learners undertake in the course of working with knowledge in practice (Gunasekara and Gerts, 2017). Authentic assessment does not fall directly under a community engaged learning approach, and less attention has been given to the role of external partners in assessment and in the co-design of new knowledge with students within the assessment process. These are the areas that we seek to address within this chapter. To educate the built environment practitioners of the twenty-first century and to further understand critical postmodern pedagogies, research is needed to improve our understanding of authentic assessment when both external partners and students are involved in the knowledge production process. By addressing the research and practice gap of what are the ingredients of assessment when external partners are involved, we hope to: a) encourage further practice from built environment educators; and b) enrich pedagogical literature on authentic and engaged assessment.

In this chapter, we focus on the pedagogies of engagement, specifically related to educational assessments with students and external partners. We provide a context to the evolution of thinking behind the concept of community engaged learning and our approach uses the lens of knowledge democracy and knowledge co-design. This chapter contributes to the theme of *'teaching' – moments for developing specific intellectual capacities and/or co-production skills* of this book. We draw on a case study within the UK higher education sector, UCL, to outline how these ideas can be applied in practice, involving a collaboration between external partners (e.g., public bodies, voluntary and community organisations, grassroots and corporate partners, among others) and students within educational assessments. UCL makes an interesting case study for zooming in and out (Design Council, 2021), as we can switch between a focus on the micro (an example of community engaged learning in a master's module) and the macro (an institutional-level community engaged learning service), to help understand the wider context in which the module fits.

Starting with the macro level, the UCL Community Engaged Learning Service (CELS) provides a centralised service to support an institutional approach to community engagement in teaching. CELS is part of a wider infrastructure within UCL to support and share knowledge on engaged pedagogies and research underpinned by the Connected Curriculum Framework (UCL, 2015), which promotes research-based education and real-world learning. We outline key principles for community engaged learning generated through a university-community curriculum co-design workshop, held in June 2019 and attended by 41 participants: UCL students, representatives from London's voluntary and community sector, and UCL's academic and professional staff. The workshop employed a co-design approach aligned with the epistemological underpinning of an inclusive curriculum (Healey *et al.*, 2014). The principles used included the management of expectations, opportunities for formative feedback, re-thinking grading systems and the value of transferable skills.

We 'zoom in' on an example of engaged approaches to education assessments in the module on the MSc titled 'Health, Wellbeing and Sustainable Buildings' at the Institute for Environmental Design and Engineering at the Bartlett, UCL. The assessment is designed around real-world problems, with students as researchers conducting a health impact assessment of a proposed development. This used a process of action research where formative assessment opportunities were integrated into the curriculum design. These were also designed to enable active participation of different stakeholders in knowledge production.

This chapter outlines the key areas that have emerged from our experience and reflections on bridging between principles and practice of community engaged learning. The chapter starts with a brief introduction to the concepts of knowledge democracy and co-design within educational assessments. This section is followed by an outline of community engaged learning at UCL, including the development of principles for engaged assessments. We follow this with an example from practice at UCL, which is explored in depth. We then compare and reflect on how the principles of community engaged learning can be applied in practice, drawing out challenges and opportunities for practitioners and educators. We aim to provide a guide for those interested in university-community collaborations to co-design education assessments that results in the co-design of new knowledge. There was a range of contributors to this work, including 41 workshop participants, four cohorts of MSc students, and a range of community groups who we worked in partnership with. We acknowledge their role in this process, and the knowledge and experience that they contributed to our practice. Our account pays attention to their efforts. We bring together valuable and collective knowledge from our work on engaged pedagogies.

Knowledge democracy and co-design within educational assessments

Engaged pedagogies are teaching and learning approaches that bring students and external stakeholders together to co-design new knowledge and bring social change through social action (Fuller, 2003) as part of the formal curriculum. Engaged pedagogies are a vehicle for the promotion of knowledge democracy where students and partners co-produce new knowledge by working together on a problem or project and by bringing in their own knowledge and positionality. According to Hall and Tandon (2017) 'knowledge democracy acknowledges the importance of the existence of multiple epistemologies and the knowledge of the marginalised or excluded everywhere, or what is sometimes called the subaltern knowledge'. The contemporary university is often characterised as working with colonised knowledge, often excluding the epistemologies of indigenous people or those excluded based on race, gender or sexuality. It is important to understand whose knowledge is included and whose knowledge is excluded to avoid reinforcing colonised relations of knowledge power.

Knowledge democracy draws on Dewey's transactional approach that as living beings we are always already in transaction with the world (Dewey and Nagel, 1986; Dewey, 1996). Based on Dewey's theory, Biesta argues (2007) that we cannot accept scientific knowledge as better than everyday knowledge and that the university's knowledge cannot be the only valid knowledge. Not allowing for other epistemologies (outside the knowledge economy) to infiltrate the higher education curriculum is a threat to democracy. This is a sociological perspective on knowledge that draws on Foucault (1980) and Apple (1996) responses to the question, 'whose knowledge is of most worth?'.

For Hall and Tandon (2017), knowledge democracy is about understanding that knowledge is a powerful tool for taking action in social movements to deepen democracy. It is also about open access for sharing knowledge, so that all those who need it have access. Building on this, a range of voices and perspectives must be included in the knowledge production process. This aligns with Freire's call for 'openness to approaching and being approached, to questioning and being questioned, to agreeing and disagreeing' (Freire, 1998: 119). Delanty (2003) suggests that universities should become sites of public discourse rather than sites of exclusive expertise, so that they can become important agents of the public sphere who not only respond to social change, but (also) initiate it. Giroux presents a similar view when he makes the case that higher education institutions can and should function as 'a vital public sphere for critical learning, ethical deliberation and civic engagement' (Giroux, 2003: 196). These views also align with the underpinnings of the Third Mission that promotes the engagement of higher education institutions with the wider society (Compagnucci et al., 2020; Molas-Gallart et al., 2002) for the promotion of mutual benefits (Krčmářová, 2011). Third Mission is strongly linked to knowledge production and co-production (Pinheiro et al., 2017).

Goddard and Vallance (2013) suggest that universities use community engagement to identify challenges and opportunities in the society and ensure to inform their teaching and research agendas respectively. Within Third Mission discourses, governments incentivise and encourage higher education institutions to also become economic engines translating knowledge into products and services for the market (Bourke, 2013). This confirms Jongbloed et al.'s concern (2008) that a university can promote innovation but can also promote commodification of education by serving private interests rather than the public good. Thus, there can be tension between the democratisation of knowledge production.

According to Hollander (2011), it is not easy to align community needs with the university agenda and student needs during community engagement teaching or research projects. Another challenge is that many universities do not have the capacity to work with communities and translate the new knowledge that they co-produce into an applicable solution with positive social impact (Perry and May, 2006). Therefore, this public investment in knowledge production with communities does not necessarily result in social benefit, despite the creation of new knowledge to address challenges within specific contexts. There are also communities who are underrepresented and do not have access to resources and are therefore excluded from universities' Third Mission (Humphrey, 2003). Higher education institutions around the world are being encouraged by governments to assume greater responsibility for economic development and to translate knowledge into products and services for the market, while simultaneously being tasked to work with communities in alleviating the social and economic excesses of the market (Bourke, 2013).

Our work acknowledges the above tensions and seeks to explore education assessment through the lens of knowledge democracy and knowledge co-design to further enrich understanding of (engaged) critical postmodern pedagogies in built environment curricula, with a focus on assessment. Specifically, within the realm of UK higher education curriculum, examples in practice include authentic assessment and experiential learning. Authentic assessment aims to evaluate the application of knowledge from the classroom into different contexts, scenarios and situations (Wiggins, 1998). Similarly, experiential learning provides opportunities for students to apply their knowledge, it can also improve motivation of students by showing their relevance to real-life situations (Helle *et al.*, 2007). We argue that the philosophical approach of co-design is fundamentally aligned with the epistemological underpinning of an inclusive curriculum for knowledge democracy. An inclusive curriculum, encompassing diverse perspectives and strategies, is more rounded, relevant and meaningful (Hockings, 2010). Using the same approach, but extending it to the local community, we are also hoping to reverse the 'democratic-deficit' and decolonise knowledge (Hall *et al.*, 2017). The inclusion of community perspectives can add depth to university curricula and ensure that content has greater relevance beyond the institution (Allen-Meares, 2008).

Within built environment studies, Rafferty *et al.* (2021) note three different approaches to embedding real-life practice in planning education: 'real world' as a case study to observe; 'real world' as a process to 'plug in' to and work, exposing students to complex socio-physical contexts; and 'real world' as a 'living laboratory' for immersion and experimentation: orientated towards community activation. Furthermore, Rafferty *et al.* (2021) offer a pedagogy that moves beyond didactic teaching styles of describing participation to planning students and towards experimental ways of exposing students to the potential opportunities and complexities of real-world co-production in participatory planning through action learning. They outline stages of knowledge co-production as: co-understanding (using knowledge sharing); co-creating (by connecting knowledge); co-designing (from knowledge appropriation); and co-delivering (through knowledge application). We echo their account and argue that students benefit from engaging with a diverse range of stakeholders (and not only with powerful voices) to better consider ways of co-producing knowledge through equal relationships and co-designing community engagement to enable positive social change. There is a need to differentiate the roles of different actors in the production of knowledge, the acceptance of knowledge frameworks or ways of knowing and learning the representation of reality, which requires an understanding of power relations involved (Armitage, 2008). This awareness is key to inclusion of more marginalised stakeholders to participate in learning processes and to democratise knowledge.

Zooming out: community engaged learning at UCL

This chapter focuses on community engaged learning at one UK higher education institution; UCL. There is a complex interplay of strategies and practical actions to formalise and embed community engagement within rescarch and teaching at UCL.

Despite an institutional focus on public engagement at UCL (Chang and Moore, 2017), there was lack of an institutional approach to engaging communities in teaching (community engaged learning), as well as fragmented community engaged learning practice across higher education institutions in the United Kingdom; this is why CELS was created at UCL. CELS is one of the key institutional drivers that enables and celebrates university-community collaborations in the curriculum across UCL faculties. CELS was created in 2018 between two professional teams: the engagement team, and the academic development team (UCL Arena). UCL defines 'CEL' as experiential learning where students collaborate with external partners to address real-world challenges and opportunities as part of their assignments and research. There is no fixed definition of the 'community' – it can include any partner outside UCL that enables teaching staff to meet their learning outcomes. The partners can be local or global, grassroots organisations or corporates. The partners recruited by the CELS and matched with UCL courses are mainly from the voluntary and community sector and the public sector (e.g., local councils and schools). It can be assumed that the leaders of these organisations have the confidence to take social action, despite their potentially limited resources. CELS projects support universities and community partners to learn how to work together, produce new knowledge and address challenges and opportunities. CELS enables the delivery of the Connected Curriculum Framework and it specifically underpins dimension 3 (students make connections across subjects and out to the world) and dimension 5 (students learn to produce outputs – assessments directed at an audience) (Fung, 2017: 146).

Developing a new cross-institutional service that aims to mainstream a resource-intensive pedagogy such as community engaged learning has been a challenge, especially in a complex institution such as UCL. Some of the initial challenges in setting up CELS were to: 1) identify the exact scope of the service within the university; 2) identify the various academic, student and community needs to develop a responsive and relevant offering; 3) develop an inclusive framing that encompasses all existing community engaged learning practices at UCL; 4) demonstrating the value of community engaged learning in enhancing academic practice, student experience and societal impact by identifying and celebrating existing practice at UCL; and, most importantly, 5) identifying what community engaged learning actually means for UCL students, staff and their communities.

CELS offers training, advice and support to staff with teaching responsibilities on how to embed engagement into their teaching practice. Engaged teaching can have many formats that involve mutually beneficial relations between students-partners; for exsmple, it can be about inviting a community fellow in the classroom to work with students on a problem (problem-based learning), or it can be about students working with partners on site to co-develop an outcome (e.g., planning students working with communities to develop neighbourhood plans) (community-based research project). The CELS team has been advising academics how to prepare their students to work with partners by offering or signposting them to training on communication, conflict management, stakeholder management, cultural sensitivity and other subjects. As part of designing the service, a number of curriculum co-design workshops with partners, students and academics were organised to define community engagement and how it looks in the curriculum (i.e., within teaching strategies, educational assessments). These workshops enabled the co-design of the principles for community engaged learning at UCL.

Principles for community engaged learning (educational assessment)

This section describes a specific workshop titled 'Building Bridges and Co-designing Learning', which took place on 3 June 2019, to co-design principles for CEL. The workshop specifically explored how a partnership between students, community organisations and academic staff could enhance student experience and enrich the curriculum and assessment practice as well as benefit the community partners, also with the idea of introducing non-academic epistemologies into higher education curricula (knowledge democracy). The workshop brought together 41 participants, including UCL students of different levels and disciplines, representatives from London's voluntary and community sector and Camden Council, and UCL academic and professional staff. The breakdown of participants was: 18 students; 15 community partners; and eight academic staff/teaching fellows/staff supporting learning. The participants represented a range of disciplines including urban studies and planning. The event was organised by CELS with the support of Students' Union UCL Volunteering Service.

We first describe the workshop activities, then outline the key findings from the session. This section concludes with some principles generated through the workshop. The workshop was structured so that students, community partners and academic staff could share their own perspectives and subsequently work together to generate ideas. There were activities to encourage self-reflection, followed by an opportunity for participants to contribute their reflections into group discussions, as shown in the list below.

Workshop activity 1 – understanding skills and knowledges

Self-reflection

- Students: What skills, qualities and knowledge do you want to gain by the end of your programme?
- Community partners: What skills, qualities and knowledge do you that think graduates should have to work in your organisation and/or address some of the challenges you face?
- Academic staff/teaching fellows/staff support learning: What skills, qualities and knowledge do you want students to gain by the end of their programme?

Group discussion

- What skills, qualities and knowledge do you think graduates should have to address (local) challenges?

Workshop activity 2 – thinking about assessment

Self-reflection

- Students: How do you like to be assessed? How do you see the role of external partners in your assessment?
- Community partners: If you were to collaborate with students on a project as part of their programme, what role would you like to have in their assessment, if any?
- Academic staff/teaching fellows/staff support learning: What do you think is the most beneficial assessment for your students? How do you see the role of community partners in the assessment?

Group discussion

- What could assessment look like when students and community partners collaborate to ensure benefit for everyone involved?

The responses were analysed by one of the co-authors, and the key findings are summarised below. In the first activity, participants mostly referenced knowledge of communication and interpersonal skills, as well as expertise in a discipline and the ability to apply this disciplinary knowledge to real world scenarios (see Table 4.1). Within the group discussion, communication and interpersonal skills were still the most referenced. Problem-solving and entrepreneurial skills came second, and planning and management came third.

In the second activity, the importance of co-designing projects/ assessments came out strongly from all participants. Community organisations seemed keen to provide formative feedback, mostly about the development of students' soft skills. The group discussions reinforced the idea of co-designing assessment, while the importance of transitioning to a fail/pass assessment system (rather than a grading system) was highlighted. The findings are summarised in Table 4.2. The findings illustrate what skills students, staff and community partners considered important and what the role of the community partners may be in assessing those skills and expertise. The importance of co-designing learning activities and assessment was also strongly highlighted for a mutually beneficial relationship, as well as the use of various assessment outputs.

These workshop activities fed into the development of principles for community engaged learning at UCL, focusing on co-designing

Table 4.1 Findings from workshop activity 1

Questions	Summarised responses: key themes
What skills, qualities and knowledge do you want to gain by the end of your programme?	Students mostly referenced: 1. communication skills, interpersonal skills, networking skills, presentation skills and listening skills; 2. expertise in a discipline or variety of disciplines and the ability to apply degree knowledge to real-world scenarios; and 3. research skills.
What skills, qualities and knowledge do you think graduates should have to work in your organisation and/or address some of the challenges you face?	Community partners mostly mentioned: 1. communication skills, interpersonal skills, networking skills, presentation skills and listening skills; 2. expertise in a discipline or variety of disciplines and the ability to apply degree knowledge to real-world scenarios; and 3. proactivity, problem-solving, entrepreneurial skills and creativity, project management and project design.
What skills, qualities and knowledge do you want students to gain by the end of their programme?	Academic staff mostly referenced: 1. expertise in a discipline or variety of disciplines and the ability to apply degree knowledge to real-world scenarios; 2. communication skills, interpersonal skills, networking skills, presentation skills and listening skills; and 3. Problem-solving, entrepreneurial skills and creativity, team working, resilience, thoughtfulness, research skills and empathy.
Group discussion: what skills, qualities and knowledge do you think graduates should have to address (local) challenges?	1. communication skills, interpersonal skills, networking skills, presentation skills and listening skills; 2. problem-solving, entrepreneurial skills, creativity, innovation and resourcefulness; and 3. planning, management and time management.

educational assessments with community partners. Six principles were agreed, which covered the whole assessment process from designing the assessment brief to marking. These are outlined in Table 4.3. These principles are not focused on any discipline or level of student education

Table 4.2 Findings from workshop activity 2

Questions	Summarised responses: key themes
How do you like to be assessed? How do you see the role of external partners in your assessment?	Students seem to think that the three most important things are to: 1. design research questions together; 2. receive feedback on projects from the partners (formative assessment); and 3. work on a research question with the partner/do volunteering with them.
If you were to collaborate with students on a project as part of their programme, what role would you like to have in their assessment, if any?	Community partners referenced a number of ideas with similar weight: 1. lead a pre-planned session 2. set tasks and coursework to give students (incorporate this with the type of sector); 3. give feedback to students; 4. assessment with academic staff, not by myself; and 5. students to become part of our team/long-term partnership.
What do you think is the most beneficial assessment for your students? How do you see the role of community partners in the assessment?	Academic staff mostly referenced: 1. co-design feedback criteria with students, staff and community organisations; 2. community partners can provide feedback on students' skill development, how the project has met the outcomes and formative feedback; and 3. a range of assessments (written – essays, portfolio, reports and case studies), oral presentations (individual and group), social media output (blogs, etc.) and other art (e.g., animation and comics).
Group discussion: what could assessment look like when students and community partners collaborate to ensure benefit for everyone involved?	1. co-design assessment with communities, students and staff – criteria, skills, work to be done; 2. mutually beneficial outcomes with feedback/evaluate what all parties have learnt; and 3. assessment can be about a fail or pass, not a grading system, especially when collaborating with external partners – it is difficult to establish assessment criteria and there must be transparency as to how students get assessed.

Table 4.3 Principles for co-designing educational assessment with community partners

CEL: educational assessment principles
Co-design of the assessment brief and the parameters (partners and students)
Formative feedback by the partner (not summative)
Reflection – check-in points throughout the project (both students and partners to be giving feedback about how the partnership works)
Agreement on expectations and roles before the project starts
Transition to a fail/pass assessment system (rather than a grading system)
Supervision/mediation of the partnership by a tutor

or type of community partner or type of assessment, instead they are a guide, at an institutional level, for considering community engagement in educational assessments. The next section 'zooms in' on one specific teaching module, within built environment studies, as an example of community engaged learning in practice.

Zooming in: community engaged learning in practice

This section focuses on a specific example of a module that undertook a community engaged learning approach. We describe the development and implementation of co-designing an assessment for an MSc module Health and Wellbeing in Cities: Theory and Practice, which has been running in UCL's Bartlett Institute for Environmental Design and Engineering since 2017/2018.

Health and wellbeing in the built environment is a complex system with a range of interchangeable and interrelated factors. For instance, the air we breathe, the social networks we have, the housing we live in and sense of community all have an impact on our health and wellbeing. Health and wellbeing factors are increasingly recognised as a key part of urban design and planning decisions. The module Health and Wellbeing in Cities: Theory and Practice aimed to enhance the understanding of health and wellbeing in the built environment at a neighbourhood and urban scale. Through a series of lectures and coursework assessment the module introduced a number of factors (environmental and social) affecting health and wellbeing within the built environment. Students learn about the relationship between the design and planning of neighbourhoods and health and wellbeing, and question why certain planning and design features impact on people's health and wellbeing. The overall aim of the students' coursework was to conduct a health impact assessment (HIA). HIAs can be defined as: 'a combination of procedures, methods and tools that systematically judges the potential, and sometimes unintended, effects of a policy, plan, programme or project on both the health of the population and the distribution of those effects within the population. Health impact assessments identify appropriate actions to manage those effects' (International Association of Impact Assessment, 2006). HIAs are a tool to assess the health and wellbeing impacts from planning. Within the case study area, Camden, London, the requirement is that where a major development is proposed, the developer needs to submit an HIA with the planning application. The students worked in groups to critically and systematically assess a real-life urban development proposal, questioning how healthy it is and thinking about the potential impacts on health and wellbeing. The approach adopted aligns with Rafferty *et al.*'s (2021) call to 'plug in' and expose built environment students to complex socio-physical contexts. Each individual student submitted a 3,000-word report for the module's assessment.

The design of the module, in 2017, involved a period of scoping with teaching staff, researchers, industry and community partners to decide upon the key content and underpinning narrative of the module. This scoping stage was essential due to the broad topic and emerging research area. The module lead decided that a cross cutting theme would be participation, and the module would take an engaged approach. The module contributed to engaged learning through four key domains: experiential learning for co-understanding; participation and inclusion for co-creation; collaboration; and action and reflection. These are illustrated in Figure 4.1 and are referenced in terms of the coursework assessment.

Experiential learning for co-understanding

The module was designed to enhance the learning experience by taking students outside the classroom, both physically and mentally, through a range of voices, perspectives and locations within and for the lectures (Ward and Fyson, 1973; Kolb, 1984). The coursework assessment was designed around real-world problems and the students' role as researchers, drawing on experiential learning opportunities.

The HIA was conducted on a real-world urban development project (to date, this has included the proposed expansion of Heathrow, in west

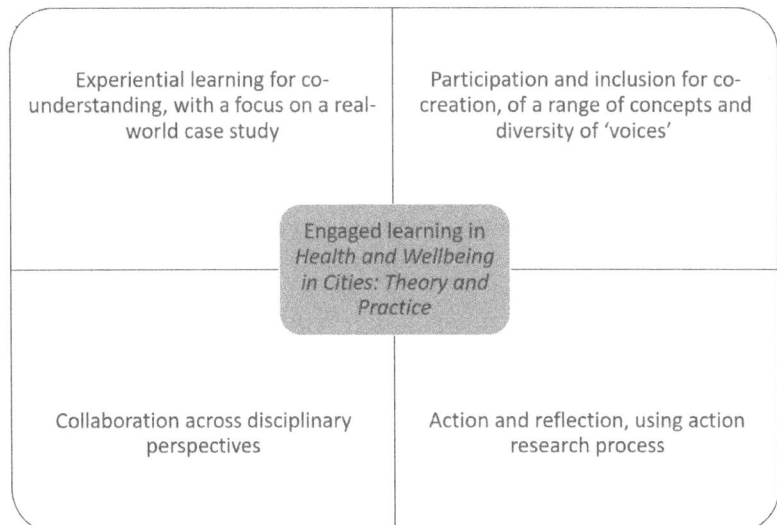

Figure 4.1 The domains of engaged learning within an MSc module.
Source: Author

London, and the UCL Centre of Excellence for Neurology and Dementia Research in Kings Cross, London). The coursework aimed to connect people who are researching health in the built environment (i.e., the students and module staff), with those who make decisions on health (i.e., planners, public health) and those who 'experience' health such as residents and community groups. The case study became a site of intersecting practices. There was building of common knowledge to understand the interests and experience of each practice. This helped to inform the production of new knowledge. This stage was crucial for the students to understand, through active learning (specifically problem-based learning) how to develop solutions to real-world problems that take account of different groups. The building of common knowledge leads to co-produced understanding. Within this example, the coursework assessment builds in ideas of the environment as the educational resource (Ward and Fyson, 1973), as it provided an opportunity for students to tackle problem-based research, rich in real world context and complexity.

Participation and inclusion for co-creation

In the field of design and planning, Pineo (2020) argues that healthy urbanism processes should be participatory, involving co-design and other methods to incorporate local knowledge. This concept was promoted in the core content of the module materials through the inclusion of theories and approaches to participation, engagement and co-design. Through the lectures and materials, students built up an understanding of the ideas behind engagement and participation, including debates that surround such practices. However, further participation is key to module delivery. The module promoted the involvement of a range of people, from inside and outside the university in the teaching. Some lectures included practitioners. For instance, the session on the role of social cohesion and networks on health was delivered with a community centre manager (in their community centre). The community centre manager shared information and reflections on the programmes they delivered to tackle issues around loneliness and isolation in the local community. The approach used gave emphasis to including a wide range of perspectives and groups involved in the module (including the lesser heard voices of community groups and local residents). Through extending the reach and diversity of those involved there is a variety of voices included in the knowledge production process. With the coursework, the tutorials, specifically the coursework, are co-delivered with community partners who ensure that local knowledge is shared with the students about the development that they are focusing on. This involved the community partner working with the module lead to plan, design and deliver the tutorial. Lectures and tutorials were designed like this to enable student active participation in the engagement of different stakeholders, to broaden their learning experience (Kemmis and McTaggart, 2000; Passon and Schlesinger, 2019). Co-delivery involved both lecturers and partners sharing information about the site and the challenges; the lecturer offered theoretical perspectives, whereas the partner offered more practical and experiential perspectives.

Collaboration

It is widely agreed that urban design and planning requires the involvement, collaboration and transfer of knowledge between a variety of people and professions. Collaboration is generally seen as a tool within urban design and planning, which is employed to minimise tensions that can prevail (i.e., siloed working, lack of ownership, bridging the knowledge-gap). Collaboration and learning through collaborative processes was therefore a useful skill to develop during the students' studies. Within the assessment, students worked in small groups (of four to five) to undertake coursework. These groups tend to be multidisciplinary, including students from engineering, architecture, geography, public policy and planning. It has been shown that group work can model professional practice, having relevance to future work and employment (Fearon et al., 2012). Built environment professionals' roles often work across disciplinary and sector boundaries; for instance, Wood states planners 'assume a far more active, entrepreneurial, cross-disciplinary and collaborative role' (2007: 78). Tutorials and support are offered to the students, who are encouraged to take ownership of the process of enquiry (Passon and Schlesinger, 2019) by collecting, collating and comparing different types of evidence; engaging with different stakeholders (including non-students) to discuss their methods and the meanings of the 'evidence' collected; and critically judging the topics and issues raised and their potential effects on health and wellbeing.

The coursework is assessed in an individual report produced by the students. Experience of running a module with a group project that turned into an individual assessment highlighted the challenges involved. This has the disadvantage that individuals in a group have the challenge of producing an individual piece of work when the data and research insights have come from working together. If the goal of collaboration is to open up decision-making to a range of voices, then it must be recognised that this itself may bring challenges; for instance, these different voices may find it difficult to find the common links to reach consensus, there may be imbalances of roles and activities. It is important to acknowledge the value of discussion, negotiation and compromise in the collaborative process. Thus, collaboration should be a supported and structured process. Within this module, the integration of formative assessment opportunities (outlined in the section below) gave some structure to the collaborative learning process.

Action and reflection

The students were specifically asked to approach the HIA through a process of action research. As part of this process, students received formative feedback from partners outside the university and were encouraged to reflect on their approach. Taking an action research approach mirrors design and planning processes, which have a number of stages, feedback loops and iterations (guided by the work of Kemmis and McTaggart, 2000). Within this module there were two clear stages of formative feedback (outlined in Figure 4.2). First, a community workshop was organised

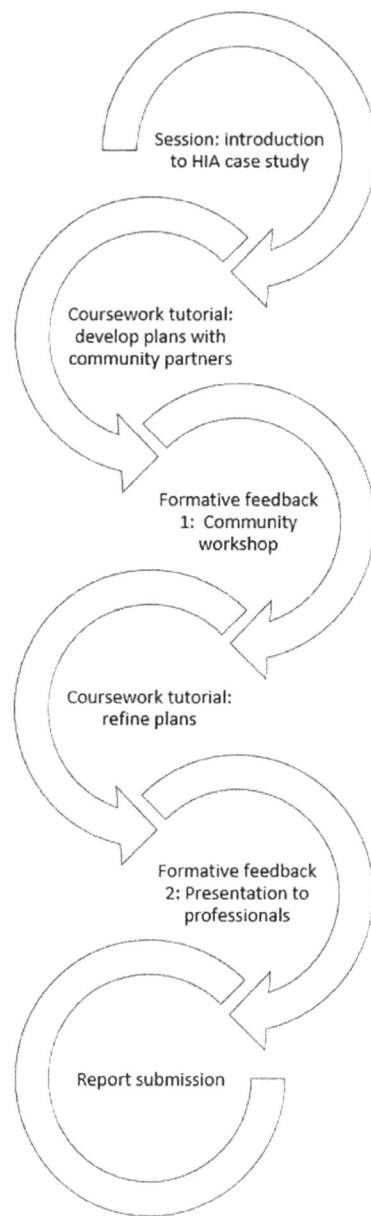

Figure 4.2 Summary of the action research process as applied in the coursework.

Source: Authors

during the module, where students presented the initial stages of their work and discussed the meaning of their findings with members of the community. It included residents and representatives who would be impacted by the proposal and would share their lived experiences of the development. This provided an opportunity for students to communicate with individuals from a range of backgrounds and cultures. The interaction encouraged the students to explore the values and ethical challenges that underpin their coursework and the experience of health and wellbeing in the built environment. Second, the students were required to present their findings (including any arising from the community workshop) to a panel of professionals – from academic, non-governmental organisations and advisory organisations, who provide valuable advice and guidance to the students. Within their submitted reports, students were marked on a reflections section, where they were asked to reflect on the action research approach and their learning through the formative feedback process.

Authentic assessment in practice

Moore and Pineo (2021) note that in practising healthy place-making, critical reflection is an instrument for progress in order to build capacity and knowledge within the sector. This module is an example of how such learning can be embedded in teaching to encourage reflective practice within built environment educational assessments. Zooming into this example demonstrates an approach to learning in built environment studies, which includes experiential and authentic assessment that involves community partners (community engaged learning). Students worked in teams, with the intention of building a common understanding between those involved, for joint recommendations on a real-world challenge of integrating health considerations in a new development project. There was value in responding to a real-world issue and contributing to a real-life process. Within one cohort (2018/2019) the students fed their assessment findings into a larger community impact assessment, run by a community organisation Just Space, and shared reflections on HIAs to the local authority (the London Borough of Camden). The assessment had a clear contribution outside of the institution, resonating with an approach to community engaged learning that Rafferty *et al.* (2021) would define as a real-world or 'living laboratory' for immersion and experimentation, orientated towards community activation.

Learning from bridging principles and practice

We have provided a more nuanced understanding of engaged learning, and although community engagement is context-dependent (Laing and Maddison, 2007), we hope that zooming in and out of our case study can help inform wider educational practice. Our learning – bridging principles and practice – contributed insights into how engaged pedagogies can be achieved in practice for built environment students, providing them with experiences that, we hope, will shape their professional practice. Our intention is to demonstrate an approach to add depth to university curricula and ensure that content has greater relevance beyond the institution (Allen-Meares, 2008). Our experience has highlighted specific strategies to push built environment education beyond the boundaries of classic knowledge systems. Table 4.4 compares the institutional principles – developed in the workshop – to practice, bringing in the reflections outlined above.

Our comparison between the institutional principles and practice offers strategies for embedding engagement with educational assessments. Our reflections reveal three tensions from translating the principles to in practice: institutional marking frameworks; dealing with flux and fluidity; and power shifting. First, despite calls to rethink the value of different knowledges (and the grading structures), there can be a need and requirement to fit into wider institutional systems of criteria and marking. Within the MSc example, it was not possible to change the grading system or have those outside the academy involved in the marking processes. Second, embedding real-life practice in education requires an ability to deal with flux and fluidity, as plans change. What we found, in practice, was that despite planning an engaged process, both barriers and opportunity arose, leading to shifts in plans. Dealing with such fluidity requires management of expectations for all parties (i.e., both students and community partners) to ensure that the collaboration is genuinely a mutually beneficial relationship, and if not, then working out how it can be. Finally, it is important to acknowledge where power lies in such processes. For a teaching programme to be approved, it must go through the Academic Partnerships Framework (UCL, 2021), which is a specific quality assurance process that defines the partnership between UCL curricula and external partners. External partners can be included (or excluded), as they need to have specific characteristics to be formally approved as 'quality assured' partners in a programme. These policies reveal where power lies in terms of deciding ultimately who is involved within teaching.

Table 4.4 Co-designing assessments with community partners – principles and practice

Assessment principles Community engaged learning	Assessment practice Community engaged learning	Alignment between principles and practice Key: ***aligned completely **aligned in part *not aligned
Co-design of the assessment brief and the parameters (partners and students)	Developed a space for co-understanding: involvement of community partners and stakeholders for the case study selection, not the brief	**
Formative feedback by the partner (not summative)	Set points made for formative feedback (i.e., workshops and presentations) during the assessment process, to ensure that community voices are included in the feedback	***
Reflection – check-in points throughout the project (both students and partners giving feedback about how the partnership works)	Built-in time for reflection in and on practice, to encourage preparation to deal with things going differently from plan	***
Agreement on expectations and roles before the project starts	Before the teaching started, we informally agreed what outputs would be created from the assessment and discussed the potential outcomes (for the university, the students and the community partner)	**
Transition to a fail/pass assessment system (rather than a grading system)	The example followed a grading system, but effort was made to regularly communicate achievements within the wider process	*
Supervision/mediation of the partnership by a tutor	Before the teaching started, the module leader set out a structure to support collaboration and collaborative learning for the students	*

Concluding remarks

Community engaged learning as an element of critical postmodern pedagogies can take many forms and produce outcomes that range from positive social action to communities, through skill development of students, to changes in educational practice. To bring about such outcomes the facilitators of engaged teaching navigate a range of tensions to translate principles to practice. Our experiences of employing knowledge co-design methodologies at both an institutional and module level illustrate several important points. First, they reveal the ingredients of authentic assessment when partners are involved, which can inform built environment educators. They also reveal the tensions between conventional teaching practice and engaged pedagogies in terms of shifting knowledge power dynamics while following university policies, building mutually beneficial relationships while working in flux, and fitting into wider institutional systems of criteria and marking.

Our example, we hope, is of interest for built environment educators who are keen to open up their teaching practice and build in spaces for engagement. The experience has demonstrated that this is possible through the creation of opportunities to apply learning in the real world; the inclusion of diverse perspectives and knowledges; structures for collaborative learning; and consideration of the importance of reflective practice from a multi-loop learning perspective. The example was an educational assessment; however, it was more than that for the students; the experience enabled the development of capacities and capabilities (e.g., to be participatory as a practitioner, to merge different forms of knowledge), which are needed in the production of spaces and places.

We propose that those motivated, interested and open to innovation might pilot new ways of undertaking co-design in assessments. Piloting and then scaling up these initiatives to other modules and courses, can be facilitated by sharing the learning (both positive and negative findings) from such initiatives. By adopting a critical approach and being reflective it is possible to engage learning to promote knowledge democracy.

References

Allen-Meares, P. 2008. 'Schools of social work contribution to community partnerships: the renewal of the social compact in higher education', *Journal of Human Behavior in the Social Environment* 18: 79–100.

Andreotti, V. 2010. 'Global education in the "21st century": two different perspectives on the "post-" of postmodernism', *International Journal of Development Education and Global Learning* 2(2): 5–22.

Apple, M. W. 1996. *Cultural Politics and Education*. New York: Teachers College Press.
Armitage, D. 2008. 'Governance and the commons in a multi-level world', *International Journal of the Commons* 2(1): 7–32.
Biesta, G. 2007. 'Towards the knowledge democracy? Knowledge production and the civic role of the university', *Studies in Philosophy and Education* 26(5), 467–79.
Bourke, A. 2013. 'Universities, civil society and the global agenda of community-engaged research', *Globalisation, Societies and Education* 11(4), 498–519.
Brand, R., and H. Rincon. 2007. 'Tackling six common dilemmas in "Live" planning projects', *Journal for Education in the Built Environment* 2(2), 36–60.
Casey, E. S. 2013. *The Fate of Place: a philosophical history*. Berkeley CA: University of California Press.
Chang, M., and G. Moore. 2017. 'Enabling conditions for communities and universities to work together: a journey of university public engagement'. In A. Ersoy (ed.), *The Impact of Co-Production: from community engagement to social justice*. London: Policy Press.
Compagnucci L., and F. Spigarelli F. 2020. 'The Third Mission of the University: a systematic literature review on potentials and constraints', *Technological Forecasting and Social Change* 161.
Delanty, G. 2003. 'Ideologies of the knowledge society and the cultural contradictions of higher education', *Policy Futures in Education* 1(1): 71–82.
Design Council. 2021. 'Beyond Net Zero Systemic Design Approach', https://www.designcouncil.org.uk/resources/guide/beyond-net-zero-systemic-design-approach (last accessed 30 November 2022).
Dewey, J., and J. Nagel. (1986) *The Later Works of John Dewey, 1925–1953, Vol. 12: 1938, Logic: The Theory of Inquiry*. Carbondale IL: Southern Illinois University Press.
Dewey, J. 1996. *Essays in Experimental Logic*. Chicago IL: University of Chicago Press.
Dovey, K. 2010. *Becoming Places: urbanism/architecture/identity/power*. London. Routledge.
Fearon, C., H. McLaughlin and T. Yoke Eng. 2012. 'Using student group work in higher education to emulate professional communities of practice', *Education and Training* 54(2–3): 114–25.
Freire, P. 1998. *Pedagogy of Freedom: ethics, democracy, and civic courage*. Oxford: Rowman & Littlefield.
Foucault, M. 1980. *Power-Knowledge: selected interviews and other writings, 1972-1977*. Brighton: Harvester Press.
Fuller, S. 2003. 'Can Universities solve the problem of knowledge in society without succumbing to the knowledge society?', *Policy Futures in Education* 1(1): 106–24.
Fung, Dilly. 2017. *A Connected Curriculum for Higher Education*. London: UCL Press, https://discovery.ucl.ac.uk/id/eprint/1558776/1/A-Connected-Curriculum-for-Higher-Education.pdf (last accessed 30 November 2022).
Giroux, H. A. 2003. 'Selling out higher education', *Policy Futures in Education* 1(1), 179–200.
Goddard, J., and P. Vallance. 2013. *The University and the City*. London: Routledge.
Gunasekara C., and C. Gerts. 2017. 'Enabling authentic assessment: the essential role of information literacy', *Journal of the Australian Library and Information Association* 66(4): 393–405.
Hall, B. L., and R. Tandon. 2017. 'Decolonization of knowledge, epistemicide, participatory research and higher education', *Research for All* 1(1): 6–19.
Healey, M., A. Flint and K. Harrington. 2014 *Engagement Through Partnership Students as Partners in Learning and Teaching in Higher Education*. York: The Higher Education Academy.
Helle, L., P. Tynjälä, E. Olkinuora and K. Lonka. 2007 'Ain't nothing like the real thing: motivation and study processes on a work-based project course in information systems design', *British Journal of Educational Psychology* 77(2): 397–411.
Hockings, C. 2010. *Inclusive Learning and Teaching in Higher Education: a synthesis of research*. York: The Higher Education Academy.
Hollander, J. B. 2011. 'Keeping control: the paradox of scholarly community-based research in community development', *Community Development Journal* 46(2): 265–72.
Humphrey, L. 2013. 'University–Community Engagement'. In P. Benneworth (ed.), *University Engagement with Socially Excluded Communities*. Dordrecht: Springer, 103–24.
International Association for Impact Assessment. 2006. *Definition of HIA*, https://www.iaia.org/wiki-details.php?ID=14 (last accessed 30 November 2022).
Jongbloed, B., J. Enders and C. Salerno. 2008. 'Higher education and its communities: interconnections, interdependencies and a research agenda', *Higher Education* 56(3): 303–24.
Kallus R. 2021. 'Planning with the community: engaged professional education in ethno-nationally contested city'. In A. I. Frank and A. da Rosa Pires (eds), *Teaching Urban and Regional Planning*. Cheltenham: Edward Elgar Publishing, 74–93.

Kemmis, S., and R. McTaggart. 2000. 'Participatory Action Research'. In N. K. Denzin and Y.S. Lincoln (eds), *Handbook of Qualitative Research*. London: SAGE Publishing.

Kolb, D. A. 1984. *Experiential Learning: experience as the source of learning and development*. Englewood Cliffs NJ: Prentice-Hall.

Krčmářová J. 2011. 'The third mission of higher education institutions: conceptual framework and application in the Czech Republic', *European Journal of Higher Education* 1(4): 315–31.

Laing, S., and E. Maddison. 2007. 'The Cupp model in context'. In A. Hart, E. Maddison and D. Wolff (eds), *Community-University Partnerships in Practice*. Leicester: National Institute of Adult Continuing Education, 8–20.

Lamb, T., and G. Vodicha. 2021. 'Education for 21st century urban and spatial planning: critical postmodern pedagogies'. In A. I. Frank and A. da Rosa Pires (eds), *Teaching Urban and Regional Planning*. Cheltenham: Edward Elgar Publishing, 20–38.

Millican, J. 2007. 'Student community engagement – A model for the 21st century?'. Paper for workshop on Models of Student Community Engagement, for the Global Citizens Conference at Bournemouth University. Poole: Global Citizens Conference.

Molas-Gallart J., A. Salter, P. Patel, X. Scott and A. Duran A. 2002. 'Measuring Third Stream activities'. Final Report to the Russell Group of Universities. SPRU Science and Technology Policy Research Unity, University of Sussex, Brighton.

Passon J., and J. Schlesinger. 2019. 'Inquiry-Based Learning in Geography'. In H. A. Mieg (ed.), *Inquiry-Based Learning – Undergraduate Research*. Cham: Springer.

Perry B., and T. May. 2006. 'Excellence, relevance and the university: the missing middle in socio-economic engagement', *Journal of Higher Education in Africa* 4: 69–92.

Pineo, H. 2020. 'Towards healthy urbanism: inclusive, equitable and sustainable (THRIVES) – an urban design and planning framework from theory to praxis', *Cities & Health* 0: 1–19.

Pineo, H., and G. Moore. 2021. 'Built environment stakeholders' experiences of implementing healthy urban development: an exploratory study', *Cities & Health*, https://doi.org/10.1080/23748834.2021.1876376 (last accessed 30 November).

Pinheiro, R., P. V. Langa and A. Pausits. 2015. 'The institutionalization of universities' third mission: introduction to the special issue', *European Journal of Higher Education* 5(3): 227–32.

Pinheiro, R., J. Karlsen, J. Kohoutek and M. Young. 2017. 'Universities' Third Mission: global discourses and national imperatives', *Higher Education Policy* 30: 425–42.

Polster, C. 2007. 'The nature and implications of the growing importance of research grants to Canadian universities and academics', *Higher Education* 53(5): 599–622.

Rafferty, G., G. Concilio, J. Carlos Mota, F. Nogueira, E. Puerari and L. O'Kane. 2021. 'Collaborative and innovative participatory planning pedagogies: reflections from the Community Participation in Planning project'. In A. I. Frank and A. da Rosa Pires (eds), *Teaching Urban and Regional Planning*. Cheltenham: Edward Elgar Publishing, 125–41.

UCL. 2018. *Community Engaged Learning Service*, https://www.ucl.ac.uk/teaching-learning/teaching-resources/community-engaged-learning-cel (last accessed 30 November 2022).

UCL. (2021). 'Chapter 8: Academic partnerships framework'. In *Academic Manual (updated)*, https://www.ucl.ac.uk/academic-manual/sites/academic-manual/files/chapter-8-academic-partnerships-framework-2018-19.pdf (last accessed 30 November 2022).

Urdari, C., T. Farcas and A. Tiron Tudor. 2017. 'Assessing the legitimacy of HEIs contributions to society: the perspective of international rankings', *Sustainability Accounting, Management and Policy Journal* 8(2): 191–15.

Ward, C., and A. Fyson. 1973. *Streetwork: the exploding school*. London: Routledge.

Wiggins, G. 1998. *Educative Assessment: Designing Assessments to Inform and Improve Student Practice*. San Francisco CA: Jossey-Bass.

Wood, J. 2007. 'Synergy city; planning for a high density, super-symbiotic society', *Landscape and Urban Planning* 83(1): 77–83.

Yonder A., M. Mercedes Narciso and J. Camilo Osorio. 2021. 'Pedagogy built on working with communities: a first semester core course'. In A. I. Frank and A. da Rosa Pires (eds), *Teaching Urban and Regional Planning*. Cheltenham: Edward Elgar Publishing, 57–73.

5
Engaged pedagogy, informality and collaborative governance in South Africa

Stuart Paul Denoon-Stevens, Lauren Andres, Martin Lewis, Lorena Melgaço, Verna Nel and Elsona van Huyssteen

For many years South Africa has modelled its urban planning practices on Northern systems, reinforced by the education and training provided to urban planning students in higher education institutions. Concerns have been raised about these methods' relevance and applicability when planning African cities (Watson, 2003, 2009). The UN-Habitat's Global Report on Human Settlements: Planning Sustainable Cities (2009) emphasises the role of urban planning in addressing urban dysfunctions and stresses the relevance of urban planning education in Africa. The South African Council for Planners (SACPLAN), which acts as the accrediting body in the country, clearly positions planning education as a way to raise the awareness of graduates and practitioners about core urban challenges. Indeed, urban planners in South Africa play a meaningful role in the development and transformation of the country (Andres *et al.*, 2020; Denoon-Stevens *et al.*, 2022). However, many crucial changes need to be made to ensure that planning and planners can help address sustainability challenges (Oranje, 2014) in a context of resource scarcity (including the number of planners and their ability to train beyond graduation). Addressing these challenges has pedagogical implications as aspiring planners need to grasp all the complexity of a profession that is evolving quickly. This requires employing diverse and innovative methods to engage students in unwrapping rapidly changing formal and informal urban contexts.

This chapter engages with the tension between planning processes that purport to be collaborative but whose legislative design limits and undermines the ability of planners to undertake collaborative and participative planning actions, and the consequences this holds for urban dwellers, particularly those living in informal settings. It explores the implications for higher education pedagogy in this context. Many of these supposed participative processes are often captured by an elite, who use such processes to further their own agendas and as such are highly exclusionary. This chapter asks: what are the challenges limiting collaborative governance in South African planning and how can planning education contribute to tackling such challenges? By doing so, this chapter responds to the need to further explore the frustrations that planners experience as a consequence of such dynamics, but also queries how such tensions can be partially resolved, particularly from an engaged pedagogical perspective. This includes, for example, exploring how planners may develop social skills to influence powerful stakeholders in this process or gain the means to trigger systematic changes to planning legislation and legislative structures that enable a more inclusive approach to governance.

Relating this to the themes and connections dealt with in this book as a whole, this chapter speaks to the notion of reviewing curricula – reflecting on how the knowledge taught in planning schools acts as a foundation for future professional development, and thus through engaging with planning professionals we create a feedback loop back in planning pedagogy. This chapter speaks in particular to the risk that occurs when normative ideals taught in universities encounter the harsh terrain of practice, and how we create a base of 'ethical stamina' that encourages future planning professionals to endure through the challenges of practice.

We draw on the results of an ESRC/NRF[1] project looking at the appropriateness, usefulness and impact of the current planning curriculum in South African higher education. The project was a collaboration between the University of Birmingham/UCL and the University of the Free State. The research team encompassed researchers with in-depth knowledge of the research and education landscape in the country, including experience of working at the Council for Scientific and Industrial Research (CSIR) and SACPLAN. The project consisted of two stages of data collection. The first included a survey conducted in 2017 with 219 planning practitioners across South Africa, with questions ranging from concerns relating to work satisfaction, to a ranking of the usefulness of planning competencies learned in accredited planning courses. During the second stage, in 2018, 89 planners across the country in both metropolitan and non-metropolitan areas were interviewed, working in the public (n = 36), private (n = 21) and education (n = 13) sectors or with a mixed portfolio of activities (n = 19). The interviews were conducted to acquire more in-depth views on some of the topics flagged as relevant in the surveys, spanning from the current state of planning, challenges and achievements, including informality; relevance of planning education and the existing curriculum; and the conditions of work in the field. The latter included available resources and preparedness of planners. While the interviews were coded by one researcher for consistency, the process was undertaken in collaboration with other members of the research team to ensure relevance. For the purpose of this chapter, reflections from practitioners are used to demonstrate (1) their experiences in working with low-income communities, especially in a township[2] setting, and hence accounting for informal uses and practices and/or (2) their experiences in working with vulnerable communities, as well as on (3) their perception regarding the appropriateness of their planning curriculum.

The chapter is structured as follows. First, it starts by contextualising the planning profession in South Africa and the wider issue of informality and poverty in both planning education and planning practice. Second, it builds on the concept of inclusive collaborative governance by highlighting the challenges related to implementing such governance as mentioned by interviewees and reflecting on the implications thereof for planners' education. Third, it discusses and reflects on the pedagogical implications involved in tackling the challenges identified before concluding on the broader lessons that the South African case may offer to the wider Global South.

Contextualising the planning profession in South Africa

The planning profession in South Africa is not only relatively young, but is a profession that has faced a huge task in turning around the profession's association with the Apartheid State (Harrison, Todes and Watson, 2008; Oranje, 2014), its largely white, male membership (Mabin and Smit, 1997; Muller, 2000) and its primarily technical approach to education (Nel and Lewis, 2020) after the change to democracy in 1994. This immediately provides a key challenge for state-citizen engagement, given that for the majority of South Africans, the state, and by proxy, planning, was an entity that historically worked against their best interests, and thus invoked an understandable distrust of the state. Planners also face the challenge of having to address the spatial and socio-economic legacy and disparity of colonialism and apartheid (Schensul and Heller, 2011; Madlalate, 2017), materialised in continuing endemic poverty, extreme economic inequality and spatial division (Denoon-Stevens et al., 2022).

Inclusive, democratic and collaborative planning has been positioned as a central tenet in post-apartheid South Africa, with extensive public participation processes systematically being implemented through a new suite of planning policies and legislation, namely the Development Facilitation Act 1996, the White Paper on Local Government 1998, the Municipal Systems Act 2000, and the Spatial Planning and Land Use Management Act 2013 requiring redress and community collaboration. However, urban and regional planning is also a small profession in the country, with 2,885 registered professional and technical planners by June 2021 and an additional 1,721 planners in their candidacy phase of training (SACPLAN, 2021). To put this in perspective, the number of registered professional and technical planners equates to a ratio of one planner to 20,847 (13,058 if including candidates) of the population, and this number is not likely to increase anytime soon. The distribution of planners is also not geographically uniform, as metropolitan areas mostly have a larger number of registered planning staff (42 on average), whereas smaller municipalities are often understaffed, with an average of three planners per municipality in secondary cities, and an average of one planner (not necessarily a registered professional planner) or less in all other municipal categories (Municipal Demarcation Board, 2012).

These significant discrepancies in available resources between large and smaller cities, and rural areas, as well as pressures towards competing agendas and investment strategies mean that planners have to tackle very complex and diverse problems 'some familiar to practitioners in the global North, some relating to broader questions of development in the global South and cutting across both public and private sectors, and some very specific to the South African context' (Denoon-Stevens et al., 2022). This has some reflection on the skills, competencies and ways to train South African planners, which has been at the core of scholars' interest for more than a decade (Todes et al., 2003; Denoon-Stevens et al., 2022).

Despite these challenges, results from the South African Planning Education Research project demonstrated that overall, planning education in South Africa has been meeting its expectations, with the majority of professionals surveyed noting that they were well prepared for practice. There were, however, a significant number of areas for improvement identified, which differed in 'conventional' (elite) universities and technical universities. A commonality that was found was the difficult balance between practice and theory and the importance of localising the learning in order to bridge gaps between theory and practice in socio-culturally distinct contexts (Denoon-Stevens *et al.*, 2022). Part of the problem is the lack of opportunity for continuing professional development along with ongoing mentoring to allow more interactions between practitioners and academics, particularly in the first five years after graduation (Andres *et al.*, 2018). This need for lifelong capacity development, as part of the learning curve, is particularly significant when planners must engage with informality (Oranje, van Huyssteen and Maritz, 2020) and navigate within the unplanned nature of fast-growing towns and cities.

As a legacy of apartheid, South African cities are characterised by extremes. They display very distinct urban landscapes ranging from the planned suburbs of middle and upper-class areas quite similar to suburban areas in Europe and North America, to informal areas with few services and no formal planning. However, the proportion of households living in formal dwellings has increased from 68.5% in 2001 to 79.2% in 2016, which is a growth of more than 5 million households in absolute numbers. Two other significant trends relate to backyard dwellings and traditional housing. The absolute number of households living in a formal or informal backyard unit, or a room/flat let on a property, has also increased from almost 1 million households in 2001 to almost 2.2 million in 2016. Of the approximately 2.2 million households in 2016 living in a backyard dwelling on a property, just over 900,000 were living in informal structures, about 1.1 million in formal structures, and about 133,000 in a room/flatlet on the property (Statistics South Africa, 2002, 2016).

The number of traditional dwellings (houses typically made out of natural building materials following African customary practices) has decreased from 1.65 million in 2001 to 1.18 million in 2016. The number of households living in informal settlements and flats has remained relatively steady over this time compared to those in backyard and traditional dwellings. These key figures denote the importance for planners to address and understand the challenges and vulnerabilities often related to forms of living largely relying on informality. Roy (2005: 149) states that informality 'must be understood not as the object of state regulation but rather as produced by the state itself ... The planning and legal apparatus of the state has the power ... to determine what is informal and what is not'. Informality thus also refers to the range of processes and systems, often highly credible, through which housing, and resources and services are provided, often due to the inefficiencies and even inappropriateness of 'formal' institutions and systems (Oranje, van Huyssteen and Maritz,

2020). It is also worth noting that while informality is most widely studied in the Global South, informality also occurs in the Global North. However, in the North, informality is more evenly distributed between 'informality of need' versus 'informality of desire', such as deviations from regulations merely for leisure and other purposes (Devlin, 2019).

Consequently, engaging with informality is a key issue for planning education as it connects to much more than just the problems related to land development and land use management, or land ownership and building regulations. The challenge for planners in South Africa is thus to develop systems compatible with residents' lived reality, rather than systems based on a fictional notion of what urban life is 'supposed' to be (Robins, 2002). It is of critical importance for planning students to engage with such realities, the implications thereof, but also with the limitations of the formal planning system and thus often the value of informal processes and development. This challenge also relates to a wider issue of inclusive collaborative governance which is explored next by understanding how planners engage and struggle with such processes in their daily activities. This chapter builds on such everyday realities to reflect on pedagogical implications.

Perspectives on inclusive collaborative governance and urban planning in South Africa

The concept of inclusive and collaborative governance draws upon the work of Ansell and Gash (2008) and rests on the involvement of a wide range of public and private actors, from different backgrounds and different interests, with the objective of promoting consensus-orientated decision-making. In spite of high ideals for a collaborative and integrated planning system in South Africa, the practice realities have suffered from the impact of a highly bureaucratised and compliance-driven system. In such a context, consultation processes for a wide range of integrated, spatial and sector plans at ward, municipal, regional and provincial scales, take place within incredibly tight timelines – in most cases requiring the development of plans every five years and reviews on a yearly basis. In addition to the above, spatial transformation, integration and collaborative planning are impacted by performance management systems where individual performance and/or departmental performance is often more important than collaboration (SACN, 2020). Recently, calls have been made to transform government and civil society engagement, 'especially to facilitate the inclusion of marginalised groups' (NDA,

2020: 78). Co-governance and the effectiveness of civil society is considered here as a way for the government to be effective and responsive, requiring a policy review to encourage quality engagement (NDA, 2020). This imperative is of great relevance when considering informality, and an ongoing issue that planners have been keen to engage with but have struggled to date.

Several planners interviewed acknowledged the need for a more collaborative approach to governance, pointing out the many ways in which the current system prevented it. One issue mentioned was that participation tended to occur in silos, while communities' issues are obviously not silo-based and often beyond the scope of the specific process, leading to high levels of frustration. This was described as follows by a respondent:

> And planning can't solve all those problems. Obviously, when you go into public participation processes around planning exercises, people target that process to try and address all those problems. And it can become very frustrating and kind of demotivating because you can't respond to all those problems … There is all sort of other sector-based issues that just drive agendas, that you don't have so much control over. (Female, mid-career, experience in the public sector and currently at the private sector)

Furthermore, local plans and participation processes are merely cogs within a wider governmental apparatus. While purporting to be participative, such processes often result in being more focused on informing the general public, or merely collecting needs than truly enabling collaborative governance. This was exemplified by an experienced planner who framed the issue as follows:

> When you speak to informal settlement communities, of course some of them demand a lot from the municipalities. But, I get the feeling … the municipality officials come there and say this is what we can do. Not like, how can we change what we can do to accommodate you. It's more like you know ja, we hear you but actually rule is we come here to relocate you and then we're gonna create this and that and that. (Black, male town planner, private sector)

This frustration and seemingly lack of ability to effectively influence processes are also reflected in opinions that speak to how plans are being used as 'window dressing' to make a government entity appear compliant and progressive, while the views of residents are disregarded in practice. A mid-career female planner working in the public sector at a large municipality noted that:

> South Africa's got a very bad pattern of public participation and consultation: it's just a compliance thing; I published an ad in the newspaper; I had one public meeting. Not just the planners, politically if we review the Integrated Development Plan (IDP)'s, we approve the budgets; it's a tick box exercise and after 20 years of IDPs, there's also a process of people don't participate and there's just wish lists. (White, female senior town planner, public sector)

The role of politics was also cited by participants as one of the issues impacting collaborative planning. Many respondents felt politicians were irresponsible, making promises that were not achievable, and changing plans to suit their agenda:

> And sometimes you know you still get hit in the end with problems because obviously these processes take one, two, three years, sometimes, to go through and what you decided three years ago with your social agreement with those people could change in a year when a new political figure comes up and tells these people 'No, they are trying to mess around with you'. So yes, it's a very volatile, ever-changing situation. But we like to learn from other experiences and as planners we try and do the right thing, I think, but it's not always politically the right thing because you know politicians blow things up and make promises that you can't achieve obviously. (White, male senior town planner, public sector)

The wider consequence is not simply disruptions to planning processes, but disillusionment with the atate, given the constant failure to deliver what was promised. This is not specific to the South African situation, yet the impact can be dramatic in a context of limited resources and selective strategies. It has wider consequences in the ability of planners to understand and appropriately engage with the everyday realities of townships, their diversity along with the complex informal processes that characterise them. And, given the low-income status of the majority of households residing in townships, these households are far more reliant on the state than middle-income households, as the latter are usually able to establish parallel processes to that of the state, effectively filling in the gaps created by state failure (e.g., private schooling, security, basic services, among other things).

The political nature of planning and power relationships shaping local planning processes and participation connect with the wider failures of the planning and governance system, evident in the often-unrepresentative nature of organisations such as ward committees and civic organisations, leading to limited engagement with the private sector. Ward committees comprised only up to 10 people, who are supposed to represent the ward (noting the average size of a ward in South Africa in 2011 was 12,104 people), but the actual composition of the committee is heavily dependent on the whims of the politically elected ward councillor, often with no democratic process behind the selection of members (Piper and Deacon, 2009). Although civic organisations purport to represent the 'community' in an area, they often only represent a small group of property owners, in many cases with particularly conservative views. They are often associated with being anti-development, resisting new developments and attempts to densify new areas, typically using arguments such as development eroding the character of the area, and parking and traffic issues (Anciano and Piper, 2018; Appelbaum, 2019). As a respondent described it:

> And then the rate payers who have the luxury of living there in the apartments with over 50 million think they can say what can and can't be. One of my big bugbear[s] is how much voice is given to the rich and the government of the city. (Female, mid-career, experience in the public sector and currently at the private sector)

In such contexts, identifying and addressing the realities of everyday informal needs is not a priority.

Thus, many respondents appeared to be frustrated about the public's lack of participation and subsequent lack of input into shaping (often abstract) spatial and long-term plans for urban settlements:

> And I think in terms of spatial planning, forward planning they actually need to have general meetings with the public … we should actually educate them why it is important to attend such meetings to understand what we want to achieve, specifically for their communities rather than just deciding or following theories to develop a settlement which will not work in their case. (Female, white, mid-career planner, public sector)

Unfortunately, views such as this could also point to a belief about 'us' and 'them' and a perception that it is the public who needs to be 'educated', while it might be 'planning' that requires to be more context relevant.

This issue translates into exclusionary dynamics as privileged groups may use participation and planning processes to further their agendas, often at the expense of the city as a whole, with dire disadvantages for the poorer communities, particularly those living in townships. This issue was evident in the comment of an experienced, male planner at a medium-sized municipality who has had an unusual opportunity to guide the development in an urban area after a major wildfire:

> Part of my job is to oversee the reconstruction of [_____]. And now I'm sitting with an interesting scope to say, 'Hmm, okay, let's do a mixed typology integrated housing project.' And everyone looks at me like 'What? What is that? We don't want low-cost housing in [_____].' Well … So, I'm finding it very interesting to engage and bring some of what I've learned elsewhere, here. But it's a very conservative mind-set, and you have to convince on a small scale before you can start to do so on a big scale. (White, male, senior town planner, public sector)

Such concerns were also shared by respondents about issues that arose when trying to navigate between the complexity of policy positions (and good practice) and experiencing opposition from privileged groups, while not necessarily being accepted by communities and individuals that these policies are supposed to 'benefit'. One respondent clearly underscored the desire of individuals living in township for low-density development, contrary to what is accepted as 'good planning practice': 'They don't want anything denser; they don't want a different house type. They also want to stay here but if the other people have to move for them to get a bigger plot, the people must move' (black, male town planner, private sector). This response highlights not only the concern regarding collaborative governance and the planner's desire to ensure buy-in for planning objectives, but also the fact that these objectives unfortunately remain uncontested in planning education and practice.

Even in projects where there has been extensive collaboration, promises may not be fulfilled: 'A number of years ago … we helped a particular community … to participate in the upgrading of informal settlements. And those plans were developed and approved by the municipality, but they've not been implemented' (white, male senior planner, NGO sector). Failure to implement plans, the continual review of plans and the extent of residential growth that happens outside the scope of the formal land development processes may lead to disillusionment with planning by planners and communities alike. This can result in citizens being excluded materially while creating a perception of inclusion in governance and decision-making (Miraftab, 2009), thus losing the trust of all parties involved, including residents, industry, politicians and planners (from government or private sector).

South African planners find it extremely difficult to achieve inclusive and collaborative planning among the numerous and complex challenges, not only in more affluent areas but more importantly in townships where informal living, adaptations and coping prevail. These challenges have pedagogical implications regarding the exposure planning students have to the realities, complexities and experiences in tackling such crucial issues.

Collaborative governance in planning education and pedagogical implications

Teaching planning to students requires a subtle balance between what can be referred to as hard skills (i.e., understanding planning regulations and land uses) and softer skills (being creative, learning how to communicate and to navigate within a highly complex and diverse environment). Betts *et al.* (2009: 102) quoted the Australian Council of Deans Education stating that 'skills of collaboration will supersede the competitive skills required in the old industrial economy and the focus will shift to interpersonal relations and communications'. Collaboration and communication are indeed eminently linked and go back to Davidoff's (1965) advocacy and pluralism planning principles. Collaboration and consensus building have been identified by SACPLAN as one of the underlying generic competencies required by urban and regional planners (SACPLAN, 2014; Lewis and Nel, 2020). As a result, South African planning educators must adopt the relevant methods and techniques to train aspiring planners.

Following Davidoff and further on, Healey's collaborative planning, planning theorists have insisted on the need to involve and empower communities in planning processes (Todes, 2009; Boraine, 2021). Such narratives, though, have been principally designed in a context which is not the one characterising South Africa and many other urban settings where the (formally) planned co-exist with the (formal) unplanned.[3] Engaging with those living in informal settings entails more than just technical skills and know-how, and includes the sensibility and wisdom to understand what is required, having empathy and being willing to create conditions that exceed what is specified by legislation. This is strongly connected to the importance of local context and localised practice experience, as well as requiring high levels of personal and emotional maturity to engage in complex and diverse political environments. These are crucial soft skills. Because planning is essentially a process of negotiating trust, hope and the allocation and sharing of scarce resources (e.g., public funds, land), it is of critical importance that such issues are not merely 'discussed' but that aspiring planners are also afforded opportunities to practice base interactions and transformative experiences (Taşan-Kok *et al.*, 2017).

As noted in the previous section, this ties into a wider issue for planners of the state being willing to listen, and work with, the communities that the state serves. If legislation requires participation, but the state is unwilling to listen, then the planner is forced into the role of creating the façade of a participative state, which is not backed by the reality of actual governance practices. Pedagogically, this begs the questions of how to prepare planning students to cope with such situations, and how to equip them to act in such scenarios to subvert the dialogue and force the state to truly engage with residents.

The complexity of such a task underscores how, in a highly unequal and diverse country such as South Africa, pedagogy must consider the limitations of (even technically proficient) collaborative processes. Thus, discussing planning education needs to transcend 'what' is to be taught, towards understanding the requirements for an engaged, inclusive and collaborative pedagogy where opportunities are created for students to engage with diversity (i.e., in backgrounds, culture and expression) but also in perspectives (i.e., private sector, traditional leaders and to collective learning). Bell hooks (1994: 13) cited in Berry (2010: 20) felt that students should be taught 'in a manner that respects and cares for' their souls rather than using 'a rote, assembly line approach'. Fostering a diverse learning environment also requires diversity in the classroom as a way to expose students to learning and practice experiences that inspire listening and dialogue, showing the importance of remembering 'to go in, before going out'. For students, it is a matter of engaging and contributing to each other's overall development (Danowitz and Tuitt, 2011), and to have an interactive relationship between student and teacher.

This education approach involves acknowledging that diversity can contribute towards teaching and learning (Danowitz and Tuitt, 2011). These transformational experiences often require vertical learning time and relationship building. Furthermore, fostering such experiences demands a pedagogy sometimes contrary to approaches followed in curricula and qualifications focused on a magnitude of knowledge and skills-based competency requirements (Van Huyssteen, 2018). It needs to be more agile and such engaged pedagogy must be embedded within creativity and adaptability. However, this does not suggest that all planners need to be highly skilled facilitators, but rather that they are able to connect with people and be humble and respectful enough to solicit appropriate support.

While facilitating skills are essential, in isolation they may fail to achieve expectations due to a struggling system. As the previous section showed, many planners raised concerns about their ability to engage with collaborative practices and were unable to achieve change due to the inherent challenges, complications and bureaucracy of the South African planning and political system. The complicated multi-sphere architecture of the South African governance system dependent on intersectoral support is poorly designed to accommodate meaningful and collaborative sense-making, decision-making and delivery of citizens' needs. In this context planners may feel alone and ill-equipped to glimpse social change.

Notwithstanding the above, the strategies of the powerful are themselves subject to negotiation (Andres *et al.*, 2020). Planners are not merely passive recipients of legislation and policy, rather statutory strategies are produced through co-construction between powerful actors, whose interests often are at odds. This is an important lesson to share with students to build their confidence and ability to negotiate and work within the structures of power, everyday temporalities and to find ways to gain additional training once in the field. From an engaged pedagogy perspective, this means that planning educators need to teach planning students to be creative, to enable planners to think beyond tried and tested methods and approaches to planning, and identify and embrace alternative practices in planning and regulation better suited to the South African context. At the heart of this is recognising that a successful planner should be able to balance hard and soft skills.

This balanced skills approach is essential to develop planners' ability to think critically and question the current South African planning system, particularly regarding the persistent belief that the public needs to be 'educated' about the value of planning, as opposed to encouraging planners to reflect on how the profession needs to change to be relevant to the public. Until this is addressed, collaborative governance will continue to be limited to isolated exceptions and will not become the norm.

Thus, pedagogy needs to include a critical and constructive reflection and practise engagement with relevant planning systems, regulations and institutional environments that inhibit and/or support inclusive and collaborative governance. This is by no means a new argument, as noted by Reece (2018). Unfortunately, challenging practice contexts, limited opportunity for practice mentoring, the demands for career growth allied with short-term orientated performance management agreements, escalating needs and trauma in communities, and personal expectations of what 'a planner' should be able to do could result in disillusionment and significantly impact the confidence and agency of planners in South Africa. The pedagogy of practices that are future-orientated require a changed approach to acknowledge the complexity, paradox and ever-changing nature of context and process (van Huyssteen, 2018).

Lastly, as noted in the previous section, part of the challenge faced by planners in pursuing collaborative planning is the actual design of the system, such as the undemocratic nature and small size of ward committees. The alternative would be that the modes of participation that have insufficient consideration of the realities of townships and low-income households, and which end up privileging the voices of the wealthy. This emphasises the importance of planners advocating for changes in the legislative structure, and governance norms, in the public sector, to create the pre-conditions needed for collaborative governance. Pedagogically, the emphasis is on the importance of ensuring planning students are taught systems thinking and equipping them with the advocacy and lobbying skills needed to effect such changes, for example, by incorporating change management as a formal skill taught in planning education programmes.

Chapter synthesis

In this chapter, the challenges faced by planning education and practice in navigating among the complex tensions inherent to the planned and the unplanned nature of South African cities has been discussed. The post-apartheid planning system in South Africa is a system that has been overtly designed to be transformative. Inadequate consideration of the realities of participative planning and the demands placed on the state has strained attempts to promote collaborative governance and achieve inclusive, participative planning. This chapter has delved into the frustration of practising planners and considered how new forms of engaged pedagogy during the early stages of planning education could facilitate participative planning. Planning students should be equipped with both hard skills and soft skills that should allow them to overcome such inefficacies in the system. Soft skills rest on an ability to be agile and creative and more importantly to communicate and engage in dialogue in a way that allows the planner to adapt to the reality of local governance and those of informal living, particularly in the monetary poor townships. This is far from easy. Aspiring planners must be taught about the difficulties of practice, and be aware of the challenges they will face and their ability to deliver transformative change, even at a small scale. Planning educators here play a crucial role, and this has important consequences in the way planners are taught not only in their home country but also in the international landscape of international planning education (Adams et al., 2020). Crucially, engaged pedagogy founded on agility and adaptability is a starting point to help planners to build stronger, inclusive and sustainable places.

Two key practical takeaways from this chapter are:

1. The level of diversity in societies globally differs, and in highly diverse and unequal situations there are limits to what can be achieved by collaborative planning practice. Pedagogically, we must ensure that what is taught in planning education sets a realistic bar in terms of what can be achieved. In such cases, teaching students how to appreciate small wins can be critical for future work satisfaction, given that big wins may often be unattainable.
2. Planning students need to be made aware of how collaborative planning processes are used by some states to present a façade of compliance, while in practice they retain a technocratic approach that is hostile to collaboration. In planning schools, students need to be prepared for how to manage the ethical, professional and personal tensions of being put into situations where they are used as part of this façade, and what options are available to them in such situations.

Notes

1. Economic and Social Research Council, UK (ESRC) and National Research Foundation, South Africa (NRF).
2. As noted by Donaldson (2014: 267), townships during apartheid were areas for exclusive occupation by people classified as 'Black', 'Coloured' and 'Indian', and since 1994 'have undergone dramatic transformation from a homogeneous to a differentiated urban landscape', where formal and informal coexist in various ways. The term is still largely used to refer to low-income areas where a substantial portion of the housing is (typically) provided by the state, with recent usage also including low-income housing areas built by the post-apartheid government. In the South African setting, 'coloured' is the appropriate terminology as this is

the term that this group identifies with, we are cognisant that this term in other countries can be perceived as offensive.
3. Noting that such spaces, while formally unplanned, many often are planned according to unrecognised informal or traditional approaches to settlement building.

References

Adams, D., L. Andres, S. Denoon-Stevens and L. Melgaço. 2020. 'Challenges, opportunities and legacies: experiencing the internationalising of UK planning curricula across space and time', *Town Planning Review* 91(5): 515–34.

Anciano, F., and L. Piper. 2018. *Democracy Disconnected: participation and governance in a city of the South.* London: Routledge.

Andres, L., S. P. Denoon-Stevens, M. Lewis, E. van Huyssteen and V. Nel. 2018. *Matching Needs: planners in local government.* SAPER Briefing Note. Unpublished.

Andres, L., P. Jones, S. P. Denoon-Stevens and L.Melgaço, L. 2020. 'Negotiating polyvocal strategies: re-reading de Certeau through the lens of urban planning in South Africa', *Urban Studies* 57(12): 2440–55.

Ansell, C., and A. Gash. 2008. 'Collaborative governance in theory and practice', *Journal of Public Administration Research and Theory* 18(4): 543–71.

Appelbaum, A. 2019. 'The micro-politics of state-led spatial transformation: the suburban middle class in a municipal tribunal'. In M. T. Myambo (ed.), *Reversing Urban Inequality in Johannesburg.* London: Routledge.

Berry, T. 2010. 'Engaged Pedagogy and Critical Race Feminism', *Educational Foundations* 24(3–4): 19–26.

Betts, K., M. Lewis, A. Dressler and L. Svensson. 2009. 'Optimizing Learning Simulation to Support a Quinary Career Development Model', *Asia-Pacific Journal of Cooperative Education* 10(2): 99–119, https://www.ijwil.org/files/APJCE_10_2_99_119.pdf (last accessed on 1 December 2022).

Boraine, A. 2021. Question and Answer Section – Session 2: Recalibration and innovation of post-pandemic governance – Urban Festival 2021 – The Rebuilt City. Zoom Webinar (27 October 2021). SACN.

Danowitz, M. A., and F Tuitt. 2011. 'Enacting inclusivity through engaged pedagogy: a higher education perspective', *Equity & Excellence in Education* (44)1: 40–56, https://doi.org/10.1080/10665684.2011.539474 (last accessed 1 December 2022).

Davidoff, P. 1965. 'Advocacy and pluralism in planning', *Journal of the American Institute of Planners* 31(4): 331–8.

Denoon-Stevens, S. P., L. Andres, P. Jones, L. Melgaco, R. Massey and V. Nel. 2022. 'Theory versus practice in planning education: the view from South Africa', *Planning Practice & Research*, 37(4): 509–25, https://doi.org/10.1080/02697459.2020.1735158 (last accessed 1 December 2022).

Devlin, R. T. 2019. 'A focus on needs: toward a more nuanced understanding of inequality and urban informality in the Global North', *Journal of Cultural Geography* 36(2): 121–43.

Donaldson, R. 2014. 'South African Township Transformation'. In A. C. Michalos (ed.), *Encyclopedia of Quality of Life and Well-Being Research.* Dordrecht: Springer, 267–8.

Harrison, P., A. Todes and V. Watson. 2008. *Planning and Transformation: learning from the post-apartheid experience.* London: Routledge.

Lewis, M., and V. Nel. 2020. 'Setting standards and competencies for planners'. In Carlos Nunes Silva (ed.) *Routledge Handbook of Urban Planning in Africa.* London/New York: Routledge, 162–76.

Mabin, A., and D. Smit. 1997. 'Reconstructing South Africa's cities? The making of urban planning 1900–2000', *Planning Perspectives* 12(2): 193–223.

Madlalate, R. 2017. '(In)Equality at the intersection of race and space in Johannesburg', *South African Journal on Human Rights* 33(3): 472–95, https://doi.org/10.1080/02587203.2017.1395166 (last accessed 1 December 2022).

Miraftab, F. 2009. 'Insurgent planning: situating radical planning in the Global South', *Planning Theory* 8(1): 32–50.

Muller, J. 2000. *Deconstructing Differences: the transformation of the planning profession in South Africa*. Paper presented at the Millennium Conference of the South African History Study Group, Planning for Reconstruction and Development, 29–31 May 2000, University of Natal, Durban.

Municipal Demarcation Board. 2012. *State Municipal Capacity Assessment 2010/2011: national trends in municipal capacity*, https://municipalmoney.gov.za/static/state_of_municipal_capacity_assessment_2010_11_national_trends_report.a5b5a4d2722e.pdf (last accessed 1 December 2022).

NDA (National Development Agency). 2020. *Requirements for Transforming the Civil Society Sector in South Africa*. Research Report. December 2020.

Nel, V., and M. Lewis, M. 2020. 'The resilience, adaptability and transformation of the South African planning profession'. In Carlos Nunes Silva (ed.), *Routledge Handbook of Urban Planning in Africa*. London/New York: Routledge, 141–61.

Oranje, M. 2014. 'Back to where it all began …? Reflections on injecting the (spiritual) ethos of the Early Town planning movement into planning, planners and plans in post-1994 South Africa', *HTS Theological Studies* 70(3): a2781.

Oranje, M., E. van Huyssteen and J. Maritz. 2020. 'Rapid urbanisation to non-metropolitan urban South Africa: a call for accrediting credible "informal" life-enhancing responses and institutions', *Cities* 96: 102487.

Piper, L., and R. Deacon. 2009. 'Too dependent to participate: ward committees and local democratisation in South Africa', *Local Government Studies* 35(4): 415–33.

Reece, J. W. 2018. 'In pursuit of a twenty-first century just city: the evolution of equity planning theory and practice', *Journal of Planning Literature* 33(3): 299–309.

Robins, S. 2002. 'Planning "Suburban Bliss" in Joe Slovo Park, Cape Town', *Africa: Journal of the International African Institute* 72(4): 511–48.

Roy, A. 2005. 'Urban informality: toward an epistemology of planning', *Journal of the American Planning Association* 71(2): 147–58.

SACN (South African Cities Network). 2020. *Built Environment Integration Practice*. Johannesburg: SACN.

SACPLAN (South African Council for Planners). 2014. *Guidelines for Competencies and Standards for Curricula Development*. Document number 8/4/1/C&S/Curr/12-2014. Midrand: SACPLAN.

SACPLAN. 2021. 'Total Registration Statistics', *Newsletter* 8: 18.

Schensul, D., and P. Heller, P. 2011. 'Legacies, Change and Transformation in the Post-Apartheid City: Towards an Urban Sociological Cartography', *International Journal of Urban and Regional Research* 35(1): 78–109.

Statistics South Africa. 2002. *South African National Census of 2001* (Dataset), https://superweb.statssa.gov.za/webapi/jsf/login.xhtml (last accessed 1 December 2022).

Statistics South Africa. 2016. *Community Survey* (Dataset), https://superweb.statssa.gov.za/webapi/jsf/login.xhtml (last accessed 1 December 2022).

Taşan-Kok, T., E. Babalik-Sutcliffe, E. van Huyssteen and M. Oranje. 2017. 'Mismatch between planning education and practice: contemporary ethical challenges and conflicts confronting young planners'. In T. Taşan-Kok and M. Oranje (eds), *From Student to Urban Planner: young practitioners' reflections on contemporary ethical challenges*. London/New York: Routledge, 15–32.

Todes, A., P. Harrison and V. Watson. 2003. 'The changing nature of the job market for planning in South Africa: implications for planning educators', *Town and Regional Planning*, 2003(46): 21–32.

Todes, A. 2009. 'City planners'. In Johan Erasmus and Mignonne Breier (eds), *Skills Shortages in South Africa: case studies of key professions*. Cape Town: HSRC Press, 246–61.

UN-Habitat. 2009. *Planning Sustainable Cities: global report on human settlements 2009*. London: Earthscan.

van Huyssteen, E. 2018. *Being, Becoming and Contributing in (and through) Planning*. Doctoral dissertation, University of Pretoria.

Watson, V. 2009. '"The planned city sweeps the poor away…": Urban planning and 21st century urbanisation', *Progress in Planning* 72(3): 151–93.

Watson, V. (2003). 'Conflicting rationalities: implications for planning theory and ethics', *Planning Theory & Practice*, 4(4): 395–407.

Section II
Providing teaching

In this second section, the focus is on those 'participatory' practices that happen within the direct provision of teaching in universities. We learn about the involvement of non-academics in delivering education, using two well-established techniques (guest talks and field work) and two new technologies (podcasts and online co-design). Those providing teaching are not only academics and teaching staff, but also lay and professional folk who are active within the world of planning and place-making practice. Reflections in the chapters, including voices of contributors and students, help understand the positionality of the actors involved. The chapter authors define the nature and purposes of participation of the various non-academics in their work, share their own rationales about the value and challenges of the teaching activities. It is apparent that the bounds of roles and responsibilities are critical in the different techniques of delivery, and part of new reflexive cultures of learning in engaged urban pedagogy. Key points are briefly summarised here about the teaching provision at the university which offers a platform for moments of exchange where student experiences are co-produced within processes that are managed by those working in higher education.

The section opens with a chapter about guest talks from practitioners (Chapter 6), which is a common contribution in classroom-based teaching. Natarajan and Raco share their reflections on the involvement of guest speakers in their teaching on urban regeneration, and how it can help to unsettle students' thinking around financialisation processes, and planning challenges involved in 'value capture', austerity and developer negotiation. They explain how exchanges with non-academics provide students an 'intellectual sandpit', where students can 'play' with conceptual problems about urban development. They argue that this is key in readying students to engage with real-world challenges.

The guest speakers are planners and other built environment professionals, and they co-shape moments of teaching. The academics select and brief a suitable speaker, for an experience where students can listen carefully and discuss content of talks with the guests. In this way, they work as a team, within a carefully curated learning space where the non-academics contributors share knowledge and students are able to be reflexive. For Natarajan and Raco, the real-world challenge at hand is the variable level of attention given to specific actors' roles in city-making. Their teaching goal is to develop students' skills in critical enquiry and think about 'who does the ethics'. The students develop awareness of the powers of actors' rationalities and skills of analysis about the effects of this in city-making. To this end, the guest speakers help enormously by providing live articulation of approaches to urban development and engaging in reflexive discussions in the classroom. At the same time, these educational exchanges are guided by academics, and Natarajan and Raco emphasise that the research-led culture of the university is reproduced.

Next, in Chapter 7, Besussi and Brownill share details of teaching around neighbourhood planning, which involves non-academics in practical activities with students. The teaching teams in two universities have, independently, adapted their courses to include projects about plan-making and enable students to work alongside communities who are involved in local planning for their neighbourhoods. The teaching goals of this 'field work' with community planners centres on developing students' skills of research. Students encounter the system of planning as it operates, and are able to 'see policy', which helps them practise critical enquiry. Working alongside people who are involved in live processes, requires attunement to the concerns of communities and reflection on ethical issues, in view of the inevitable moral judgements around planning decisions. There are also opportunities for students to practise soft communicative skills of planning, for interpersonal interactions and working with members of the public.

Besussi and Brownill reflect on the 'co-learning' with communities in planning processes, and what it means for learning. They highlight how they may adapt to the plan-making timelines and needs of communities, but they must deliver on the teaching goals. Besussi and Brownill argue that it is critical to be reflexive about the in-kind support provided via student engagements to the very planning system being studied. They stress the need to carefully manage the processes to focus student energies on learning about planning rather than getting absorbed in doing work for others.

Following on from Chapters 6 and 7, which explore how face-to-face interactions between students and non-academics reshape learning opportunities in lectures and fieldwork, Chapters 8 and 9 take us on to teaching where the involvement of non-academics is mediated by digital communication technologies. Communication is vital for teaching, planning and place-making, and the digital mode of exchange can introduce new dimensions to students' experience. This adds a layer of intrigue as it may open up new 'participatory' spaces relevant for planning and place-making and can enhance students' enjoyment and attentiveness. Digital tools may have become more prevalent with increased social distancing during the recent pandemic, and it is noteworthy that they can be beneficial in terms of remaining connected with people, and hence student well-being. The implications for active learning in built environment higher education are of great interest to engaged urban pedagogy. Like the other two chapters, they demonstrate the creativity and flexibility needed on the part of teachers, and how communicative exchanges stimulate active learning within students. In Chapter 8, Gullino *et al.* discuss a 'research-teaching nexus' enabled by student podcasting, and in Chapter 9, Sendra and Di Siena present a student-community group work mode of civic co-design via the online platform 'Miro'.

As Gullino *et al.* explain, podcasting is a relatively novel educational resource, where audio files provide educational material in a highly accessible form. This was harnessed for teaching on sustainability challenges of planning and place-making, with students listening to existing podcasts and producing their own open access podcasts. In these assignments, students also become engaged in the sharing of knowledge, rather than digesting it purely for their own learning. In doing so, they could not hide behind passive learning but were obliged to communicate their approach to evidencing potential new 'sustainable solutions' and make their learning visible. This experience gives students a great sense of control over the gathering and dissemination of information. The digital mode of 'broadcast' engages curiosity and motivates students towards knowledge exchange beyond the classroom. It places emphasis on engaging the creativity of students, via control over 'voice' and materials, and the social element of collaborations with their peers help sustain enthusiasm in a time of great stress.

Podcasting allows creative space for student exploratory work, which is valuable in the search for innovations in sustainable development, but as Gullino *et al.* explain, the students work needed to be guided towards higher education purposes. Mirroring the analogue exchanges with guest speakers and neighbourhood planners, the focus was on developing research skills and boosting critical thinking. As students were proactive in disseminating findings, they could also develop soft skills of group work and technical skills of digital communication. The non-academics helped to unlock this with IT specialisms, as well as knowledge of current debates in planning media. Importantly, the teachers' role was to steer the students towards deeper learning and to understand the means of rigorously testing evidence and structuring investigations.

At the end of the section, Chapter 9 also concerns how the use of digital technologies might support students' creativity and intellectual development. Sendra and Di Siena have been working with an online platform called Miro, and are interested in the ways this connects into a 'local ecosystem' of knowledge about places. Having employed Miro 'boards' to co-design online during the pandemic, these practice-orientated boards were adapted for collaborative design work of groups of students and communities in the university.

Sendra and Di Siena's work is concerned with reflexivity around a real-world challenge of participation. Neighbourhood planning education included lessons on how to account for community knowledge, and likewise designers need the capacity to understand grassroots concerns and build them into their proposals. Working with others was a means to develop students' technical and relational skills, as they saw first-hand how urban designs about places could be understood differently by local people living and working there. This enabled them to gain experience of making proposals and critically analysing other people's designs, as well as developing their awareness of the situatedness of all urban knowledge.

Together the four chapters of Section II provide insights from experiences of teaching that affords students opportunities to connect with urban development stakeholders and live processes of planning and place-making. However, those providing the teaching stressed that it was important to ensure that immediate urban development experiences and concerns of contributors didn't overshadow the opportunities for deeper learning. We noted in Chapter 1 the forms of knowledge involved in our own fields are highly relational, and therefore the ways to active learning are full of communicative and political challenges. Lessons from the book on the different channels and spaces of exchange with people from outside the university demonstrate the practical concerns. Educators spend time in retooling and, as we learn in the next four chapters, need to diligently encourage students' critical thinking, particularly about the planning system, place-based practices and the politics of knowledge production, as well as reflecting on the co-learning of urban 'others' within educational processes. For instance, guest speakers affirmed how stimulating they find this thinking space that is at one remove from their daily activities, and they can of course feed new ideas back into their practices. This underscores the need for reflexivity about the wider effects of participatory forms of teaching, which provide learning both in *and around* built environment higher education, and the expectations of academics.

6
Planning imaginations and the pedagogic value of external guest speakers

Lucy Natarajan and Mike Raco

The practice of engaging guest speakers from the 'real world' of planning as contributors to teaching at universities is commonplace and seems at first to be a fairly simple activity. It is a moment of learning in its own right, which has become prominent in planning education. Despite its ubiquity, this practice has not received the attention given to other forms of wider engagement within urban pedagogy such as service learning (see, e.g., Forsyth, 2000; Dearborn, 2011). Broadly speaking, the premise is to hear directly about the latest activities and thinking, and this may offer a practical live connection to action, problems and frameworks in play. The chapter recognises that guest contributions can play a part in the delivery of course material for built environment courses, but argues that the implications for learning and the details of the practices of teaching deserve much closer attention.

The discussion assesses the rationales for engaging practitioners and reflects on the collective experience of teaching undergraduate and postgraduate level students in the Bartlett School of Planning, UCL. The courses are research-led and draw on a range of deep theoretical links between urban concepts and topical, up-to-date empirical research on urban development and planning practices. The chapter sets out three dimensions of involving guest speakers, discusses how they shape moments of engagement and modes of learning, and explores the purposes and outcomes in relation to pedagogy. These are: the process of curation; the nurturing of reflexive practice and knowledge sharing; and the reproduction of research-led teaching cultures. It develops the argument that this form of pedagogy is a fundamental component in the development of a relational planning imagination among and between students, research active academics, and those beyond the university sector working in the planning field. This can be defined more precisely as the construction of a set of imaginary frames of reference and ways of thinking within which understandings of planning are used to shape broader outlooks and approaches to real world problems. A planning imagination can also be used to shape the development of broader conceptual/explanatory frames of reference, many of which remain abstracted and thus appear remote from the life-worlds of people in planning practice and their experience.

Moreover, it demonstrates that in the fields of built environment education, the role of the academic lecturer is *re-centred* in the careful process of curating and giving a platform to external voices, with a view to promoting critical thinking around specific sets of knowledge within the nexus of societal controls. By drawing on academic research, critical understandings of planning systems and contemporary writings, course directors are ideally placed to act as a conduit for communicating multiple viewpoints and establishing methods and techniques to make the diverse perspectives visible while offering critical and research-led insights. This re-centring, in turn, reflects and reproduces the fundamental importance of research-based teaching in universities, led by academic experts in the field. It also enables research-led propositions and ideas to be tested and discussed in the classroom, both furthering the educational quality of taught courses and generating new forms of knowledge that can feed into future research and help inform practice. The process of interaction might therefore act as a creative moment both in terms of pedagogy and in encouraging new reflections and insights within the practitioner community. The framing lends weight to the importance of external guest speakers. It establishes a bounded and clearly defined pedagogic site for exploring and contesting epistemic controls, or an intellectual sandpit in which multiple perspectives are shared and challenged. There is no predetermined outcome expected from such processes, but it plays a role in fostering a culture of critical enquiry, underpinned by a planning imagination.

The chapter draws on an example of broader trends observed in the teaching of urban development and the governance of contemporary planning, both of which are increasingly being undertaken in a context of creeping financialisation or the 'ingraining of financialised metrics and reasonings into [governmental] spaces and situations where they were previously non-existent or less common' (Chiapello, 2015: 15).

In countries such as England, financial metrics and viability-based economic calculations are shaping planning deliberations and practices in unprecedented ways, with public policy seeking to both expedite the delivery of urban projects and encourage enhanced private sector investment in all aspects of urban development processes (Colenutt, 2020). This is increasingly reflected in the topics covered by external guest speakers and the priority they give to specific practices surrounding value-capture, contractual negotiations and the determination of project viability. The observation of this phenomenon is in itself a type of research finding and has influenced subsequent curriculum development, so that students are better equipped to understand and (within their potential future careers and/or forms of active citizenship) directly influence planning deliberations and outcomes. This exemplifies the broader interactive reflexivity that can emerge through engaged pedagogy, with the potential for building of new forms of critical and participatory citizenship.

The chapter starts with an exploration of the processes of curation around external guest speakers and the associated development of reflexive forms of practice and knowledge-sharing. It then turns to the ways in which speakers represent a fundamental element in the propagation of research-led teaching cultures. It finishes with the example of how understandings of financialisation have expanded within urban regeneration teaching and as a topic that increasingly dominates the reflections and insights of external guest speakers. It argues that it is through exposure to a range of perspectives that critical practice emerges and active, insightful planning imaginations can be fostered. Silencing voices that might conflict with pre-determined agendas represents an abdication of responsibility on the part of lecturer-academics and leaves students (and researchers) ill-equipped to confront the types of real-world challenges that planners and citizens face.

Curation

The process of curating involves the deliberate and purposeful sampling and presentation of the subject material under investigation and its core components. A broad range of literature exists in studies of museums and exhibition spaces that discusses the ways in which curators use selected objects and artefacts to present coherent narratives and windows on the world (Clover *et al.*, 2018). As with university teaching, these narratives are, of course, power-laden and represent expert-led 'takes' or cuts on what is being displayed, even where the experiences are 'visitor-centred' or curators seek co-produced dialogue about the materials. These in turn are shaped and bounded through a combination of actor-centred knowledge and institutionalised constraints. Curations of the planning field similarly move beyond simply presenting descriptions of places and populations; they play a role in bringing them into existence, by creating objects of attention and transforming them into 'realities', subject to discussion and analysis (Raco and Taşan-Kok, 2020). It involves the normative process of making scholarly decisions over the types of knowledge and planning voices that *should* be included in a course.

While there is much writing on the importance of bringing marginalised voices into the teaching and delivery of planning courses, there are also strong pedagogic and political reasons for encouraging *intellectual* engagement with the range of actors who have power within and over urban development. All forms of urban knowledge carry political weight and are reflexively shaped by decision-making processes (Wynne, 1996, Grundmann, 2017). But the chapter contends that, particularly within the built environment sectors, the level of attention paid to the views and perspectives of professional actors has tended to be shaped by political ideologies. This is a form of symbolic control (Bernstein, 2001). The power of voices of professionals beyond (public sector) planning departments deserve to be paid more attention. Longer-term traditions in the planning sector have focused on its role as a state-led form of public practice, in which practitioners are told to be reflexive and work towards the implementation of collectively agreed public interests (Schön, 1983). Such thinking presents the state as the key agent of control and downplays the importance of other agents and their various logics, including civil society groups and private sector actors who also play a key (and growing) role in governing cities and places.

What matters for curation therefore is to engage explicitly with the politics of knowledge and make visible the bounds of thinking. Whatever the voice of an external guest speaker, they are inevitably *engaging in* an educational space. Likewise, academic lecturers in urban education cannot hope to represent the world in its entirety. Instead, there are only ever choices over whether and how different types of speaker might contribute, which shape the possible scope of critical engagement. Where knowledge exchange within education merely mimics the range of voices prevalent within the world of practice, it risks reproducing those (often tacit) frames of reference and reifying their power. In other words, the fundamental pedagogic concerns relate to how voices and knowledge shape epistemic boundedness and the consequent curation of external contributions.

The development of reflexive forms of practice and knowledge-sharing

Urban development is a complex field of practice, with specific exigencies for the development of reflexive forms of knowledge-sharing. Its subject matter often captures the broad public imagination through the sensational stories that are live in the media, many of which are highly critical of the costs of projects and/or act as a showcase for associated political projects. Take, for instance, the contestations around the urban megaprojects that are the Olympic Games, where increasingly global media coverage combined with the universal appeal of human progress have produced an expansive 'discourse arena' (Cottrell and Nelson, 2011; Andranovich and Burbank, 2021) over the impacts and costs of investments in host cities and whether there are public benefits. Consequently, academics will generally aim to bring less visible elements to life and do so in a way that promotes critical thinking and rigour in evaluation.

The primary purpose for engagement with external guest speakers might be seen as fairly instrumental, in that these professionals can provide a live demonstration of particular subject matter for students. However, drawing on the experiences of teaching in a planning school, it relates more to the key areas of 'learning outcome': familiarity with the empirics of practice; and intellectual capacities around the techniques of enquiry. Of course, the categories of student in higher education, external guest speaker and academic researcher are not mutually exclusive, and as noted practitioner-speakers are by definition former students, academics sometimes contribute to practice and students will sometimes possess earlier (or contemporary) practice experience, especially at the postgraduate level. Nonetheless, there is a certain underpinning 'delivery rationality' that grows from an assumption of those roles.

External guest speakers are invited to share their experiences with a broad sweep of research directions in mind. While these external practitioners are neither staff members nor remunerated for their teaching contributions, they provide more than one-off demonstrations and often return year on year and appear as a regular part of the delivery team. This suggests that there may be a deeper connection to learning and encourages exploration around their role in higher education. Billing guest talks from external speakers to students as 'hearing from practice' downplays the importance of critical engagement with them and underplays their significance in the development of broader planning imaginations. First, as already indicated, students in higher education need to be developing reflexive skills and critical insights in respect of the subject matter, but they may already be exposed to dominant urban political discourses. Second, to broadly characterise the area of study, there is an enormous diversity of socio-economic, cultural and political processes and outcomes of development. Students are expected to engage with the complex interlocking dimensions rather than a single area of expertise. Third, urban guest contributors have particular types of professional expertise and experience. This suggests that the external guest speaker might offer an empirical 'resource' for spaces of critical enquiry and help explore new ideas.

Typically, external guest speakers who work in urban planning and development provide presentations based on their real-world experiences, and students have opportunities to discuss with them. Although in discussion with professionals, educators tend not to be prescriptive, lecturer-academics always advise them in scoping out their contributions and set the parameters for their inclusion. As such, the particular contributions are selected as a means not just to provide detailed descriptions from recent experience with meaningful current empirics that can speak to the more recent types of potential change or conservation at hand, but more importantly they are positioned carefully as a means to open up an avenue into practitioner deliberations. In the United Kingdom, planners from local government are involved in the majority of the work, but speakers may also come from private sector bodies, from across the multiple tiers of government and from local and international non-governmental or voluntary associations. In effect, guest speakers are pressing pause on their external activities and tacitly inviting reflections from students around as yet unresolved issues. Even where plans or decisions are already made, speakers may highlight the critical forks in the road of their judgements and the options involved. They can share their insights into current dilemmas and reflect on their own approaches to planning. They have the opportunity to engage with students freely, either *ad hoc*, or fielding question and answer sessions, something that also acts as a useful moment for their own reflections.

The selection of external guest speakers contributing to teaching is constantly under review, but understanding who is now a 'planner' and who is shaping agendas and outcomes in cities has become an increasingly complex question and one that course curators must confront. Planning systems are coming under structural pressures of reform. In countries such as England, private sector planners and consultants, acting on behalf of the state or other interests, now play an expanding role in the development and delivery of policy programmes and place-building. Nearly half of all planners work for private companies (Raco,

2018). As recent research has shown, their activities are often focused on market-building and profit-making rather than the establishment and delivery of public interest projects (Linovski, 2021). Moreover, the growing influence of private sector involvement in the delivery of planning programmes and, in particular, the greater reliance on private finance for new projects, has given financial actors and knowledge practices a much stronger role in the building and governance of cities (Penny, 2021).

With a view to the development of knowledge-sharing, a carefully curated course should involve and include voices, with a critical pedagogy focused on in-depth understandings of how the planning system works and the knowledge now required to shape processes and deliver outcomes. Undertaking meaningful curation in this regard requires an in-depth understanding of the evolving landscape of contemporary processes and trends. Identifying who and what should be curated is a skilled and highly politicised task. Similarly, with a view to developing reflexive forms of practice, educators must exercise their own professional judgement around how best to facilitate higher learning. The pedagogy is focused on the engagement within lecturing sessions and involves briefing both students and external guest speakers on the purposes and necessities of the moment as well as on-the-fly moderation of discussions. In this way, the educators are positioned as guides, who not only curate lengthy deliberative exchanges between students and external guest speakers, but also draw on their area of research expertise to set up a space of critical enquiry that they consider relevant and invite participants to relate within that space.

The (re)production of research-led teaching cultures

Across the higher education sector there have been growing moves towards what is described as 'research-based' teaching. While the term itself is highly contested (see for instance, Schapper and Mayson, 2008), in a university teaching environment research and teaching are structurally interconnected and relational. A core part in the development of a planning imagination is the instilling of a culture of research based on the rigorous assessment and analysis of evidence and arguments. Research expertise is what differentiates university teaching from that undertaken elsewhere – the lecturer acts as a producer of knowledge, an expert in their field of study, and a teacher. The inclusion of external voices reflects and reproduces a set of conscious professional choices and judgements made over the relationships between the curation of external voices and contemporary debates and understandings in the academic fields of planning and urban studies. The presence of different voices also opens up possibilities for the questioning and challenging of established positions and gives students an insight into how qualitative research processes operate in practice.

Undergraduate and postgraduate programmes generally attract a diverse cohort from across spatial planning, housing and urban design programmes. Many students are prospective built environment experts, but they may be undertaking courses for a variety of reasons. Urban development is a potentially challenging object of study and may be especially daunting for an aspiring future professional. In addition, the softer skills required for regeneration, such as negotiation and partnership working across teams (Bailey, 2005), have been a matter of particular debate in the United Kingdom. They are commonly viewed as vital to interdisciplinary built environment work. Charismatic urban professionals can offer a demonstration of the presence and confidence that are needed in the role.

As discussed above, on one level the reasoning for engaging external guest speakers is somewhat instrumental. However, live engagement is a social activity and promotes deeper learning through enquiry. The guest speaker has an insider position within external epistemological networks and this has enormous potential in relation to wider and evolving urban studies. Only through a combination of critical discussion and questioning can rationalities be understood. Students have the chance to engage with speakers' insights, and critically reflect on them via their own questioning and hearing them debate with others, including their lecturers. At the same time, external guest speakers provide educators with the chance to reflect back on context. This does *not*, of course, mean that these understandings lead axiomatically to uncritical agreement with established positions – ethically or politically. Instead, the development of a critical planning imagination requires the input of multiple forms of knowledge and frames of reference. As with all qualitative research, it is at the intersection between conceptual knowledge and insights from practice that new understandings are forged (Sayer, 2000).

While course materials for students are carefully curated to set up programmes of learning, the stores of knowledge that come from research into urban development, its social purposes, multiple practices and future development orientations, are constantly evolving. There is a constant co-evolution between curations and research findings and engagement with external guest speakers. In most universities, lecturers' research will run alongside their teaching. Academics are in this sense eternal students, and those of us with an interest in urban development and planning seek to develop new approaches to study as well as to uncover deeper structures, trace meanings and review the evolution of sociopolitical, cultural and other systems around urban renewal. As such, the moments of engagement with urban professionals that emerge from their guest speaker contributions has intellectual uses beyond delivery of teaching, and by extension may be part of the evolving studies that underpin university education.

Educators seek to bring empirics to life, yet pay careful attention to alignments with (and challenges from) theoretical insights. Professionals may not have been in university for some time. Thus, the contributions of an external guest speaker are a matter for careful negotiation in relation to the content of the course and providing accounts of continuation of developing understanding. They also provide a unique opportunity to pick up on potential new lines of research – the force of changes on the deliberations and tones and skills and the moment for reflection for all those involved. Intended as a point of critical reflection for students, there is also a much wider critical reflection on practice through discursive moments with students. The chapter now develops these points by turning to the example of recent shifts in the English planning system and the growing prominence of financialisation and private sector knowledge-practices. The example is used to shine a light on the ways in which the inclusion of external speakers from practice can act as a springboard for more effective modes of pedagogy and the development of new research trajectories.

Financialisation and the remaking of the English planning system

During the 2000s, before post-financial crisis austerity cuts hit many planning departments, planners were generally more optimistic about their roles and capacities to shape urban development. Under successive Labour governments, planning as a way of thinking and governing found new impetus. Sustainable communities' agendas of the early 2000s evolved into broader deliberations over how planning could be used to deliver community well-being and the formation of inclusive, well-designed places. While there were growing concerns over the availability and delivery of decent affordable housing and the quality of urban environments (Edwards and Imrie, 2015), there was a recognition that planning mattered and that the planning profession was in a pivotal position within broader government programmes and projects.

Since 2010, there has been a shift in both the types of narrative that planners are delivering to student groups and a broadening in the base of what the planning sector as a whole now consists of. Most significantly, there is an evolving orthodoxy that city governments have become more dependent on inward investment and the availability of global finance to generate new development and sustain welfare services (Penny, 2021). In England this has involved a wider shift towards viability-led planning and the introduction of market-led value-capture mechanisms to both promote new housing and use some of the surplus value generated to invest in social infrastructure and welfare services (Ferm and Raco, 2020; Latham and Leyton, 2019). For practitioners these changes have ushered in fundamental changes in the types of knowledge practices that are required within the planning process. In particular, there is a greater importance given to *calculative practices* or the conversion of qualitative demands into financial metrics and market-type coordinates, such as profits, returns, risks and rewards (Crosby, 2019). All traditional planning activities – such as community engagement or the promotion of quality urban design – must increasingly be converted into financial metrics before they become deliverable and valid forms of input into planning deliberations. There is a process of commensuration (Espeland and Stephens, 1998) whereby planners are forced to convert qualitative, place-based demands for quantitative spaces of financial action.

The skills and knowledge now required by professional planners must reflect this wider set of changes and this in turn raises pedagogical challenges for those delivering courses. There is a need to develop understandings of how financial negotiations and contractual relationships operate within the private sector and to develop more critical reflections on how planners may be able to develop their negotiating techniques to try to obtain a 'better deal' from contractual discussions. As much of the critical literature on viability planning demonstrates, planners are often losing out within such negotiations, as they privilege the knowledge-practices and expertise found in the private sector (see Colenutt, 2020). As noted above, this is being compounded by the growth of private consultancies and their growing influence(s) in shaping the planning process.

For non-state actors, these wider changes also have profound effects. Civil society groups have increasingly had to engage in technical deliberations over financial viability calculations and been confronted with 'commercially confidential' contracts when trying to contest spending decisions. As deal-making processes have moved beyond the public gaze and into the realms of financial expertise, so modes of activism and conflict have had to seek new mechanisms through which to try to influence planning decisions. An associated trend is a move towards judicialisation, or a growing tendency for planning policies to be negotiated through the legal system and in debates over how financial data has been acquired and used, again requiring all actors to develop new forms of knowledge and skills.

There has been a growing tendency for external speakers, of all types, to discuss the changing form and character of planning practices in the wake of these changes. University courses on planning and place-making need to explore issues of societal progress and social justice. Indeed, this is an increasingly explicit institutional expectation (Sen *et al.*, 2017), which has long since been bound up with the interlocking challenges of globalisation and diversity (Friedmann, 1994; Hemmens, 1998; Sen 2005) and the introduction of a broader range of voices (Ritzdorf 1993). However, the overarching societal mission of planning in intervening in an uncertain future is a messy business without instrumental or normative rules and famously prone to wicked feedback loops (Pipkin, 2019). These forms of uncertainty have always haunted planning research and teaching, but since the global financial crisis in 2008 and the subsequent attack on the legitimacy of planning, they have become a form of state practice, and the very existence of planning has been called into question in ways unprecedented in the post-war era.

Perhaps most significantly, traditional planning literatures that focus on communicative dialogue and negotiation (e.g., Forester, 1989; Healey, 2006) look naïve and dated when confronted with real-world stories and narratives of how contemporary and financialised planning deliberations operate. The tensions between different interests are manifest, with planners often highlighting the structural challenges they face in negotiating with financial interests that are intent on maximising returns and limiting potential risks and the costs of planning obligations. The latter can often draw on international (and expensive) consultancy expertise to make their case, in the full knowledge that any increase in the financial costs of deliberation can then be weaponised and converted into fewer value-capture payments in order to maintain profits and ensure the viability of new developments (Bradley, 2020).

At the same time, the introduction of private sector voices and other civil society groups enables broader exchanges to emerge that open up new avenues for both research (by academics *and* students) and teaching, and contribute to the development of a reflexively produced set of active planning imaginations. While there is a corpus of literature that analyses community-based activism and social movements, there is a paucity of writing on the multiple types of private sectors that exist, the ways in which they operate and the political and ethical codes that they follow. As Özogul and Taşan-Kok (2020) argue, in their comprehensive review of the planning literature on urban development, there is a lack of attention given to the diversity of and within the 'private sector'. In urban development writings, for example, investors and developers are frequently discussed interchangeably, despite growing evidence to show that they are increasingly in conflict and possess very different needs, time frames and outlooks (see Brill, 2021).

In talks and communications, private sector speakers argue that the provision of social infrastructure is something that planners and governments should take primary responsibility for – an ethical as well as practical argument. They are not equipped, they claim, to engage in political discussions with the range of interests that have a stake in contemporary urban planning and development. This is the role of planners and/or politicians. In London, for instance, developers are now required to engage in local ballots with residents when redeveloping estates and must get local approval, but this they claim should not be their responsibility. Such insights, whatever the wider ethical questions they raise, demonstrate clearly the structural limitations created by wider planning system reforms in which the roles and responsibilities of market actors and state actors have become intertwined in unprecedented ways. Private sector speakers question why they should be expected to provide funds for state spending through their development activities, and why these are not raised through general taxation. This in turn raises fundamental questions for students to consider beyond the standard critical critiques that exist around gentrification and/or assumptions that private elites seek out and demand more powers and responsibilities.

It is in developing such insights that the incorporation of external guest speakers has opened up new ways of thinking among student groups and broader research agendas, especially concerning the growing tensions embedded in contemporary forms of planning governance and regulation. In undertaking this type of work the quality and contemporary value of teaching has been enhanced, as has the ability to curate and select external speakers to illuminate these themes to classes of students. It also facilitates more relevant and engaged classroom discussion by framing the types of question and topic that are covered. These are more relevant than those embedded in traditional planning texts that were written in a very different era and lend themselves to idealised constructions and understandings of deliberative processes. The curriculum can therefore be used to generate critical reflections on the wider contexts within which planning is operating, and impart to students some of the knowledge practices and skills that they will require if they move into planning and development professions. It also empowers them to become better informed and more active citizens, especially in the fields of planning formation and deliberation.

For external guest speakers these educational sessions have also provided opportunities for greater self-reflection, while also imparting to students (and academic researchers) some of the core skills and knowledge practices that are now required to undertake in their work. The consequence is that teaching should now focus less on idealised discussions of communicative rationality and more on the shifting form and character of state systems and the relationships between planning, development and welfare. It should give more insight into the workings of the private sector(s) and the professional organisations whose knowledge increasingly shapes and plans the built environment. Moreover, for students the inclusion of external voices also reinforces the legitimacy of the studies they are undertaking and gives them an insight into some of the research work undertaken by critical academics. It shines a light on this dual role and encourages them to think more about their role (and the role of teaching) in generating new knowledge and insights on planning practices and processes.

Reflections and practical take-aways

The chapter has argued that the primary purpose of bringing in external guest speakers is to support the development of a reflexive and widely shared planning imagination among students, researchers and practitioners. It is a mode of pedagogy that plays an active role in embedding real-world experiences directly into the classroom, while also shedding light on the nexus of interactions that underpin teaching, research, and practice. The unfolding of engaged, relevant and topical research agendas is an ongoing process, which feeds spaces of learning and, as we have argued, is also fed by it. As discussed, there are significant pressures on planning practitioners to employ modes of thinking embedded in quantitative and increasingly financialised framings of planning. This is just one example of the need for built environment students to grapple with agendas in academic research and how this offers the opportunity to develop relevant intellectual skills and a deep and meaningful understanding of how contemporary planning processes and governance arrangements operate. More traditional understandings, founded on assumptions that a well-resourced and powerful public planning system exists, are increasingly outdated and teaching practices and research-based knowledge production must reflect this.

Greater reflexive awareness of processes of curation should be a norm that we espouse in view of the complexity and changes to planning policy and epistemologies around financialisation. As discussed, the curation of external guest speakers requires an explicit approach to knowledge production processes in recognition of their primary importance, both within the education of students and 'in the real world'. However, the processes of curation demand authenticity and openness on the part of the researcher-teacher. To be uncritical or disingenuous is to do it badly, and to disempower the student, precluding powerful learning opportunities.

By carefully curating a role for guest speakers the control of the educator is momentarily relinquished, albeit in a coordinated and structured way. This is because knowledge may not be observed, and only by being involved in the learning and exchanges may we understand it. The educator is also temporarily holding a participant role in classroom exchanges, alongside their primary role as teacher. For this reason, it is critical that they avoid defaulting to a didactic position, which can have limiting effect on students' independent thinking. Instead, they must focus on bounding the space for critical enquiry, and guiding the abstracting process within the moment. In practical terms, this means setting up a planning imagination and encouraging students to join the discussion with reference to the diverse frameworks in play.

The production of a bounded space encourages inquisitiveness and radical views, but more importantly the expertise of academics is opened up for greater scrutiny and questioning. First, research-led teaching is foregrounded in establishing the arenas of interaction in the classroom. Existing specialisms are re-centred. Second, in offering judgements to the audience, of both students and external parties, lecturer-academics are inviting others to critically engage with them. These exchanges may test both the knowledge within this space, and the bounds of the space. This matters greatly for students in achieving their learning objectives, especially in respect of ethical questions around how built environments should be governed and managed.

As a final authentic reflection on the experience, a productive external guest speaker session requires trust and intellectual reciprocity. These are softer skills that can be demonstrated to the student body, and without those a critical enquiry is meaningless.

References

Andranovich, G., and M. J. Burbank. 2021. 'Cities and the Olympics in urban politics'. In G. Andranovich and M. J. Burbank (eds), *Contesting the Olympics in American Cities*. Singapore: Palgrave Macmillan, 1–21.

Bailey, N. 2005. 'The great skills debate: defining and delivering the skills required for community regeneration in England', *Planning Practice and Research* 20(3): 341–52.

Bernstein. B. 2001. 'Symbolic control: issues of empirical description of agencies and agents', *International Journal of Social Research Methodology* 4(1): 21–33. (last accessed 1 December 2022).

Bradley, Q. 2020. 'The financialisation of housing land supply in England', *Urban Studies* 58(2), https://journals.sagepub.com/doi/10.1177/0042098020907278 (last accessed 1 December 2022).

Brill, F. 2021. 'Governing investors and developers: analysing the role of risk allocation in urban development', *Urban Studies* 59(7), https://journals.sagepub.com/doi/10.1177/00420980211017826 (last accessed 2 December 2022).

Chiapello, E. 2015. 'Financialisation of valuation', *Human Studies* 38: 13–35.

Clover, D., K. Sanford and K. Johnson. 2018. 'Museum and gallery pedagogic strategies for change', *International Journal of Lifelong Education* 37(1): 1–3.

Colenutt, B. 2020. *The Planning Lobby*. Bristol: Policy Press.

Cottrell, M. P., and T. Nelson. 2011. 'Not just the Games? Power, protest and politics at the Olympics', *European Journal of International Relations* 17(4): 729–53.

Crosby, N. 2019. 'Development viability assessment and the provision of affordable housing: a game of "pass the parcel"?', *Town Planning Review* 90: 407–28.

Dearborn, L. M., and S. A. Harwood. 2011. 'Teaching students about complexity: reflections about an interdisciplinary community service learning studio in East St Louis, Illinois', *Journal of Urbanism: international research on placemaking and urban sustainability* 4(2): 127–51.

Edwards, C., and R. Imrie. 2015. *The Short Guide to Urban Policy*. Bristol: Policy Press.

Espeland, W., and M. Stevens. 1998. 'Commensuration as a social process', *Annual Review of Sociology* 24: 313–43.

Ferm J., and M. Raco. 2020. 'Viability planning, value capture and the geographies of market-led planning reform in England', *Planning Theory and Practice* 21(2): 218–35.

Forester J. 1989. *Planning in the Face of Power*. Los Angeles CA: University of California Press.

Forsyth, A., H. Lu and P. McGirr. 2000. 'Service learning in an urban context: implications for planning and design education', *Journal of Architectural and Planning Research* 17(3): 236–59.

Friedmann, J. 1994. 'Planning education for the late twentieth century: an initial inquiry', *Journal of Planning Education and Research*, 14(1): 55–64.

Grundmann, R. 2017. 'The problem of expertise in knowledge societies', *Minerva*, 55(1): 25–48.

Healey, P. 2006. *Collaborative Planning: shaping places in fragmented societies*. New York: Palgrave.

Hemmens, G. C. 1988. 'Thirty years of planning education', *Journal of Planning Education and Research* 7(2): 85–91.

Latham, A., and J. Layton. 2019. 'Social infrastructure and the public life of cities: studying urban sociality and public spaces', *Geography Compass*, https://doi.org/10.1111/gec3.12444 (last accessed 2 December 2022).

Linovski, O. 2021. 'The value of planning: views from management consultants', *Journal of Planning Education and Research*, https://doi.org/10.1177/0739456X211051420 (last accessed 2 December 2022).

Özogul, S., and T. Taşan-Kok. 2020. 'One and the same? A systematic literature review of residential property investor types', *Journal of Planning Literature* 35(4): 475–94.

Penny, J. 2021. 'Revenue generating machines? London's local housing companies and the emergence of local state rentierism', *Antipode*, https://doi.org/10.1111/anti.12774 (last accessed 2 December 2022).

Pipkin, S. 2019. 'Dissolving "wicked" problems: beyond institutionalist and participatory approaches to land title regularization', *Journal of Planning Education and Research*, https://doi.org/10.1177/0739456X19856066 (last accessed 2 December 2022).

Raco, M. 2018. 'Private consultants, planning reform and the marketisation of local government finance'. In J. Ferm and J. Tomaney (eds), *Planning Practice: critical perspectives from the UK*, London: Routledge, 123–37.

Raco, M., and T. Tasan-Kok. 2020. 'A tale of two cities: framing urban diversity as content curation in London and Toronto', *Cosmopolitan Civil Societies* 12(1): 43–66.

Ritzdorf, M. 1993. 'The Fairy's Tale: teaching planning and public policy in a different voice', *Journal of Planning Education and Research* 12(2): 99–106.

Sayer, A. 2000. *Realism and Social Science*. London: SAGE.

Schapper J., and S. E. Mayson. 2010. 'Research-led teaching: moving from a fractured engagement to a marriage of convenience', *Higher Education Research and Development* 29(6): 641–51.

Schön, D. A. 1983. *The Reflective Practitioner: how professionals think in action*. New York: Basic Books.

Sen, S. 2005. 'Diversity and North American planning curricula: the need for reform', *Canadian Journal of Urban Research* 14(1): 121–44.

Sen, S., K. Umemoto, A. Koh and V. Zambonelli. 2017. 'Diversity and social justice in planning education: a synthesis of topics, pedagogical approaches, and educational goals in planning syllabi', *Journal of Planning Education and Research* 37(3): 347–58.

Wynne, B. E. 1996. 'May the sheep safely graze? A reflexive view of the expert-lay knowledge divide'. In S. Lash, B. Szerszynski and B. Wynne (eds), *Risk, Environment and Modernity: towards a new ecology*. London: SAGE, 1–26.

7
Co-Producing planning? Neighbourhood planning as the context for participative pedagogy

Elena Besussi and Sue Brownill

The planning profession in the United Kingdom has experienced a long-term transformation characterised by the normalisation of the notion of growth as the guiding principle of urban development, and by the parallel erosion of the relevance of a critical practice capable of challenging these ideas. In this context, it has become increasingly difficult to justify the need, in the education of future planners, to practically engage with the politics of planning and with the expectations that planning raises especially for local and impacted communities. This practical engagement requires the design of a learning experience which substantiates theory-led critical reflection with a guided plan-making experience that can explore these problematics.

This chapter discusses the authors' experiences of bringing together community groups and planning students in the co-production of neighbourhood development plans (NDPs).[1] Co-production is here defined as a process of collaboration between communities and 'experts' which has the intent to transform pre-existing understanding of the position and expertise that both parties represent (Durose *et al.*, 2012). The process of co-production is considered able to produce shared and more robust evidence to support plan-making, and to overcome the democratic deficit of 'instrumental' participation (Ellis, 2000: 214).

For these reasons, co-production in the context of planning can be seen as a pedagogical route to expose students to (more) reflective practices (Schon, 1983), to explore the contradictions that the contemporary political environment imposes on the purpose of planning (Rydin, 2011) and on the role of planners and the public (Clifford and Tewdwr-Jones, 2013), and to develop an understanding of planning knowledge and evidence that is plural and locally articulated (Ferm and Raco, 2020).

The analysis and reflections are framed in terms of the relationship between co-production in the pedagogical *process* and co-production in the *context* of (neighbourhood) planning. In the pedagogical process, co-production of the content and format of learning between community groups, students and teachers can be transformative of existing understandings of how learning happens, what learning is, who the learner is and what is to be learnt. In the context of neighbourhood planning, co-production can be seen as the pedagogical route to possibly transform pre-existing understanding of the roles and definitions of planners, experts and evidence. However, the chapter also shows how this context also acts to limit the potential of co-production within both the pedagogical and planning processes. These categories are further explored in the discussion of teaching practices and of the participants' experiences.

What is neighbourhood planning? The context

Neighbourhood planning was established in England as part of the Localism Act 2011 and since then has remained an opportunity for communities to write the planning policies and plans that shape the future development of their neighbourhood (Brownill and Bradley, 2017). Results from the past 10 years have made us cautious about how effective neighbourhood planning is at steering local development (Davoudi and Madanipour, 2015), but there is no doubt that it has encouraged community groups to engage with planning and in many cases also challenge or question existing planning practices and strategies (Brownill and Bradley, 2017). Since its inception more than 2,000 neighbourhood planning groups have been formed and more than 1,000 NDPs have become a statutory part of the planning system (MHCLG, 2020). The premise behind neighbourhood planning was to 'revolutionise the planning process by taking power away from officials and putting it into the hands of those who know most about their neighbourhood – local people themselves' (DCLG, 2010).

What is different about NDPs is, unlike previous hyper-local plans that were advisory only, NDPs become part of the statutory planning framework by setting out policies for the use of land in defined local areas which are then taken into consideration when decisions are made on planning applications. Neighbourhood plans carry legal weight, which is a major part of their attraction to communities. To achieve this status (or to be 'made' in planning jargon) plans must be drawn up by a recognised body; either a town or parish council or in largely urban areas without these a neighbourhood forum approved as representative by the local authority. They must also go through a regulated process including consultation with residents and stakeholders, the production of a draft plan and a 'light touch' examination that ensures they meet a set of conditions including being in conformity with other statutory plans and meeting environmental and other standards. If the plan is approved, it goes to a local referendum and must be approved by over half of those voting. Those eligible to vote are people registered on the electoral roll. Within this process, NDPs are required to be in conformity with all other planning policies, the first of many other contradictions which will emerge through this chapter.

In addition to the right to prepare neighbourhood development plans, the Localism Act 2011 introduced a range of 'community rights' that allow voluntary and community groups, and parish councils to take a more direct initiative and control over development and the provision of local services. For example, the Community Right to Build Order can be used by neighbourhood forums to propose a development in their local area and obtain permission to build it, without having to go through the planning process. Although often considered under the umbrella of neighbourhood planning, the exercise of community rights requires technical expertise and knowledge different from planning, including architecture, management and development finance.

Government funded support is provided for neighbourhood planning groups in the form of funding and technical support. Groups can apply for (up to £10,000 in 2021) basic funding each year over five years, rising to £18,000 if certain conditions are met. Technical aid in the form of tailored packages linked to certain aspects such as site allocations is available from consultants AECOM. Both of these are administered by Locality (a government supported non-governmental organisation), which also provides information sharing on its website.[2]

Why choose neighbourhood planning for exploring co-production in planning pedagogy?

There are several reasons why neighbourhood planning is of value in learning and teaching planning in the framework of co-production. First, it is underpinned by the principle that anyone can plan and it materialises the aspiration of breaking down the barriers between experts and non-experts in the planning process and in the production of knowledge that supports planning decisions. The 2011 legislation was based on a pamphlet called Open-Source Planning (Conservative Party, 2010), which set out the view that, as with open-source programming, anyone with the right tools and information can plan.

Second, NDPs are based on bounded geographical areas of intervention (the neighbourhood area), which, in the context of teaching and learning, facilitates the development of a sense of competence and allows teachers and students to gauge the resources needed to complete a project within a set amount of time.

Third, it provides a single point of reference within the community (the neighbourhood forum or parish or town council). And finally, it can be seen as a microcosm of key planning issues. It provides an opportunity to explore the nexus between local interests, supra-local drivers of development and strategic planning agendas in the determination of development decisions. It also makes real the different approaches to and styles of planning that often exist in an uneasy tension within any planning system; particularly between a growth-led and a more inclusive and socially orientated agenda. This enables students to see these relations and processes as they play out on the ground in bounded examples and to reflect critically on policy and practice.

Some possible limitations

However, for all these positive reasons there are also some limitations to the exploration of co-production through neighbourhood planning. The first is that it is well established that neighbourhood planning is more likely to happen in affluent areas (Parker, 2017) and there are also questions about the representativeness of neighbourhood planning groups (Davoudi and Cowie, 2013). Therefore, there is a risk of supporting groups who already have resources and presenting a one-sided view of planning. We must remember that neighbourhood planning is not immune to the uneven nature of participation in planning, to control by the 'usual suspects' or to the hidden and not so hidden power differences between the interests involved.

Second, although the legislation has remained static, central government regulation of neighbourhood planning has changed over time. Tait and Inch (2016) write about different phases of localism, starting with the earlier years of 'Big Society' Localism during which NDPs emerged that stressed a citizen-led approach, this was replaced by growth localism that sought to nudge activity to promoting growth (i.e., housebuilding), and later 'muscular localism' where central government began to set stricter guidelines and recentralise power (see Table 7.1). The result of this has been to restrict the spaces of neighbourhood planning, affecting the scope of what neighbourhood planning groups can do and their power to influence planning outcomes.

Finally, there are some inherent contradictions in neighbourhood planning, some of which have been implied above, while others will emerge through the discussion. Of particular significance for the work presented here is the still quite heavy legal and technical requirements and processes that neighbourhood planning groups must follow. The fact

Table 7.1   Phases of localism (adapted from Tait and Inch, 2016)

Big society localism (2010–12)	The Localism Act, the National Planning Policy Framework, and open-source planning	New statutory powers introduced encouraging neighbourhood planning, power of neighbourhood planners reinforced by ministers and legal rulings
Growth localism v big society localism (2012–15)	The Planning and Infrastructure Act, and regeneration to enable growth	Favouring growth (housing developments)
Rolled-back, austerity or 'muscular' localism (2015–19)	Amendments to legislation and the National Planning Policy Framework; re-centralisation; changes to neighbourhood planning regulations (e.g., housing-needs methodologies); and further reliance on private-sector funding	Presumption in favour of development strengthened; less ministerial intervention in support of neighbourhood planners, tightening of regulations in relation to local plans
Levelling up and rediscovery of localism (2019–)	Planning white paper post-Brexit settlement, and levelling up	Retention of neighbourhood planning but potential shift to focus on design and character; and loss of power to allocate sites

that the Department for Communities and Local Government (DCLG) was itself promoting links between neighbourhood planning groups and universities was in part a recognition of this gap and raised further warning signs for the possibilities of 'true' co-production in the context of neighbourhood planning. Related to this the support for neighbourhood planning groups, which until 2015 was spread between a range of community and planning based organisations, has been concentrated (and relatively professionalised) within the Locality/AECOM partnership.

These shifts in the *context* of neighbourhood planning impacted on the pedagogic *processes* discussed here. The earlier years of neighbourhood planning are characterised by a diverse range of interpretations and approaches to the formulation of NDP content and process. This diversity can be explained by the absence of a predefined model for neighbourhood planning, its uptake by community groups coming from different experiences of local campaigning and community planning and the availability of publicly funded technical support from a wide range of national organisations and was mirrored in the range of interests for collaborative projects with students. Later, the adoption of regulatory and implementation legislation and the convergence of government funding for technical support into one consultancy firm, led to the consolidation of neighbourhood planning towards a more standardised approach where planning policies and planning technical language are central to the production of the plan. This is reflected in a shift in the content of collaborative initiatives with neighbourhood planning forums towards a type of technical expertise focused on policy writing or, alternatively, in the support for the implementation and management of small urban projects. This has led some to suggest that neighbourhood planning, rather than being locally/community driven, is an example of a form of 'co-production' of planning where different interests come together in the production of a plan (Parker *et at.*, 2015)

As discussed later, the shift in focus towards more technical aspects of plan-making can be an opportunity to develop skills that are close to the demands of the planning profession, but it also puts tension on and constrains the opportunities for mutual transformative learning of which co-production is the underlying vehicle.

Creating the space for co-production for students and community groups in the context of neighbourhood planning

Many planning schools independently used the advent of neighbourhood planning as a way of continuing the commitment to engaged pedagogy that has long characterised planning education. Here, two such examples initiated in the Bartlett School of Planning (UCL) and Oxford Brookes University are discussed. While they share similar aims in the sense of putting into practice the objectives of engaged pedagogy set out above (such as bringing students and community planners together, supporting community groups, exploring the possibilities for co-production and developing a critical perspective on planning practice among students), they also differ in terms of timing, the level of the course students were on and of course geographical context (see Table 7.2).

At the Bartlett School of Planning, the introduction of a new MSc programme in urban design and city planning offered the opportunity to redesign the core teaching on planning practice and plan-making as a collaborative project with London's communities. A new module was introduced in 2014 based on a close collaboration between the school, London's emerging neighbourhood planning forums, and Just Space (a network of community groups established to coordinate participation and responses to London planning issues). The decision to work with neighbourhood forums was inspired by the experience of Oxford Brookes University and the reasons set out above, as well as by the aspiration to close the gap in technical expertise that, at the time, appeared to be at the roots of a lower uptake and lower completion rate for neighbourhood planning in London.

The pedagogical model involves an initial collaboration between academic staff and the community partners to identify a project brief that meets the partner neighbourhood forum's agenda as well as the requirements of the school's planning curriculum. Once a brief is agreed, students develop a response which usually involves a combination of urban analysis, review of the local policy and institutional context, and recommendations, either as neighbourhood plan policy options or as direct interventions (which broadly correspond to the Localism Act 'community rights'). Together with the project brief, academic staff and neighbourhood forum members agree the type and extent of active participation of the neighbourhood forum in the teaching activities. This has ranged from support for one-off site visits to weekly feedback sessions with the students. Since 2014 the Bartlett has worked with 15 neighbourhood forums across London.

Over the years the pedagogical model has not changed although the focus of the projects has. There is of course an intrinsic variability dictated by the nature of the work being live and there is, as discussed, a transformation of neighbourhood planning towards a more standardised policy-based format. But there has also been a learning process and adaptation and the academic and teaching staff have become more

Table 7.2 The neighbourhood planning initiatives

	UCL	Brookes
Dates	2014–22	2012–18
Level	The project is part of the core teaching of a postgraduate taught programme with Royal Town Planning Institute accreditation	Adaptation of final-year undergraduate module on local plans
Timing	Over one 10-week term	Over two semesters (September–March) Neighbourhood planning project formed half of the work of each semester
Process	Neighbourhood planning groups identified by module leader Project brief prepared by module leader with neighbourhood planning groups Initial meeting and site visit Students interpret and respond to project brief Meetings with neighbourhood planning groups available but not compulsory during the project Support and associated lectures given in class	Neighbourhood planning groups identified by module leader Initial meeting and site visit at start of module Themes and tasks suggested by neighbourhood planning group Student groups take on selected topics Support and associated lectures given in class
Outputs	Report and poster (term 2)	Local poster exhibition in neighbourhood planning area (semester 1) Report to neighbourhood planning group (semester 2) Individual student reflection Assessed as part of module
Context	Fewer neighbourhood planning groups available in London, especially at early stages of plan preparation	Limited neighbourhood planning groups in and immediately around Oxford, largely in more affluent areas with a history of engagement in planning

aware of what works and what doesn't in the classroom. First, this is due to becoming more sensitive to engaging students on project briefs where the initial expertise required to complete the project was not available within the student cohort. Students are not 'experts' when the project starts. Second, as a consequence of this and of the changing nature of neighbourhood planning, the demands from neighbourhood forums have become less diverse, due partly to the establishment of government regulations and partly by the emergence of government funded technical support concentrated within one organisation.

The initiative at Oxford Brookes established close links with neighbourhood planning groups in the city and surrounding county from the time the legislation was passed. The university campus is itself located in one of the first neighbourhood planning areas in Oxford and this provided the springboard for including project work on a final year double module on the undergraduate planning degree between 2012–18. As this was an established module, it was not possible to focus a new module around co-production as at UCL, instead an existing group project element had to be adapted to enable students to produce a report with a neighbourhood planning group. This represented 50 per cent of the work that students were doing on the module that semester. Briefs were drawn up in discussion with the groups, students were given lectures and seminars around key concepts and practices, group members came along to talk to them, and field visits were carried out. The work was reported in stages, including an initial presentation of ideas to the staff and neighbourhood planning group and a final poster presentation held in the neighbourhood area. Between 2012 and 2018 we worked with all three neighbourhood planning groups in the city and one in a neighbouring village.

Despite the Barlett example being part of a wider course review, the fact that both initiatives were linked to single modules and therefore to the experiences and enthusiasm of particular module leaders raises questions about how such initiatives are embedded, or not, in the curriculum and about their sustainability. This point will be returned to in the reflections.

Co-production in practice?

This section brings together the authors' experiences and reflections from the initiatives outlined above focusing on the contradictions and issues both in the *process* of doing co-production/live pedagogy and in the *context* of co-production in neighbourhood planning. It highlights a range of ways in which specific intellectual capacities and co-production skills have been developed through the work.

When (how) co-production happens

If we see co-production as transformational both in the context of the classroom and planning, then we would argue that breaking down barriers can be seen in a variety of ways in the examples that we have been involved in.

The first is where co-production becomes co-learning, for example, through students and community groups working out a project brief together. Significantly this process becomes more than just a set of aims and outputs, as agreeing the brief means discussing differing understandings and expectations of planning which emerge. This relates to where ideas come from. Often, up to this point in their education, students have seen planning largely from the point of view of the formal planning system and the actors within it. Postgraduate students may also be professional planners on a part-time course. Hearing from and working with community groups whose aim is to make the planning system work for them provides a different perspective. Similarly, the opportunity for community groups to have access to students' existing knowledge of skills, programmes and other examples of what does and does not work can help in reframing their objectives. For both sides, the idea that planning processes are to be discussed and considered rather than one side or the other determining it is a key learning point. At the Bartlett School of Planning, the pedagogical approach to co-production draws on the recommendations of the 'Protocol for research collaboration between community/activist groups and university staff', formulated initially by Just Space and UCL to improve the experience of all those involved in collaborative projects (Just Space, 2018). The protocol articulates in principle and, most importantly, in practice the importance of understanding and valuing different perspectives on planning, and of recognising the relative nature of planning knowledge and expertise. For example, in the principle of co-authorship and ownership of the knowledge produced through the projects, the final student's reports, including all data collected, sources and analysis methods, are always shared with the neighbourhood forum as a long-lasting resource.

In an example from Oxford, students brought skills and approaches to carrying out character assessments to the neighbourhood planning groups. This helped the neighbourhood planning group realise that they needed to simplify their approach making it easier to implement and prioritising the elements they felt were particularly relevant rather than taking an existing methodology from the shelf. In turn, the students had to modify their methodology to these priorities but then had the benefit of implementing and evaluating it. Students commented on how the fact that the neighbourhood planning groups valued this work really increased their confidence in being able to come up with 'valid' planning solutions. This process can be assisted by students working with the same group over a number of years, as relationships build up between neighbourhood planning groups and staff and student cohorts share experiences. Nevertheless, see below for some downsides to this.

In addition, these debates can also highlight different paradigms of planning. Community groups are often challenging what Rydin (2011) refers to as the 'growth dependent' planning paradigm, which prioritises economic growth over other purposes of planning such as addressing social and environmental needs. The co-production of neighbourhood development plans in the pedagogical setting, has been able to expose all parties to the wider limitations of planning to respond to needs and aspirations that community groups identify as intrinsic to the quality of urban space but that fall beyond the legal competence of planning. This happens, for example, when traffic or public health are raised as issues of concern or when a neighbourhood forum wants to exercise one of the community rights. When both sides recognise that a development plan cannot respond to these demands, more general questions are raised and a different understanding of planning and place can emerge.

Groups are often trying to find ways to bend the existing planning framework towards other outcomes. This enables students to see that there can be other ways of doing planning and it makes real for them the debates that may seem abstract when encountered in lecture halls and articles: 'working with the neighbourhood forums was good experience and made it possible to see how planning actually works in practice' (UCL student, 2018).

At the Bartlett School of Planning, the London context always exposes students to the impacts that growth-led strategic planning at the metropolitan scale has on local neighbourhoods, but collaborative projects with neighbourhood forums have allowed students to realise that not all local responses are negative. For example, students have built knowledge expertise to develop planning responses to manage increased densities (in North Kingston and Vauxhall) and protect community infrastructures (in Grove Park and Crystal Palace) and community groups have explored options to become proactive managing community assets in the context of intense pressure for their disposal.

Co-production can also challenge existing narratives of place. For example, taking the starting point that a local group wanted to protect local businesses from threat of redevelopment, UCL students developed evidence that supported a locally articulated understanding of the value that these businesses have in the social and economic sustainability of the neighbourhoods, offering an alternative understanding to the one provided by the local authority that often identified this area as inefficient or low performing. The rationale here was to offer evidence to alternative definitions of value that could lead to the development of a set of policies different from those contained in the local plan and aimed at achieving this alternative vision. This is doubly important, as one of the criticisms levelled at NDPs is that they merely repeat local plans and fail to develop locally distinct policies. Similarly, students at Oxford Brookes worked on re-looking at the night-time economy and what it brought to the area which challenged residents' perceptions that they wanted their place as just a 'non-party' zone. This suggested ways in which policies could be included that managed these spaces and also brought in a range of venues (e.g., school halls) to provide a variety of entertainment types.

A third area that showed some evidence of co-production was when all parties had their perceptions and practices transformed by the process. For example, students begin to understand why community members engage in planning, to respect the time and energy they put in and not to just label them 'nimbies' by appreciating that they were often articulating a different narrative of place and a different set of purposes for planning rather than merely opposing development: 'It was beneficial to engage with planning in a real life scenario, talking to those affected by it and looking to utilise Neighbourhood Planning to affect positive change' (UCL student, 2018). They could also see that planning is an emotional process rather than being solely a technical/political one, and that it has an impact on peoples' lives (Jupp, 2013). Similarly, community members could see students as young people with future possible careers in planning and engage with them to change their perspectives on planning rather than see them just as hands to get tasks done. This is linked to the willingness of all sides to open their minds and very often the 'generosity' of community planners, particularly those with experience of working with young people and in educational settings. In relation to this, some students went on to do further work in neighbourhood planning either working for neighbourhood planning consultants, doing placements with local authority neighbourhood planning units or getting jobs as neighbourhood planning officers themselves, or even, in the case of the Bartlett School of Planning, continuing the collaboration in a volunteering role.

A further positive outcome is where parties can critically reflect on neighbourhood planning as a policy process resulting from the interaction. Representatives from neighbourhood planning groups working with Oxford Brookes University commented that coming to speak to students enabled them to stand back and reflect on the neighbourhood planning process, including what was possible and what was not, particularly in relation to their relationship with local and national plans and agencies. It also enabled them to look back on their experience from starting a plan, what they had gained and whether it was worth it! At the Bartlett School of Planning, some partner neighbourhood forums commented that through their experience they had become more confident about what to ask and how from planning consultants or the providers of technical support. Students, perhaps inevitably as they were also being asked to engage critically with planning in their courses, were also able to see some limitations in neighbourhood planning, particularly in terms of the representativeness of the groups that they were working with as already outlined. At Oxford Brookes, students were also asked to write a critical reflection on their experience, highlighting one area of neighbourhood planning. At the Bartlett School of Planning, a final session is used by students and teaching staff to develop a collective critical reflection on the experience, often highlighting a mix of frustrations with the limitation of the planning systems and the gap between the statutory provisions of a plan and the needs and aspirations posed by neighbourhood forum.

These outcomes are evidence of how knowledge and skills produced through these initiatives have transferred outside the university and can potentially have long-term effects for how groups see themselves as experts.

In reaching these positive outcomes there were some practical issues. The process of co-production works better at some stages within the neighbourhood planning process than others. It is especially effective when groups are in the early stages or articulating issues and gathering evidence. For example, in Oxford the first Brookes project in 2012 linked students to plan working groups around transport, green spaces, the high street and housing, among other things. Student groups worked with the chairs of those committees to set briefs and carry out work such as a survey of retailers and bringing in good practice from other neighbourhood planners. Brainstorming sessions and initial reports set out ideas of what the plan could do. Another group undertook an analysis of participatory methods and what would work in the context of Headington. Some neighbourhood planning groups have used these as part of their evidence base for the NDP.

The later stages of a plan, however, proved more difficult in the Oxford Brookes example, as groups were often looking for specific skills such as writing policies or undertaking environmental statements, which were beyond the competence of undergraduate students. Linked to this is the closing down of the spaces for neighbourhood planning influence through the changes in regulation brought about by the government. This put greater emphasis on the 'robustness' of plans in being able to stand up to legal challenges and restricted the areas in which student planners could become involved. Similarly, at the Bartlett School of Planning there were projects where the technical expertise required from students was either unavailable or beyond the scope of the planning course. When this happened, project briefs would include, for example, requests for technical support in the preparation of funding bids or in the application of the new community rights enshrined in the Localism Act 2011 (right to bid, right to challenge, right to build, right to reclaim land). These are important tools in the agenda of neighbourhood forums but often require skills that planning students do not have in advance and do not develop in the space of their programme of studies.

This is where the *process* of doing live pedagogy with neighbourhood planning groups conflicts with the context of doing neighbourhood planning itself and shows some of the contradictions in a process that is meant to enable residents to plan for themselves, but which is regulated in a way that requires specific competencies and skills. While this can initially open up spaces for involved pedagogy it can also close those spaces down. As a result, while positives are possible, it is necessary to question whether this is co-production and the conclusions will return to this question after looking at what does not go so well.

When (how) co-production does not happen

There were also situations where co-learning and co-production did not emerge for a variety of reasons. Within the pedagogical *process* the most significant one is where the transformation of each sides' views, both of each other and of planning, does not occur. An example of this is where part-time students who engage with neighbourhood planning groups in their day jobs, carry this experience and framing into the learning setting. This can mean that, for example, they bring with them the planning cultures of some local authority departments that see neighbourhood planning groups as obstructive to development or unrepresentative and are not open to having this view challenged. Alternatively, other students may see neighbourhood planning groups as not being challenging or representative enough, questioning why they should be working in areas that could access resources from elsewhere while others are unsupported. On the other side, some members of neighbourhood planning groups, especially in a university town such as Oxford, may see students as part of the problem that they are trying to plan away or that they are there to carry out what the group wants rather than agreeing an agenda through a process of negotiation. There are therefore different expectations and motivations between students, researchers/tutors and neighbourhood planning groups. Students may not share the same ideals as their tutors, particularly in terms of promoting alternative community-led approaches to the growth oriented and procedural forms of planning that are promoted by current policy and practice in England (see comments below about professional identity and careerism). These differences can be widened if the work is part of a compulsory module, as was the case in Oxford and London. Some students may then adopt an instrumental attitude, seeing the project as just another piece of coursework, and become less open to the encounter, although there are still examples of some students leaving this behind as the work progressed.

There are also different timescales. Universities are bound to semesters and courses are run within set periods with fixed assessment points that may not fit with the neighbourhood planning group. The Oxford Brookes projects worked best when there was a double module enabling the work to be carried out over a longer period (between October and March). When course changes resulted in this being turned into a single module, the flexibility was lost. The Bartlett School of Planning projects were always bound to the short period of a 10-week term. This has been a significant constraint on what kind of projects students could do, challenging the teaching staff to identify and isolate elements of the plan-making process at the expense of a more realistic plan-making experience. Then, of course, students can be students; missing sessions, undertaking last-minute work and encountering problems with group work despite the efforts put in by module leaders. As a result of these process factors, perceptions are not challenged or altered – sometimes they are even reinforced, and what is produced does not necessarily meet community needs or move their neighbourhood planning process along, and does not challenge students to learn new things.

These experiences increasingly demonstrate the need to be aware of the politics of co-production and power differentials. If co-production is about breaking down the barriers of power and transforming agendas, does this happen in practice, and, if so, where are the barriers? These issues of power become more important when the impact of the pedagogical *context* to neighbourhood planning is taken into consideration. Besides the contradictions of the technical and legal requirements of what is meant to be a non-expert form of planning and the difficulties of these requirements being met by students, neighbourhood planning groups could also access the government technical support, and some chose this as being able to better meet their needs.

There is also the wider context of the planning profession. To some student planners, neighbourhood planning can be seen as a challenge to a professional and disciplinary identity that they have been developing in response to other elements of the course, their career expectations, their sense of the key principles and practices that the planning profession is currently adopting or their existing work in planning. Students might therefore find it difficult to embrace a community-led agenda that challenges a growth-orientated planning strategy, since this position is seen to be against the principle of "positive planning", but they might find it less problematic to support a consensus-driven model of community participation.

Part of this wider context involves the agendas of other agencies and the use made of these examples. In the early days of neighbourhood planning, the DCLG actively promoted university involvement in neighbourhood planning, as a way of illustrating its support for neighbourhood planning groups and providing a 'good news' narrative. Department representatives came to student presentations and tutors gave presentations to national neighbourhood planning events. However, as the support package became more developed there was less need for this. Universities keen to show their community credentials also promoted these activities, although in the case of Oxford Brookes this was complicated by a campus redevelopment that put them in the role of the planning 'enemy', showing how different parts of the university can have different agendas. The raising of student fees in England to £9,000 per year in 2012 also produced a more instrumental and career-focused attitude among students, leading some to question the value of this type of activity – and the nature of some planning courses has changed, perhaps reflecting the changes in the nature of the established planning profession itself. For example, at Oxford Brookes, the bespoke planning course has been changed to one that includes property development, attracting a different type of student.

The changing spaces and content of neighbourhood planning also pose challenges to co-production. Arguably, there was more opportunity in the 'Big Society' localism stage or 2011–15 for 'co-production' to occur when neighbourhood planning groups had more room to manoeuvre and be creative. Further, it has become clearer that neighbourhood planning is 'still planning', institutionally isomorphic and strategically compliant to pre-existing planning practices, policies and aims. This 'bounded recognition' (Porter, 2015) of neighbourhood planning has made the opportunities for co-production more limited over time, for example where national growth agendas considerably reduce the scope of neighbourhood planning, like in the case of Drummond Street under the shadow of HS2. As a result of these limitations and contradictions both of our attempts to undertake engaged pedagogy through working with neighbourhood planning groups have come to an end. Increasingly, the extensive time invested by tutors, students and in particular neighbourhood planning groups, did not seem to be resulting in commensurate positive outcomes. Arguably, the shifting power relations, policy context and expectations meant that the possibilities for co-production outweighed the limitations.

Conclusions: but is it co-production?

The two initiatives at UCL and Oxford Brookes have now been paused and the obvious conclusion to take from this experience is that co-production in engaged pedagogy (at least in this context) does not work or is too difficult. However, there is room for 'critical optimism' when it comes to neighbourhood planning and to reflect that the situation is more complex than this initial reading would suggest. This reflection is articulated in four main points and six practical takeaways.

First, that live pedagogy and neighbourhood planning have both to be seen as contradictory processes. The examples discussed here show that there are tensions in the way neighbourhood planning has been regulated by government (e.g., between autonomy and conformity) there are also dynamics of power and differing expectations within any example of engaged pedagogy. It is not possible to assume that initiating a project such as the ones outlined here is a 'good thing' without being aware of potential possibilities and limitations and taking these into account when designing such projects.

Second, within this there needs to be consideration of the dynamics between the pedagogical processes and the context within which they are practised. Third, these practices suggest the need to re-examine the meaning of co-production focusing on: co-learning; challenging perceptions of place and the purposes of planning; and the way that all sides are transformed through this. And this is not just an issue for those engaged in designing such projects. It is a valuable experience for students to be exposed to the fragmented democratic processes in planning and to see how publics and planners are constructed within these.

Third, these practices suggest the need to re-examine the meaning of co-production focusing on co-learning and on challenging perceptions of place and the purposes of planning that is of value and the way that all sides are transformed through this. As such, there is value in doing this work and the initiatives presented here have shown when it can work well and what can be achieved. The focus is then not on the products that might emerge from a collaborative process through a range of interests in the shape of a plan or a report that could have the co-production 'tag' attached to it. It is therefore uncertain and maybe unhelpful to see these engaged pedagogy examples as co-production. It is more useful to focus on how some of the contradictions in these examples can be recognised and overcome, to try to be aware of the politics and power differentials, and on how different purposes of planning can be promoted through these practices.

Finally, the fact that these initiatives were paused shows their vulnerability when they are dependent on the energy of particular staff and are not fully embedded in the wider curriculum or fully supported by the institution. Once staff move on or can now longer provide the extra time and effort needed for these types of module, co-production can slip down the agenda of the curriculum unless it is included in course aims and objectives and is reflected in the resources provided both to staff and to individuals and organisations outside the university.

These experiences highlight six practical takeaways for those involved in developing engaged pedagogy initiatives. First, do not be afraid to stop what could become an 'institutionalised' pedagogical initiative (i.e., a course that runs year after year) if you feel it is no longer able to achieve its aims. Second, take time to talk with the groups beforehand to enable them to clarify what they would like out of the project and to be clear that what the group wants is within the possibility of students to deliver – be aware that this could take time and cover issues such as timescales, expected outputs and skills needed. Third, ensure that the final brief for each group of students within the course is agreed between the students/university and the community groups to avoid unmet expectations. Fourth, have a 'debrief' afterwards to reflect on what went well and what could be improved and feed this back into future collaborations.

Fifth, set up the opportunity for students to present preliminary ideas so they can get feedback from the community before the final work is completed. Finally, consider translating your experience into a protocol of collaboration (see Just Space, 2018) that extends to how community groups relate to the students.

Notes

1. Throughout this chapter, NDPs are distinguished from neighbourhood planning (i.e., the statutory process for their production).
2. See https://neighbourhoodplanning.org/about/grant-funding/#basicgrant.

References

Brownill, S., and Q. Bradley. 2017. *Localism and Neighbourhood Planning: power to the people?* Bristol: Policy Press.
Clifford, B., and M. Tewdwr-Jones. 2013. *The Collaborating Planner? Practitioners in the neoliberal age*. Bristol: Policy Press.
Conservative Party. 2010. *Open Source Planning Green Paper*. London: The Conservative Party.
Davoudi, S., and P. Cowie. 2013. 'Are English neighbourhood forums democratically legitimate?', *Planning Theory and Practice* 14(4): 562–6.
Davoudi, S., and A. Madanipour (eds). 2015. *Reconsidering Localism*. London: Routledge.
Durose, C., Y. Beebeejaun, J. Rees, J. Richardson and L. Richardson. 2012. *Towards Co-production in Research with Communities*. Arts and Humanities Research Council (Connected Communities).
Ellis, H. 2000. 'Planning and public empowerment: third party rights in development control', *Planning Theory and Practice* 1(2): 203–17.
Ferm, J., and M. Raco. 2020. 'Viability planning, value capture and the geographies of market-led planning reform in England', *Planning Theory and Practice* 21(2): 218–35.
Jupp, E. 2013. '"I feel more at home here than in my own community": approaching the emotional geographies of neighbourhood policy', *Critical Social Policy* 33(3): 532–53.
Just Space. 2018. *Research Protocol*. London: Just Space, https://justspace.org.uk/history/research-protocol/ (last accessed 2 December 2022).
MHCLG. 2020. *Notes on Neighbourhood Planning No 24*, https://assets.publishing.service.gov.uk/government/uploads/system/uploads/attachment_data/file/890528/Notes_on_Neighbourhood_Planning_-_June_2020_Newsletter.pdf (last accessed 2 December 2022).
Parker, G. 2017. 'The uneven geographies of neighbourhood planning'. In S. Brownill and Q. Bradley (eds), *Localism and Neighbourhood Planning*. Bristol: Policy Press, 75–92.
Parker, G., T. Lynn and M. Wargent. 2015. 'Sticking to the script? The co-production of neighbourhood planning in England', *Town Planning Review* 86(5): 519–36.
Porter, L., and J. Barry. 2015. 'Bounded recognition: urban planning and the textual mediation of Indigenous rights in Canada and Australia', *Critical Policy Studies* 9(1): 22–40.
Rydin, Y. 2011. *The Purpose of Planning: creating sustainable towns and cities*. Bristol: Policy Press.
Schon, D. A. 1983. *The Reflective Practitioner: how professionals think in action*. New York: Basic Books.
Tait, M., and A. Inch. 2016. 'Putting localism in place', *Planning Practice and Research* 31(2): 174–94.

8
Podcasting and collaborative learning practices in place-making studies

Silvia Gullino, Simeon Shtebunaev and Elodie Wakerley

This chapter explores the value of podcasting in undergraduate planning programmes in the United Kingdom. It presents the findings of a research project carried out from Spring 2020 (at the start of the first COVID-19 lockdown) by an interdisciplinary research team of academics, an education developer[1] and students[2] on the use of podcasts[3] in urban planning studies in higher education.[4] The starting point for this project, funded by an internal grant from the Faculty of Computing, Engineering and Built Environment at Birmingham City University, had been the experience of teaching on a final-year undergraduate planning module devised pre-COVID lockdown. In this pre-pandemic module, named 'Drivers of Change', podcasts were for the first time introduced both as an innovative teaching and learning method (in the form of freely available podcasts from various digital platforms)[5] and as a form of assessment (in the form of student-generated podcasts).[6]

The initial aim of the project was to introduce novelty to the learning experience of students in their final year of studies. However, in the wake of the COVID-19 lockdown and the need to rapidly shift to online learning (Crawford *et al.*, 2020), the use of educational technology (edtech) such as podcasts gained new currency. The need to switch to online learning offered exciting opportunities to rethink how to reconfigure blended learning (online/offline, synchronous/asynchronous and active/passive methods) to ensure engaging and creative students' experience, but also to experiment with new practices.

In recent years, podcasts have moved beyond recreational listening to contribute to higher education, demonstrating use and purpose that is innovative and effective (Guertin, 2010). The rationale behind their use is multifold: podcasts are an innovative, time-efficient form of communication to deliver teaching/research content; they enable asynchronous[7] learning that can potentially support community building; they can meet students' propensity to study and learn using a variety of digital equipment; and they can enthuse students as an innovative method of teaching and assessment.

Existing literature suggests that podcasts in higher education have been used across different disciplines and mainly in the form of a classroom lecture recording or revision, supplemental course materials or students' feedback on assessments. The wide availability of freely available podcasts on various educational topics on different digital platforms makes them easy to access and include as external resources, which students can listen to and engage with.

The novelty of this research is twofold: first, the project explored the effectiveness of purposely teacher-generated podcasts in teaching and learning, and as a form of assessment within the context of an undergraduate planning course to encourage a more diffused use; second, the project specifically focused on the use of audio podcasts within urban planning studies, which traditionally have a distinctive visual representation dimension, by experimenting with new *audio* content, communication and a storytelling approach.

The research questions at the core of the investigation contribute to the three participatory principles (see Chapter 1) explored in relation to higher education throughout this book. What educational potential do podcasts have in learning processes in higher education? How could the use of alternative teaching and assessment methods promote inclusivity in the learning experience? Which podcast formats could better support and empower students in their independent learning?

Another clear element of originality of this research was the interdisciplinarity of the team and, most of all, the inclusion of two second year planning undergraduate students. Their involvement as research partners, rather than research assistants, resulted in a distinctive factor of this project. First, the research-teaching nexus has become a recurrent theme in higher education with great encouragement of embedding more research-based learning to enhance students' experience and intellectual development (Jenkins *et al.*, 2003, 2004). Involving students as research partners means they had the opportunity to gain relevant research experience and critical transferable skills that could be beneficial for future academic and professional careers. Second, by working as research partners, students moved from being the recipient to co-producers of knowledge: they had the opportunity to consult participant peer fellow students (through workshop discussions) and become active agents in the process, co-producing and co-disseminating knowledge (Hill *et al.*, 2013).

A multi-method research approach was taken to answer the three intertwined research questions. It included desk research and online engagement between the research team and student participants in workshops and seminars. By analysing the origin and use of podcasting in higher education, this chapter elaborates on the use of teacher and student generated podcasts specifically within urban planning studies as an important approach to teaching, learning and assessment. By engaging in podcast making, it explores how students can shift away from passive information recipients and become active knowledge creators for urban planning studies, making their knowledge more visible and generating students' agency in their learning.

This chapter argues that the value of teacher-generated podcasts in urban planning studies emerge fully when contextualised in the specific learning framework of a module and into structured tasks. The chapter discusses three major contributions that podcasting offers to this book and, in general, to higher education. First, the asynchronous nature of podcasts provides new, flexible and attractive opportunities for students' study. As students can access teacher-generated podcasts at anytime, anywhere via mobile technology, learning can take place outside the traditional classroom setting. Second, podcasts offer flexibility to create and share knowledge that transcends physical co-location. As podcasts can be recorded by using Microsoft Teams or Zoom, for example, opportunities are provided for the wider and more inclusive involvement of professionals, researchers and peer students in the world of planning and place-making. Third, using student-produced podcasts as a form of assessment can provide an opportunity for students to feel empowered and explore their interests in urban planning, providing the opportunity to work in small teams collaboratively. Student feedback from the research project suggests that producing podcasts can facilitate passionate, in-depth engagement with content that is more achievable than in traditional forms of assessment and can sustain student enthusiasm. The chapter concludes by systemising the key learnings from the project within the three core themes of the book – learning, inclusion and empowerment – and explores alternative ways for education to occur in the student's experience.

Podcasting as a medium of teaching, learning and assessing

Recently, podcasting as a form of knowledge dissemination, has increasingly gained prominence throughout academic, professional institutions and private businesses. In the planning profession and research, podcasting offers opportunities to discuss new projects and professional practice. This is the case of the Bartlett Planning Podcasts, which is an outlet to discuss planning research undertaken at the Bartlett School of Planning at UCL.[8] Other examples that all discuss issues shaping planning theory and practice include: '50 Shades of Planning',[9] which has established itself as a valuable platform for discussion and dissemination of current planning issues by academics, politicians and planning representatives; the long-standing podcast series from established planning practices such as Barton Willmore[10] and planning barrister chambers such as No5 Barristers;[11] and the APA Podcast by the American Planning Association.[12]

In this section, studies were reviewed contributing to the three main themes that this book focuses on: learning, inclusion and empowerment. This review section is not intended to present a comprehensive overview of podcast mediated learning in higher education.

In higher education, the use of podcasts has seen growing popularity since the 2000s. In principle, the use of podcasts is convenient, as all that is needed is a device (a mobile phone or a computer/tablet) an internet connection and no additional software or hardware (Zanussi *et al.*, 2012). Such a high level of accessibility makes the use, or the production of, podcasts ideal for educators and students (Hubackova, 2013).

As a result of the shift to online learning, there has been an uptake in interest in podcasting within diverse higher education contexts (Hitchcock *et al.*, 2021; Marunevich *et al.*, 2021; Donnet and Verpoorten, 2021). Research shows popularity in the use of podcasts among students because of the flexibility of the medium to support their (mobile) learning: podcasts are portable as they can be easily downloaded on personal devices (at a very limited cost as small files) and listened to offline; they can be reviewed and replayed; and they can be listened to while on public transport or walking. The latter facilitates what Evans (2008: 492) calls the 'just-in-time' learning where students can take advantage of unexpected free time (i.e., during lunch breaks, in the evenings and at weekends) (Sutton-Brady *et al.*, 2016).

Beyond the immediate COVID pandemic, podcasts can provide enrichment for distance learners; for advanced or highly motivated students; for learners requiring assistance with reading and/or other disabilities; auditory support for multi-lingual or foreign language students; and finally, podcasting caters for both auditory and visual learners (Walls *et al.*, 2010). Audio podcasts as learning tools are usually supplemented by metadata or visual material (Jalali *et al.*, 2011) and can encourage further research into a topic. Emerging research further identifies the potential inclusion role of podcasting in enabling visually impaired students to engage within higher education (Kusumastuti and Supendra, 2021).

However, Walls *et al.* (2010) highlight some potential drawbacks: podcasting could result in cognitive overload when added on top of a large pre-existing workload for both teachers and students. The making of a podcast means engaging in new learning material, but also conveying it using a communication style that is different from a written essay or a verbal presentation. In addition, some students could deem listening to a podcast as a replacement for a lecture, rather than complementary, risking affecting other forms of engagement resulting in poor academic performance. Finally, as students use mobile devices for entertainment, it may require some adjustment before students use their devices for learning purposes, resulting in mobile devices causing a distraction to the learning process.

Depending on how podcasts are used in teaching and learning, Zanussi *et al.* (2012) suggest that as students tend to learn better in groups and listening to podcasts tends to be a solitary exercise (at least in the learning, less so in the assessment), podcasting may not be the best supplement to traditional teaching methods. Additionally, podcasting is often referred to as passive learning, as there is usually no opportunity for feedback or questions. Moreover, there is little research into the added value that podcasting provides, there is still a concern that podcasts could be viewed as a form of entertainment, not a tool, which is helpful for only some subjects or courses.

However, podcasts allow students to be more receptive due to the assimilation and re-presentation of content (Evans, 2008). Gachago *et al.* (2016) suggest that podcasting can lead to deeper learning as students feel more involved in their learning. Such an argument is compounded by Lonn and Teasley (2009) who suggest that podcasts amplify a students' sense of contact with their lecturers (in the case of teacher-generated podcasts), resulting in increased students' motivation. Reflecting teacher enthusiasm in the delivery of a podcast is another factor that can increase students' motivation when engaging with the subject (Konig, 2021). Such positives can certainly benefit students when engaging in distance learning.

Advantages seem to arise not only when podcasts are generated by teachers, but by students as well. Lazzari (2009) states that the student learning experience can be vastly improved when involving students in podcast-making: engaging students in the co-creation of podcasts enhances subject knowledge, skills development and fostered community building (Killean and Summerville, 2020). However, for podcasting to be successfully employed it must be integrated into structured tasks to foster deep learning, where students have an active understanding of the learning material's meaning and significance (Drew, 2017; Pegrum, Bartle and Longnecker, 2014). Pegrum *et al.* (2014) also discuss that inclusion of creative podcasting in the learning process had no negative effect and it fostered better retention of the material included in creative podcasting at exam level.

If podcasting has received some attention within teaching and learning processes and practices, the use of podcasting as a form of assessment (student-generated podcasts) is more limited. However, podcasting does have the potential to be a strong form of assessment: evidence suggests that student-generated podcasts as a form of assignment encourage the use and improvement of transferable skills like communication, creativity, teamwork, professionalism and organisation (Powell and Robson, 2014; Besser *et al.*, 2021, Killean and Summerville, 2020).

During the development of a podcast, students must fully appreciate and understand the subject matter involved to deliver a strong podcast, which listeners enjoy (Wall, 2019). Podcast-making can generate enthusiasm in students: the over-reliance on conventional essay formats or problem question has become stale as a form of assessment (Wall, 2019). McSwiggan and Campbell (2017) point out that podcasts may engage students in assessment guidance and feedback, thus creating the opportunities for better interactions with lecturers and deeper understanding of feedback.

Research methods

As already mentioned earlier in this chapter, the opportunity to carry on a podcasting project to support students' learning experience and to enable innovative practices while learning remotely was certainly ignited by the sudden start of the pandemic. However, the use of podcasts as both teaching/learning and assessment methods had already been experimented by two of the authors (Gullino and Shtebunaev) in teaching Drivers of Change in its pre-pandemic format (Autumn 2019).

In this section, the authors will discuss the learning context of this module in more detail as, by its own nature, it is conducive to experimenting with contents, delivery and assessment. By identifying local-scale actions/projects/innovation in European cities, this module aims to explore multiple ways in which urban problems are identified and addressed through local practices. The module explores case studies of existing initiatives confronting contemporary global problems and how such activities can transcend the local scale and generate broader impacts. Through the analysis of these activities, the module interrogates the extent to which planners can engage in drivers of change and offer alternative responses to global challenges. By engaging with radical ideas and practices, the module offered opportunities to experiment with innovative teaching/learning/assessing methods.

In its pre-pandemic version, freely available podcasts were initially employed as a method of enquiry and assessment. Students were invited to use technology that was straightforward: mobile phones and easily accessible software (e.g., Anchor) were introduced in class. As discussed earlier in the chapter, reasons for using podcasts include the following: they are an innovative, time-efficient form of communication and are an accessible means to engage with research content. On the one hand, pre-existing and easily available podcasts allow students to engage in contemporary debates and ideas, and on the other hand, simple technology allows students to design content, experiment with new software and innovatively aim to convey messages to the listeners by simply using voice and sounds.

The feedback of 100 per cent student satisfaction at the end of the module, as students felt that podcasts were influential in their learning and, concurrently, the start of the pandemic and a new 'unknown' dimension, were both key factors that motivated the authors to start a research project on podcasting in higher education. Considering what has emerged from the literature (see Zanussi 2012; and Walls, 2010), three intertwined questions demanded attention: what is the educational potential of the use of podcasts in higher education; what is the podcast format that can best support students in their learning; and what learning activities and support do students need to make podcasts a form of assessment.

The core team that led this research project comprised two academics in urban planning (Gullino and Shtebunaev), one education developer (Wakerley) and two second-year undergraduate students in planning, all from the same institution. The interdisciplinary nature of the team was essential to this project. The two planners played the role of experts in place-making, coordinating the phases of the projects and keeping the communication style accessible. The role of the education developer was to provide rigorous support on the learning, teaching and assessment-related complexities. The two second-year students were the core of the team acting as paid research partners. The core team ensured their integration into the entire process as valuable research team members, rather than just supporting us with *ad hoc* tasks. The students were involved in each phase, and they received support throughout the process: in the weekly team meetings, in reviewing the literature and podcasts, in generating primary data through workshop and finally in preparing a joint conference paper presented at an international planning conference (UK-Ireland Planning Research Conference, UCL, 2020). Despite the awareness, the risk of being subject to unequal power relations was still a possibility, as Gullino was the students' course leader. However, such asymmetrical relations were mitigated by Wakerley and Shtebunaev, whose age was much closer to the two undergraduate students, and by Shtebunaev and his dual role of academic and PhD student. Students' experience was monitored and, through their feedback, was largely positive.

The research, which underwent Faculty Ethical approval, was structured through five main phases (see Figure 8.1). Due to the COVID-19 restrictions, the field research for this project and all the weekly communications between the team were undertaken online using Microsoft Teams. The five research phases consisted of: first, a literature review and a seminar with a professional planner expert in communication via podcast; second, an online workshop with undergraduate planning students' recipient of this teaching/learning/assessing module before the pandemic; third, a review of the module delivery from freely accessible podcasts to designing and developing *ad hoc* ones; fourth, an interview with the two students partnering in the project to review their experience as researchers and students recipient of a reviewed version of Drivers of Change; and finally, the integration of the podcasts in the teaching and learning context of the module.

In phase one (Spring 2020), the team reviewed the historical experience of podcasting in the existing literature and identified significant

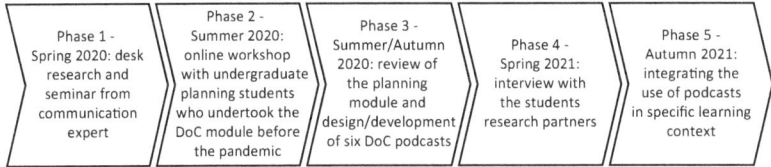

Figure 8.1 Workflow with timeline and main phases of the project.

Source: Author

emerging issues to consider during the workshop (phase two) with the cohort of final year students who had already experienced this mode of learning in pre-pandemic. A consultant expert, Sam Stafford convenor of the 50 Shades of Planning podcast series and an urban planner himself, was also invited to hold a seminar on communication via podcast. This seminar was important in establishing best practices in preparing, recording and disseminating podcasts, informing the research team about the practicalities of generating podcasts and sharing expertise.

Phase two (Summer 2020) consisted of an online workshop organised with the cohort of final year planning students. The aim was to gauge their learning experience of the module delivery in the pre-pandemic, in the teaching/learning/assessment, in light of reviewing the module delivery. All final year students were invited and offered a presence voucher. In phase three (Summer/Autumn 2020), the research team used the data that emerged from both primary and secondary research to (a) review the Drivers of Change module delivery approach and (b) design and develop six teacher-generated, short and urban planning-focused podcasts to replace the freely available podcasts to support the delivery of the module from September 2020 as part of a blended-learning approach. By identifying and interviewing scholars involved in local-scale actions/projects/innovation in European cities, each of these podcasts was based on original material and explored multiple ways in which urban problems are identified and addressed in practice within the module learning context. Phase four (Spring 2021) offered the opportunity for the student research partners to discuss and reflect through an interview on their dual experiences as researchers and students in the module. Finally, phase five (Autumn 2021) consisted of working towards integrating the podcasts, which had been produced and published (Gullino *et al.*, 2021), within the specific learning context of the Drivers of Change module.

Towards an effective integration of podcasts in the learning context

In this section, the significance of our findings is discussed in relation to the key elements emerging in the literature and new insights into the use of podcasts in teaching, learning and assessing in higher education.

In the initial phases of the research, the team reviewed existing literature on the use of podcasting in learning. Existing research shows clear evidence on the expansion of e-learning and the inclusion of new learning technologies (Nielsen *et al.*, 2018). It also shows increasing use of audio podcasting in specific curricula, for example, health, psychology, social work, but less so in urban planning studies where, as pointed out earlier, the visual component is still strong and traditional pedagogies seem to prevail.

Podcasts allow learners to engage easily in contemporary debates and ideas. Existing literature also highlights the benefits of deeper learning from students as motivation levels can increase and wider learning where podcasts can serve as an entry point to diverse topics (Gachago *et al.*, 2016; Lonn and Teasley, 2009). Furthermore, learning can develop outside of the traditional classroom setting as students can access podcasts and engage in their learning anytime and anywhere via mobile technology.

Overall, existing literature emphasises the role of podcasts as a supplementary and inclusive learning tool in education (teaching and learning, and summative and formative assessment), which can be suitable for a diverse range of learners. Podcasts can in fact meet learners' diverse needs (i.e., listening rather than reading or watching). Furthermore, the asynchronous nature of podcasts offers new, flexible and attractive opportunities for students' study and potentially improves students' learning experience. Students can pause, rewind and listen to a podcast several times (also during unexpected free time) to better understand complex material. Such features allow students to control the pace and frequency of listening to course content, which can be extremely important for English as a second language students and students with learning disabilities (Guertin, 2010).

In addition, podcasts can foster collaborations and community building. Video calling platforms such as Microsoft Teams or Zoom can facilitate virtual engagement by offering students possibilities to share/create knowledge in new podcasts that transcends physical location. Opportunities are provided for the broader and more inclusive involvement of professionals, researchers and students in planning and placemaking. This aspect is particularly significant at a time when travelling and movement could be significantly affected or even restricted, but also when trying to collaborate with people at a distance. Yet, the literature also points to potential barriers to technological adoption from teachers and learners based on cultural values, entertainment perception and cognitive overload (Ifedayo *et al.*, 2021).

Finally, exciting research shows that podcast development has the potential to empower students and even involve them in the learning process (Merhi, 2015). Podcasting can in fact enhance students' empowerment by fostering collaborations, but also by enhancing the development of new communication skills and providing a mobile and easy to access format of learning.

New insights emerged from the empirical research reported here within the context of place-making studies in an undergraduate UK planning course. The final-year students were invited to an online workshop to retrospectively recount and share with the research team their experience of the use of freely accessible podcasts[13] and the making of podcasts as part of their assignments. The aim of the workshop was that of generating data to: (1) develop purposely designed podcasts for the module (in terms of content exploration, formats, lengths, style); (2) better understand how to effectively embed them in the teaching and learning to encourage active learning and creativity yet limiting cognitive overload; and (3) shape effective support to students in their podcasting and podcast-making.

Changes to the future module delivery of Drivers of Change and the support to students were discussed. When used as a teaching and learning method, as Zanussi *et al*. (2012) claimed, podcasts risk encouraging a passive learning approach. It emerged as crucial to enhance the interactive role of teaching and learning by associating their use with exercises and leading questions for students to adopt an active and engaging listening approach. Pre-existing podcasts in planning currently tend to be long, between 30 and 90 minutes.[14] The relatively short and snappy nature of podcasts (15 to 20 minutes) was also beneficial to keeping students' attention focused. The innovativeness of podcasts as an assessment method was valued for its challenges as well as the opportunities to encourage creativity:

> Innovative podcasts had not been a feature of Uni assessments prior to this module. Using podcasts did offer some unique challenges in terms of structure, flow, and line of questioning. However, I did value this because if the assessment was another bog-standard, 'write an essay with an intro, research, findings, etc', I don't think I'd have engaged with the topic or material anywhere near as in-depth. (Student 1, workshop, 24 August 2020).

The innovative component of podcast-making was reinforced by the possibility for students to choose their own topic. Students felt enthused by the freedom to explore a topic they felt passionate about without constraints of word count or style:

> [Podcasting] is new but familiar as everyone has had conversations before! It was not intimidating. Working on a podcast allowed me not to focus on word count. It allowed us to go more in-depth into a chosen topic, as there was no concern over words count. It was also less fragmented compared to work on a (group) assignment like an essay. (Student 2, workshop, 24 August 2020).

From the workshop, it emerged that students built up academic confidence and a sense of empowerment by working in small teams and developing a podcast on an innovative topic seen as a driver of change. In the specific context of the module, an innovative, pro-active response to problems within an urban context:

> It felt natural in terms of how the conversation flowed, and whilst we were working to a time limit, it gave the chance to explore the topic. It is very important to choose a topic as it allows you to feel more passionate about it (Student 3, workshop, 24 August 2020).

The element of innovativeness was also seen as a potential career-advancing opportunity serving as a promotional tool in interviews, in a similar way that portfolios might supplement an applicant's ability to demonstrate knowledge. Students felt that employers would find the podcasts an engaging way of assessing a candidate.

The critical review of existing literature and the data generated during the workshop with the students led the research team to define specific features (see Table 8.1) around the creation and use of podcasts (phase 3). As a result, six teacher-generated episodes were designed and developed and adopted in the Drivers of Change module from September 2020. At the core of each episode was an interview-based discussion with an urban scholar on a relevant topic pertinent to the learning context of the module.[15]

Two undergraduate students played the dual role of researchers and students. Their role as research partners shifted to students in September 2020 when they undertook the Drivers of Change module in its reviewed version with the inclusion of six teacher-generated podcasts. Through the interview, their views and reflections were captured, providing useful feedback when further contextualising the use of podcasts in the learning context of a module. Podcasts must be integrated into structured tasks to encourage deep learning (Drew, 2017; Pegrum, Bartle and Longnecker, 2014).

From the interview, new insightful points emerged through their experience with new innovative content, communication and synthesis skills. In terms of teaching and learning, students discussed the value of teacher-generated podcasts recorded between lecturers and experts in a specific field as an opportunity to supplement blended learning approaches. It allowed students to step away from reading as a way of receiving information to a listening mode, accommodating different learning needs. The reading versus listening way of learning was highlighted as a benefit: 'Change it up a bit, spice it up! Many people get bored by it [reading]' (Student Partner 1).

Podcasts were also seen as a tool to bring relevance to the classroom. Podcasts can present students with topics which are emerging and, often, are yet to be fully explored in academic texts: 'The podcasts let you dip your toes … where you can be introduced to a new topic' (Student Partner 2), have an exploratory approach to new subjects and enthuse students to further research. This innovative feature was seen as a key appeal by students, allowing them to feel like they are learning cutting-edge information.

A sense of empowerment emerged when talking about the engaging nature of the podcast format as part of the assessment. Often associated with entertainment topics in everyday life, podcasts, when reimagined in the academic context, were found to be more enjoyable to produce than an essay. Students felt that the podcast was a stimulating way to conduct assessments. Combining the novelty element of podcast production with the necessity to synthesise and present key insights about a contemporary topic, meant that students found the learning process engaging and exciting. Although it was felt that the podcast format suited best to the introduction of a new topic or to broaden knowledge in a bite-size manner, students commented on the fact that background research might be wider than in a traditional assessment such as an essay.

Podcasting was also seen as an essential learning tool to develop new and advanced communication skills that were not necessarily present in traditional urban planning studies. Essays allow for an in-detail demonstration of knowledge and several lines of enquiry can be conducted. In a podcast, students felt that a more conversational style was a must, yet with a clear structure acting as a frame. Whereas essays were seen as restricting and needing a clear conclusion, podcasts allowed the exploration of a topic for the student to bring different influences together and the outcome was not predetermined.

Moreover, the lack of visual backing meant that students had to balance descriptive and analytical points, to convey their knowledge. Due to the format often being informal and sometimes improvisational, confidence in the knowledge was also seen as a key prerequisite in producing a successful podcast. However, students saw the podcast format as a less stressful way of applying knowledge. The lack of predetermined expectations and academic connotations allowed students to approach the podcast in an exploratory mode, open to learning: 'The informal style of the podcast benefitted the assessment' (Student Partner 1).

Issues such as knowing when to speak, moderating tone of voice and reading invisible body language in the co-production suddenly became paramount. Voice articulation, the ability to convey meaning through audio clearly, was seen as another key skill. The audio format did not allow students to hide behind an essay or references. Instead, it exposed a nervousness in their voice, hesitation or lack of confidence, demanding that the researched topic was well understood before the podcast was recorded. Furthermore, podcasts required students to develop synthesis skills and convey key points succinctly and engagingly to fit into the time-bound nature of the format.

Overall, students saw their communication skills challenged. Such challenges, however, were highly valued as the communication style enhanced by podcasting was seen as a key skill in the post-COVID world, where the prevalence of hybrid meetings and virtual work would only increase.

Conclusions

This chapter has discussed the use of podcasting in higher education through a research project based on the students' experience of a final-year undergraduate module. The project looked specifically at podcasting as an innovative, time-efficient form of communication to deliver teaching/research content in urban planning studies. Podcasting offers multiple benefits, including asynchronous learning, community building and the development of critical professional and teamwork skills.

Students' responses from this research project suggest that podcasts bring great relevance to the classroom and, by introducing a new topic, encourage further exploration perhaps through traditional academic literature. The shift from freely available podcasts to teacher-generated ones was seen as beneficial: students felt more motivated by the meaningfulness of topics that fitted into the module context and the direct involvement of their teacher. Teacher-generated podcasts require considerable additional work: from identifying topics and scholars to timing interviews on Microsoft Teams (as was still the case in lockdown), getting scholars' time to record and consent for the publication on SoundCloud, designing specific frames for each discussion, developing and producing the podcasts. It was all time-consuming; however, it also meant that producing such podcasts ensured the preparation of resources with some longevity.

For those providing higher education looking to use teacher-generated podcasts in their practice, the project team identified specific features to encourage student engagement (see Table 8.1) and, most of all, identified that podcasts should be integrated into structured tasks to encourage deep learning. The aim and learning outcomes of a module provide a frame that is essential for the preparation of such resources aimed at a specific audience. The risk of podcasts to be seen as entertainment rather than education resource and approached passively need to be addressed too. For example, students can, to begin with, be asked to listen to a podcast while in class. It can always be listened to again at other times outside the classroom. While in class, an active approach can be encouraged by giving students some leading questions to answer (perhaps with a partner or in a small group) before opening the discussion to the class.

Producing podcasts can facilitate passionate, in-depth engagement with content that is more achievable than in more traditional forms of

Table 8.1 Relevant features emerged to guide the design and development of teacher-generated podcasts in Drivers of Change

Length	• 15–20 minutes long (coffee-break length in style)
Recording	• Recording face to face or using Zoom/Teams • Clear audio and negligible background noise
Structure	• Identification of a clear and innovative topic and a defined audience • Introduction with key elements of the podcast (e.g., specific focus, professional/academic guests) • Pre-arranged topics to discuss with all participants but not script-reading • Conclusions
Style	• Open and conversational or more formal with questions and answers • Aiming for active engagement from the audience (e.g., referencing planning projects and encouraging the audience to further explore)

assessment. When discussing podcasting as part of their assignment, students participating in the workshop mentioned that '[podcasting] allows passion for coming through' and the 'power of voice', 'less anxiety for words limit' and showed appreciation for 'the go/innovative/novel assessment'. Student-produced podcasts can provide an opportunity for students to feel empowered and explore their interests in urban planning while working collaboratively. It allowed students to experiment and creatively design content, experiment with new and easily accessible software, and innovatively convey messages to the audience by simply using voice and sounds and enthuse them to contribute to creating Open Sources.

Acknowledgements

The authors are extremely grateful to the Faculty of Computing, Engineering and Built Environment for the research grant received; to Archie Wotton and Conor Matthews for joining us as research partners and for their amazing participation in the project; the planning students from the BSc Property Development and Planning for taking part in the workshop and sharing their enthusiasm with us; to Sam Stafford convenor of the 50 Shades of Planning podcast series for generously sharing time and experience with us; and Colin Marx and Mark Shelbourne for their constructive comments on previous versions of this chapter. Finally, the authors feel immensely grateful to Lucy Natarajan and Michael Short for being supportive editors and encouraging them to keep writing despite these difficult times.

Notes

1. Their role was to provide rigorous support on the learning, teaching and assessment-related complexities.
2. Two second-year students joined the team acting as paid research partners.
3. A podcast, or *personal on demand broadcasts*, is any downloadable audio or video file (typically MP3) streamed via the Internet that can be downloaded and played anywhere and at any time. They can be simply developed using accessible software available on smartphones or tablets; they are easily downloadable on smartphones; they tend to engage in innovative content (topics/series) and are portable on smartphones and therefore very accessible.
4. Higher education is a third-level education leading to award of an academic degree.
5. For this chapter, we will refer to *freely available podcasts* when talking about existing podcasts already available on different platforms and websites, to *teacher-generated podcasts* when talking about podcasts developed by teachers within a specific learning context, and to *student-generated podcasts* when talking about podcasts developed by students as form of assessment.
6. The Drivers of Change module requires students to produce, together with a podcast developed in pairs, an individual essay.

7. Asynchronous in this context refers to learning that students can undertake on their own schedule rather than timetabled real-time interactions.
8. The monthly podcasts are available at: https://www.ucl.ac.uk/bartlett/planning/home/bartlett-planning-podcast.
9. The '50 Shades of Planning Podcast', created by Samuel Stafford, are available at: https://pod.co/50-shades-of-planning.
10. Relaxed discussions across the development industry are available at: https://bartonwillmore.co.uk/Knowledge/Intelligence/2022/Uncut-In-Conversation-Our-Podcast.
11. Seminars by No5 Barristers Chamber are available at: https://www.no5.com/media/podcasts/.
12. The American Planning Association's podcast delves into planning with deep curiosity, expert analysis and affecting, true-life stories and is available at: https://www.planning.org/podcast/.
13. Freely available podcasts were selected by the lecturer (Gullino) as part of the core reading specific to each topic explored.
14. Episodes from *Monocle 24: The Urbanist* tend to be 30 to 40 minutes long; *About Buildings + Cities* between 60 and 90 minutes long; and *99% Invisible* between 30 and 50 minutes. *The Urban Planner's Podcast* tend to be shorter at between 20 and 30 minutes.
15. These episodes are available as open sources on SoundCloud: https://soundcloud.com/birmingham-city-university/sets/drivers-of-change.

References

Besser, E. D., L. E. Blackwell and M. Saenz. 2021. 'Engaging students through educational podcasting: three stories of implementation', *Technology, Knowledge and Learning* 27: 749–64, https://link.springer.com/article/10.1007/s10758-021-09503-8 (last accessed 5 December 2022).

Crawford, J., K. Butler-Henderson and R. Jurgen. 2020. 'COVID-19 20 countries higher education intra-period digital pedagogy responses', *Journal of Applied Learning and Teaching* 3 (1), https://journals.sfu.ca/jalt/index.php/jalt/article/view/191 (last accessed 5 December 2022).

Donnet, B., and D. Verpoorten. 2021. 'Students' engagement with podcast during lockdown – an analysis of interaction footprints in a computer science course', *European Distance and e-Learning Network: Conference Proceedings* 459–67, https://doi.org/10.38069/edenconf-2021-ac0045 (last accessed 5 December 2022).

Drew, C., 2017. 'Educational podcasts: a genre analysis', *E-Learning and Digital Media* 14(4): 201–11, https://doi.org/10.1177/2042753017736177 (last accessed 5 December 2022).

Evans, C., 2008. 'The effectiveness of m-learning in the form of podcast revision lectures in higher education', *Computers & Education* 50(2): 491–8.

Gachago, D., C. Livingston and E. Ivala. 2016. 'Podcasts: a technology for all?', *British Journal of Educational Technology* 47(5): 859–72.

Guertin, L. A. 2010. 'Creating and using podcasts across the disciplines', *Currents in Teaching and Learning* 2(2): 4–12.

Gullino, S., S. Shtebunaev and N. Granieri. 2021. *Drivers of Change*, https://soundcloud.com/birmingham-city-university/sets/drivers-of-change (last accessed 5 December 2022).

Hill, J., V. Blackler, R. Chellew, L. Ha and S. Lendrum. 2013. 'From researched to researcher: student experiences of becoming co-producers and co-disseminators of knowledge', *Planet* 27(1): 35–41.

Hitchcock, L. I., T. Sage, M. Lynch and M. Sage. 2021. 'Podcasting as a pedagogical tool for experiential learning in social work education', *Journal of Teaching in Social Work* 41: 172–91, https://doi.org/10.1080/08841233.2021.1897923 (last accessed 5 December 2022).

Hubackova, S., and I. Semradova. 2013. 'Comparison of on-line teaching and face-to-face teaching', *Procedia-Social and Behavioral Sciences* 89: 445–9.

Ifedayo, A. E., A. A. Ziden and A. B. Ismail. 2021. 'Podcast acceptance for pedagogy: the levels and significant influences', *Heliyon* 7(3): 1–9.

Jalali, A., J. Leddy, M. Gauthier, R. Sun, M. Hincke and J. Carnegie. 2011. 'Use of podcasting as an innovative asynchronous e-learning tool for students', *US-China Education Review* A 11: 741–8.

Jenkins, A., R. Breen, R. Lindsay and A. Brew. 2003. *Reshaping Teaching in Higher Education: a guide to linking teaching with research*. London: Routledge.

Jenkins, A. 2004. *A Guide to the Research Evidence on Teaching-Research Relations*. York: Higher Education Academy.

Killean, R., and R. Summerville. 2020. 'Creative podcasting as a tool for legal knowledge and skills development', *The Law Teacher* 54(1): 31–42.

Konig, L. 2021. 'Podcasts in higher education: teacher enthusiasm increases students' excitement, interest, enjoyment and learning motivation' *Educational Studies* 47(5): 627–30

Kusumastuti, G., and D. Supendra. 2021. 'The potential of podcast as online learning media for supporting visual impairment students to introduction to education course in Universitas Negeri Padang', *Journal of Physics: conference series* 1940: 012129, https://doi.org/10.1088/1742-6596/1940/1/012129 (last accessed 5 December 2022).

Lazzari, M. 2009. 'Creative use of podcasting in higher education and its effect on competitive agency', *Computers and Education* 52: 27–34.

Lonn, S., and S. D. Teasley. 2009. 'Saving time or innovating practice: investigating perceptions and uses of learning management systems', *Computers & Education* 53(3): 686–94.

Marunevich, O., O. Bessarabova, E. Shefieva and V. Razhina. 2021. 'Impact of podcasting on English learners' motivation in asynchronous e-learning environment', *SHS Web of Conferences* 110: 03006, https://doi.org/10.1051/shsconf/202111003006 (last accessed 5 December 2022).

McSwiggan, L., and M. Campbell. 2017. 'Can podcasts for assessment guidance and feedback promote self-efficacy among undergraduate nursing students? A qualitative study', *Nurse Education Today* 49: 115–21.

Merhi, M. I. 2015. 'Factors influencing higher education students to adopt podcast: an empirical study', *Computers & Education* 83: 32–43.

Nielsen, S. N., R. H. Andersen and S. Dau. 2018. 'Podcast as a learning media in higher education', *European Conference on E-learning* 424–30.

Pegrum, M., E. Bartle and N. Longnecker. 2014. 'Can creative podcasting promote deep learning? The use of podcasting for learning content in an undergraduate science unit', *British Journal of Educational Technology* 46(1): 142–52.

Powell, L., and F. Robson. 2014. 'Learner-generated podcasts: a useful approach to assessment?', *Innovations in Education and Teaching International* 51(3): 326–37.

Sutton-Brady, C., K. M. Scott, L. Taylor, G. Carabetta and S. Clark. 2009. 'The value of using short-format podcasts to enhance learning and teaching', *ALT-J* 17(3): 219–32.

Wall, I. 2019. 'Podcast as assessment: entanglement and affect in the law school', *The Law Teacher* 53(3): 309–20.

Walls, S., J. Kucsera, J. Walker, T. Acee, N. McVaugh and D. Robinson. 2010. 'Podcasting in education: are students as ready and eager as we think they are?', *Computers & Education* 54(2): 371–8.

Zanussi, L., M. Paget, J. Tworek and K. McLaughlin. 2012. 'Podcasting in medical education: can we turn this toy into an effective learning tool?', *Advances in Health Sciences Education* 17(4): 597–600.

9
Adapting the Civic Design Method to digital learning and collaboration with communities

Pablo Sendra and Domenico Di Siena

Engaged teaching has been at the core of the Bartlett School of Planning for many decades. Having as precedent the work of Professor Michael Edwards with various communities and activists in London – which goes back to students supporting campaigns in the 1970s, such as the one to save Covent Garden (Bartlett, 2019: 100) – various lecturers, notably Elena Besussi and others whose work features in this book, have developed module syllabuses that are designed around collaboration with community groups and activists. One of the examples of such engaged teaching with communities is the Civic Design Continuing Professional Development (CPD) course and module, which the authors of this chapter – Pablo Sendra and Domenico Di Siena – collaboratively put together at the Bartlett School of Planning, UCL. The course was launched in 2018 as a UCL Summer School, which targeted mainly international undergraduate students. It became a CPD course in 2019[1] and a postgraduate module in the academic year that runs in parallel to the CPD course. The CPD course is aimed at built environment professionals who want to learn about civic engagement, and the module is for postgraduate students from UCL who can choose it as an elective. Its two aims are to equip students with methods and tools to run co-design processes, enable civic engagement and involve communities in decision-making; and to expose students to the direct experience of working in collaboration with community groups. Each year, the course coordinator establishes a partnership with a community group in London and develops the brief that the students will be working on with that community group. The brief is related to the campaign objectives of the community group and the work that the students produce is expected to be a useful document for the campaign.

The title of the course 'Civic Design' refers to an approach to working collaboratively with communities that focuses on the intersection between urban design, public engagement and exploring and experimenting with forms of governance for places and spaces. The term civic design was coined at the beginning of the twentieth century by Adshead (1910). The original concept looked at the administrative organisation of the city, democratic processes, welfare delivery, and the political dimension of the city. It had a mainly top-down approach. The way that this course approaches civic design is slightly different from the original concept. It explores how to engage with communities, new forms of governance and democracy in the city, how to co-design the built environment, and the way spaces work and are managed with communities. The CivicWise network, which collaborates with this course, also takes this bottom-up approach to civic design. It is important to note that this approach does not intend to exempt the state from its responsibility for delivering welfare and public services, but it is a means to advocate for open institutions that ensure access to public services and, at the same time, support grassroots initiatives and innovative forms of community-led governance (see Sennett, 2019; Sendra and Sennett, 2020).

Civic design is not limited to the built environment disciplines, but has also been used in other disciplines that involve rethinking democratic processes, governance and collaboration. For example, Emerson College in Boston uses a civic design approach to the pedagogy of Civic Media Art and Practice. They identify the skills of a civic designer (which they provide in their course) as 'critical perspective on democracy and participation', 'co-design practices', 'sideways thinking', 'design and prototyping' and 'measuring value' (Gordon *et al.*, 2017: 68–9). These skills resonate with some of the learning outcomes of the Civic Design CPD course – which is in the field of urban planning rather than of media and art – and with some of the processes and practices included in the Civic Design Method (see Di Siena, 2019), which is taught in the course.

The course, in its current format, has two parts. The first is a 10-week online course composed of pre-recorded lectures and live discussions on the lectures. The second is a four-day intensive face to face workshop, where students and community groups collaborate on a project. The two authors of this paper deliver most of the content of the pre-recorded lectures. Di Siena explains the Civic Design Method (Di Siena, 2019) through a series of lectures. This is an open-source method for community engagement, facilitating collaborative design processes, and for working on the intersection between (co)designing the built environment, the governance of spaces, and how people live together. The method builds on Di Siena's more than 15 years' experience working for institutions and communities in civic innovation and participatory projects. This method employs three canvases – civic realm canvas, collective intelligence canvas, and circular process canvas – that aim to facilitate collective thinking. The canvases have demonstrated to offer powerful tools for facilitating a transition from thinking individually to thinking collaboratively and co-creating ideas. They are also very flexible and allow adaptation for different contexts. Once familiar with the method, it is possible to create further canvases derived from the first three, adapted to different contexts and questions that need to be asked. Since it is an open-source method, it can be used and adapted by anyone familiar with the method, and derived versions of the canvases can be re-shared, so the process keeps evolving and improving through collaboration.

The 2020 edition of the Civic Design CPD course took place in May 2020. In that version of the course, the 10 online lectures/discussions and the intensive workshop with communities took place in the same month (with 10 lectures over two weeks and the intensive workshop in the third week). The workshop was meant to be face to face, as it had been in the previous year. However, the COVID-19 pandemic and consequent national lockdown that took effect in England from 23 March 2020 meant that the course needed to be adapted for a fully online delivery. This short-notice requirement to adapt an engaged pedagogy course that relies on close collaboration between students and community members was a significant challenge. However, it brought an opportunity to reflect on how to adapt the Civic Design Method to a digital platform so that it could be used for the collaboration between students and communities. This was also an opportunity to adapt the Civic Design Method for engaged pedagogy, better integrate the methods taught in the lectures within the practical part of the course and enhance the collaboration between students and community groups. For this purpose, the course used the platform Miro (Miro, n.d.) for digital collaboration, which at that time was not well known but became very popular during the pandemic.

This assemblage of various situations – an engaged pedagogy course on co-design, a standing collaboration between UCL and CivicWise to deliver teaching, the partnership with community groups for a learning activity, the open-source method for engagement, the global pandemic that forced teaching to go online, and the digital platform for collaborative work – created a good opportunity to adapt the Civic Design Method, tailor it for the collaboration with a community group for this particular learning activity, and create a flexible tool that can be adapted to other situations, including engaged teaching and learning, action-research, and consultancy on co-design processes.

This chapter explains the process of adapting the Civic Design Method for community engagement and collaborative design into the digital platform Miro to deliver engaged teaching and learning in collaboration with community groups. The aim is to deliver a new digital version of the Civic Design Method, which can be used for the digital engagement and collaboration between community groups, students and scholars, and which is also open source and can be adapted and used by anyone familiar with the method and with the Miro platform. The chapter is structured in four parts. First, it explains the context of the Civic Design CPD course and how it was created. Second, Di Siena briefly explains the Civic Design Method. Third, it explains the adaptation of the method into the digital platform Miro at the beginning of the pandemic, and the results from adapting it to the platform, looking at the case study that we used for the Civic Design CPD: the collaboration with Granville Community Kitchen on a Community Plan for Granville and Carlton. Finally, it reflects on how this adapted Civic Design Method has been used since then, as well as on practical take-aways for engaged pedagogies, and how students, staff and professionals have kept adapting and using it for teaching and learning, action-research and consultancy projects.

Background of the Civic Design CPD course

The Civic Design CPD course builds on multiple influences and inspirations, bringing various experiences together in a course that combines theory, methods, practice and direct experience of working with communities. First, it builds on years of engaged teaching and learning at the Bartlett School of Planning. In particular, it builds on the collaboration between UCL staff and students, and the London-wide network of community groups Just Space, which has been collaborating with UCL for around 15 years. Before starting this course, one of the authors, Pablo Sendra, had collaborated with Just Space in the postgraduate modules coordinated by Elena Besussi – BPLN0033 Collaborative City Planning Strategies and BPLN0043 From Strategic Vision to Urban Plan. Pablo had also partnered with Just Space on the British Academy/Leverhulme-funded research project 'Community-led social housing regeneration: between the formal and the informal', which resulted in the open-access book *Community-Led Regeneration* (Sendra and Fitzpatrick, 2020). These previous experiences informed the process for creating the Civic Design CPD. While developing the course, the authors met community groups and scholars with experience in delivering this type of courses to make sure the course proposed a fair partnership between universities and communities.

The second influence is the Civic Design course developed by the CivicWise network, which Di Siena launched as a fully online Massive Open Online Course (or 'MOOC') in 2015 in the early days of CivicWise. Unlike the course developed at UCL, CivicWise's Civic Design course did not engage directly with community groups, but had both a series of pre-recorded lectures and live collaborative sessions where students would work together on a project. Some of the student projects have resulted in initiatives that have been further developed and applied in practice, such as the Civímetro, which is a tool to measure civic innovation (Civímetro, n.d.).

The third influence is the authors' professional practice experience. Sendra's work with Lugadero Ltd coordinating co-design processes, including for two public spaces in Wimbledon, London Borough of Merton, fed into the content of the pre-recorded lectures and the discussions. As explained below, the professional experience of Di Siena fed into the development of the Civic Design Method that forms part of the content of the course.

Finally, the trigger to start the Civic Design course at UCL came from a community walk organised by CivicWise's London Circle. In November 2016, CivicWise member Marco Picardi, organised a walk along the area of the Westway, a fly-over motorway in north-west central London, which was built in the late 1960s and caused the destruction of many homes. Local activism during the construction of the fly-over led public authorities to give the land below the flyover to the community as a compensation. Three local activists – Edward Daffarn, Henry Peterson and Toby Laurent Belson – guided various CivicWise members along different parts of the walk. This walk is recorded in the film 'Westway: Four Decades of Community Activism' (Sendra and Civicwise, 2017). After the walk, various conversations with Toby Laurent Belson resulted in planning together a Civic Design course at UCL where academic staff and students would collaborate with CivicWise and local campaigning groups near the Westway to produce outputs useful for community campaigns. The UCL Summer School provided a good format to start the collaborative work. International students studying for three weeks at UCL would work on a brief, which had previously been developed with three local campaigns: Westway23, Friends of North Kensington Library, and Save Wornington College. The process for setting up this summer school and the results of the students' work has been explained elsewhere (Sendra, 2018). Both students and community groups provided useful feedback about their experiences of the process: students wanted even closer contact with the community, so that they could work closely with them on elaborating the coursework rather than having three collaborative sessions along the course; and community groups suggested having 'community mentors' in the group, who would accompany students along the whole course. They also enjoyed the experience of working with international students, so that they could share struggles and experiences with young people from other countries.

After the summer school, the course was revised and turned into a CPD short course. The CPD short course had a more flexible format, which enabled a blended approach consisting of digital lectures and intensive face-to-face workshops with communities. It also provided the possibility to offer registration without charge to a number of community members, so people from the community group could sign up to the course for free, take it with the rest of the students and receive a UCL short-course certificate on completion. This allowed a continuous close collaboration for both staff and students. For both the 2019 and 2020 editions, the course partnered with Granville Community Kitchen,[2] a community organisation that runs food projects in South Kilburn, including dinners before lockdown, food aid since the pandemic started, community allotments, and other food-related activities. In addition, they are involved in campaigning on various issues related to housing, regeneration, and community facilities in the area.

In 2019, Granville Community Kitchen put the course coordinator in contact with William Dunbar and William Saville Residents Association, which are two tower blocks in South Kilburn, north-west London, that Brent Council is planning to demolish and redevelop with a higher density as part of a large redevelopment scheme. Students and community members worked together on developing alternative proposals to refurbish the existing blocks and densify the site through infill housing development, avoiding the demolition of the two existing blocks and the relocation of residents. The course created a strong bond between students and community members through working collaboratively. This year, student feedback suggested that the workshop part of the course should better integrate the use of the Civic Design Method and other co-design methodologies that they had learned during the lecture part of the course; allocating time and space to incorporate the three canvases of the Civic Design Method into the engagement sessions for students and community groups, so they could experience how the canvases facilitate collaborative design and community engagement.

In 2020, Granville Community Kitchen was community partner on the course again. This time, students worked on the regeneration of the Granville and Carlton community buildings, where Granville Community Kitchen is based. The council was (and, at the time of writing, still is) planning to regenerate the site into a mixed-used development that would include workspaces, housing and community space, which would entail a loss of community spaces and of open spaces. Students and community members collaborated on alternative proposals, which also explored community-led management proposals for the buildings.

When the pandemic started, the course had to be delivered fully online, including the workshop. This brought many challenges. The bond and the spirit of collaboration between students and community members seen on the 2018 and the 2019 iterations of the course – when this interaction was face to face and allowed for in-depth discussions on site – would be very hard to achieve online, particularly in the first weeks of lockdown, when people were experiencing technical difficulties related to accessing online platforms and bandwidth capacities. However, the authors of this paper took this as an opportunity to better integrate the Civic Design Method into the practical part of the course and explore its potential as a tool for engaged pedagogy. Below, this chapter first outlines the Civic Design Method and then explains how it was adapted to the Miro platform.

The Civic Design Method

Before exploring the details of online adaptation, this section explains the Civic Design Method[3] for collaborative design and civic engagement, which is used in the Civic Design CPD course for engaged pedagogy. The Civic Design Method is a guide in constant evolution.[4]

Civic design, as a discipline, has the capacity to bring the politics and governance of a territory together with the professional, structured practices and actions of citizens interested in improving their territory. As such, it is a new sphere of territorial action, where solutions may be reached through processes and methods for enabling relationships and strategies based on collaboration within localities. However, the strength of this conceptualisation is that it goes beyond repositioning citizens in relation to the governance of a territory. While people have been living for many years with governance mechanisms that detach them from physical and local dimensions of places, the imaginary that we are building around this concept encourages people to recover their situated role as active citizens. The starting point must be the territory of which each individual is a part; without forgetting the connection and relationship of that place with the world, or 'glocal' dimensions.

Civic design is the capacity to programme and activate a process of collective intelligence thought out and developed from a specific territory, with the capacity to generate a positive impact, independent of the capacities and involvement of those who initiate it. There are multiple definitions of 'collective intelligence' (see Malone and Bernstein, 2015), a term that has been used widely in computer-based collaboration, as well as in the built environment (see Ravetz, 2020). This chapter engages with Smith's definition (Smith 1994, cited in Malone and Bernstein, 2015), who understands collective intelligence as the phenomenon that takes place when a collective of humans think as one entity, rather than as a collection of individuals.

From reflection on direct experience of different civic design processes, Di Siena defined a first version of the Civic Design Method, expounded in detail in a whitepaper (Di Siena, 2019). This is structured around a continuous cycle that is generated by the three essential actions of doing, thinking and situating, whose order may vary within from the outset and throughout. At each turn, the whole cycle is enriched with new inputs, people and objectives.

Learning in any process can be produced not only through theoretical research (thinking), but also through execution or production (doing), where situations or unforeseen conditions determine the need to act differently from what was planned and generate a discovery, or new learning that can be an essential step towards innovation. Somewhat less self-evidently perhaps, iteration between thinking and doing needs a complementary process that is centred on situating. Today, knowledge for urban design increasingly comes from places and territories that are distant from places implicated for intervention. Haraway has spoken of the need to think in terms of situated knowledge (Haraway, 1988), but we cannot ignore knowledge and experience that comes to us from beyond a specific context. Hence, the importance of a continuous cycle and the process of situating throughout the cycle, constantly re-positioning events and lessons learnt in a process that engages non-local dimensions.

Circular process canvas – doing

The circular process canvas encourages reflection on the different stages of civic design. It is structured around 10 stages, in a sequence that can be repeated or restarted from any point. Together they describe the implementation of a civic design process:

1. **Kick-off** – Creation of the initial team; definition of the objective and initial purpose of the process.
2. **Planning** – Preliminary analysis to recognise which are the communities and local actors; definition of the different phases and objectives of the process.
3. **Engagement** – Involve the communities and local stakeholders; incorporation of professionals promoting transdisciplinarity and glocality; synchronisation of the entire team and activation of the protocols and governance of collaborative, open, and transparent work.
4. **Vision** – Revision of the initial purpose involving the entire team and local communities and stakeholders. Prepare a narrative describing the objective of the process, its stages, and methodology.
5. **Spreading** – Communication of the beginning of the process in different platforms, media and formats.
6. **Welcoming** – Activation of the dynamics and devices to welcome in the process all interested people.
7. **Deployment** – Activate sets of dynamics and devices to activate collective intelligence
8. **Prototyping** – Realisation and production of low-cost prototypes; direct experimentation with one of the parties that defines the final project to test the effective capacity to achieve results, to limit problems when it is time to scale.
9. **Implementation** – Moving on to the implementation of what was proposed in the previous phases. Scale-up the tests of the prototyping phase.
10. **Impact** – Close the cycle to open another one; after the implementation of the proposal, we look for ways to replicate, sustain or connect with other realities or processes so that it continues to generate positive effects and regenerate itself.

Collective intelligence canvas – thinking

As already noted, the basis of the Civic Design Method is the activation of a collective intelligence process. Therefore, an essential tool for immersion in this method is to focus on the definition and understanding of collective intelligence, specifically connected or developed from a territory.

The collective intelligence canvas invites reflection on which are the actors, connections and situations that can facilitate the activation of a collective intelligence process. Users must understand the canvas as a tool that suggests key questions, while focusing primarily on designing the process rather than its result and bearing in mind the territorialised perspective.

This tool enables us to reflect on the people, resources, dynamics, scenarios, strategies, timing, and the necessary relationships between all these elements needed to activate a collective intelligence process from a territorial perspective. The canvas enables connections to be drawn between: team and driving group (those involved in designing and delivering the civic design process); purpose, people, and communities; communication and documentation; spaces, physical-digital hybridisation; times, rhythms and cycles; and prototyping, funding, and governance.

Civic realm canvas – situating

This tool enables reflection on the activation of infrastructures, resources or commons capable of engendering a civic realm. Civic realm is understood as the context, environment or ecosystem where domestic, market, social, and institutional dimensions come together. It mixes protocols and imaginaries, practices, and resources, and generates impacts and commons that constitute the infrastructure capable of strengthening or promoting the construction, transformation, and collective management of a territory.

The canvas has the double objective of helping to understand the essence of civic realm and to reflect on the basic elements that allow us to generate a synergistic ecosystem, which is expected for good processes of situated collective intelligence. For this purpose, it uses a matrix with two axes. On one axis, the focus is on the degree of interest, from the most particular to the most general; and on the other axis, the focus is on the levels of interaction, from the most personal to the most global. Their intersection provides four domains of domestic, market, institutional, and social dimensions, and four vectors that indicate integrated, autonomous, local and global character. In addition, three specific rings help to define the people, the spaces, and the types of organisation (governance) that exist within the specific territory, and which can be brought into activation of collective intelligence.

Adaptation of the Civic Design Method to Miro

The civic design method is not a one-size-fits-all method, since such a thing does not exist. It is instead a guide to create your own method to work collaboratively with communities. The course's lectures introduce the methods that the authors have used in their practice to the students; Di Siena introduces the Civic Design Method, while Pablo Sendra explains some of the co-design methods and recommendations on working responsibly and ethically with communities. Through mixing these methods and approaches, as well as thinking about the case study of the Carlton and Granville community buildings in South Kilburn, the authors came out with a process to work collaboratively with students. Students were divided into two groups, and various community members were allocated to each group who would work collaboratively with them. Each group would develop three tasks: drafting a co-design route map; co-producing evidence with residents; and co-designing proposals. One of the groups would work on the activities and services that residents would like to see in the buildings and the physical infrastructure needed to develop them. The other one would work on the community-led governance of the Carlton and Granville buildings. At the end, both groups would come together and combine their work in a single collaborative report.

Since this was a four-day workshop, and it was the first time that it was run fully digitally, it was particularly important to structure these tasks well and relate them to the canvases and methods seen in the lectures. Therefore, the canvases were prepared by the course teachers before the course in Miro, where participants could simultaneously write, draw and add post-it notes on previously prepared canvases online boards within that application. This is presented here as a case of engaged pedagogy, which facilitated discussion between students and communities.

Draft co-design route map

The first task was the same for both groups. The first approach to facilitating a co-design process involved thinking collectively with residents and communities about how that co-design process should be, which strategy could reach the diverse population in the neighbourhood, and which of the different stages were needed. To facilitate discussion about the process, the authors created a modified version of the circular process canvas. Sendra and Di Siena collectively reviewed each stage of the process, how it related to the case of Granville and Carlton community buildings, added new stages that were missing, removed some that were irrelevant, and changed the name of some of them to make the language more accessible. One important addition to the circular process canvas was the co-production of evidence with residents – making them participants of the analysis of the place, which we developed in the second task. The name of some stages, such as 'deployment', were replaced by other names that were easier to understand and that better reflected the process – in this case deployment was substituted by 'co-design workshops'. The geometry of the canvas was simplified so that participants would concentrate on discussing each of the stages (see Figure 9.1).

This was the first task developed in the workshop. After explaining the exercise in a plenary session, students and community members were divided into two breakout groups. The students and the community members discussed each of the step of the process, looking in particular at how the community should be involved in each of the step of the process and the strategy for reaching the diverse communities in the area. This is particularly relevant, since a process can be genuinely participatory only if the efforts concentrate on bringing and welcoming different

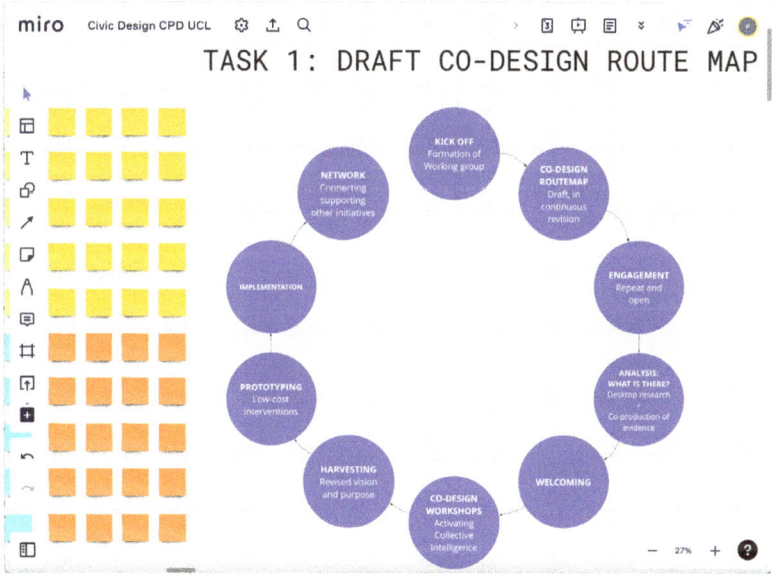

Figure 9.1 Circular process canvas in use May 2020.
Source: Author

communities into the process. It was also a good warm-up exercise, since students and community members could start talking about people living in the area and their aspirations around participating in the process.

Co-production of evidence

For this second activity, the two groups worked on two different activities. Co-producing evidence consists of involving communities in the production of knowledge about their area. This approach comes from participatory action research (Fals Borda, 1987), which takes 'grassroots communities' as 'full partners and co-researchers' (Fals Borda, 1995). This participatory action research is taught to students in the lectures and experienced with communities during the workshop. The canvases work as tools to facilitate this process of co-producing evidence, since they guide the conversation and allow collective thinking. Thanks to these tools, the co-production of evidence is not just a list of points, but a structured set of ideas where there is reflection on who it is for and how it happens. One group worked on co-producing evidence of the activities and services taking place in the building and what is needed to carry out these activities. This group used a version of the civic realm canvas. The other group looked at how the governance of the Granville and Carlton community buildings currently operates; and for that they used the collective intelligence canvas.

Activities and services
Students needed to co-produce evidence on the memories that residents associated with the buildings, the activities and services that have taken and take place in the buildings, and the physical infrastructure and management for these activities. We found that the civic realm canvas was very appropriate for this. The main advantage of the civic realm canvas was that provided a framework for discussion of who organised the activities, how they were organised, and for whom they were being organised. Therefore, when thinking about the activities that take place in a building, the output was not just a list of activities, but something much more complex that required collective reflection. This was achieved by the four quadrants of the civic realm canvas – market, institution, domestic, and social – which required participants to reflect on which quadrant each activity belongs to. Since the names of these quadrants were occasionally found to be misleading (e.g., 'market' and 'institution' do not necessarily offer differentiation between public and private initiatives) the canvases

provided further guidance with a description in the vertical and the horizontal axis. These are different from those proposed in earlier versions of the civic design method. The vertical axis goes from bottom-up to top-down activities, and so distinguishes between activities organised spontaneously and those that are more planned. This aligns with the framing of civic design explained in this chapter that combines top-down and bottom-up forms of governance and democracy. Since it is an axis, there is a gradient where participants can identify the degree of spontaneity of an activity. The horizontal axis indicates whether activities are for the benefit of the individual, the closed group or the collective. Likewise, the horizontal axis has a gradient that helps to determine whether the activity is more open to the public or more closed to a particular group. The civic realm canvas has additional layers of information. It has three rings titled 'where', 'how', and 'who'. For the course, these were removed to simplify the canvas. Instead, the course provided a series of civic realm canvases, each of which would be used to explore different dimensions, with a question given above it for discussion (see Figure 9.2).

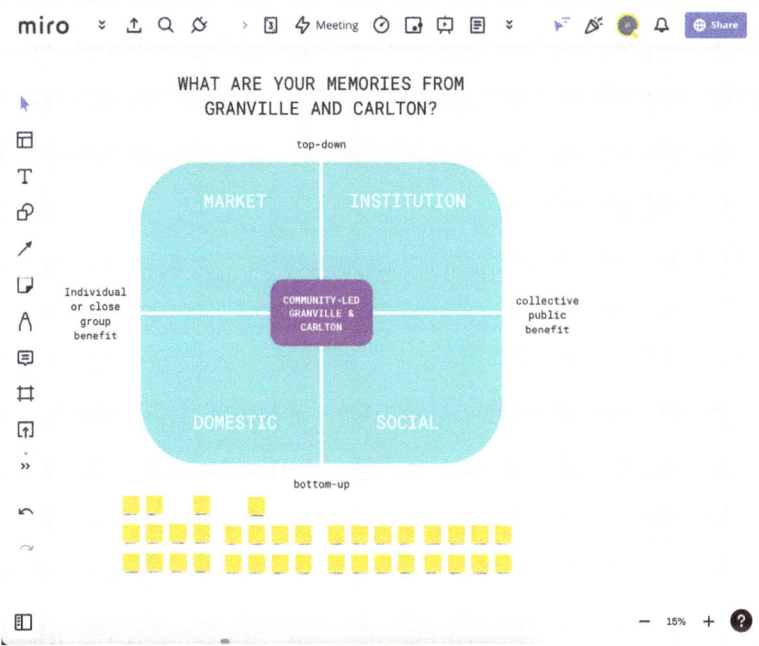

Figure 9.2 Civic realm canvas in use May 2020.
Source: Author

Governance

Along with the community members, the other group had to co-produce an analysis of how the current governance system works in the buildings. Both buildings are owned by the local authority Brent Council. Most of the Granville building is managed by the South Kilburn Trust, an organisation that was set up to manage the remaining funds from New Deal for Communities, a national funding programme to improve deprived areas that was implemented mainly in the first decade of the twenty-first century under Tony Blair's administration (see Lawless, 2006). There are also other services in the building such as the family support services and a nursery. At the time of the course in May 2020, most of the Carlton building was temporarily used by a non-for-profit organisation, Rumi's Cave, which organised cultural and social activities. The complexity of the governance of the buildings requires a tool to understanding. The collective intelligence canvas was a useful tool to understand how the governance of the buildings work. Although the collective intelligence canvas is used to propose, the activity proved that is also useful to understand how a system currently works. Again, the canvas was adjusted and simplified (see Figure 9.3), with a different geometry, removing some of the boxes that were not relevant to the case study, such as prototyping or blended realm, and re-arranging the position of the boxes so that it was easier to understand how each part relates to each other. It is important to note that this analysis was done having in mind that the next stage would consist of co-designing an alternative form of governance using the same canvas.

Co-designing proposals

For co-designing proposals, students and community members again used the civic realm canvas and the collective intelligence canvases. While the civic realm canvas remained the same, the collective intelligence canvas was re-adapted during the co-production of proposals, which demonstrate the flexibility and elasticity of the method. These canvases were followed by a collective mapping exercise on the floorplans of the buildings, where participants started to spatially map where each activity and service that they had proposed could go in the buildings, and to discuss how the proposals could be implemented. The canvases were useful tools for both analysing and for proposing, and they were easily adaptable while producing the proposals.

The use of these canvases during the workshops was followed by the elaboration of proposals based on the outcomes from the canvases.

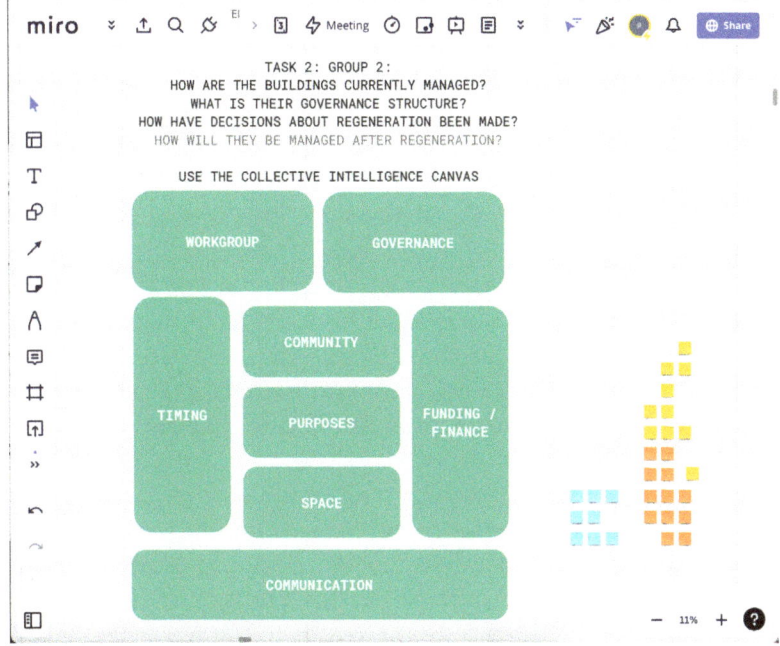

Figure 9.3 Collective intelligence canvas in use May 2020.
Source: Author

On the fourth and final day of the course, students presented the proposals to a wider community audience that came to listen what had been done in the course and offer further feedback on it.

An open-source adaptable tool for engaged teaching, learning, and collaboration with communities

The adapted circular process, civic realm, and collective intelligence canvases worked very well in the digital environment. They also had the capacity for online workshops in the early days of the pandemic when staff and students were not used to online collaboration. Since the lockdown caught everyone by surprise, and there were only a few weeks to adapt the course to the online environment, the canvases and each step of the process was planned by the teachers before the course. This meant that the students did not have the experience of adapting the canvases, except for the adaptation of the collective intelligence canvas for co-designing the proposals, which was adapted during the workshop.

In this sense, the teachers engaged in reviewing the educational design in response to the situation, in teaching co-production skills through the canvases (although the students did not experience the ability to change and adapt the canvases themselves). For 2021, which had a blended format with some students and community members doing the workshop face to face and others doing it online, students prepared their own canvases based on those provided by the course, which meant that in addition to the abovementioned skills, they also developed the capacity to adapt the canvases to different contexts and briefs. The 2021 students created a multiplicity of variations of the canvases, including them in matrixes and combining them in different ways. This once again demonstrated the flexibility of method and how powerful it is to leave these canvases as open source, so that people can keep adapting and improving them.

In the 2021 course, half the students were doing the workshop online and the other half were doing it face to face. Both the online and the face-to-face students used the canvases as tools to facilitate the discussion with communities and both used the Miro.com platform for this. This demonstrates that the three canvases in the Miro platform, which we originally adapted for digital collaboration, can be used both for digital and face-to-face collaboration with communities. In both cases, the canvases were useful tools for engaging the community groups that the course worked with, for facilitating the discussion, for co-producing evidence and for co-designing proposals with communities. However, the tools acquire a different role in their digital and in their face-to-face format. In the digital sphere, the canvases are central, since the main thing is to facilitate the discussion and activate the collective intelligence process – transitioning from thinking as individuals to thinking as a collective entity (Smith, 1994). All participants are watching the Miro board at the same time and discussing the contributions and where to locate the post-it notes in the canvases. This leads participants to create a collective piece that says how a co-design process should be (Figure 9.1) or what would be the ideal governance model for the community buildings, where it is not possible to identify the authorship of the different contributions.

In contrast, in the face-to-face collaborative sessions in the Civic Design CPD course 2021, the canvas acquired a more secondary role. In the case of face-to-face collaborative workshops with communities, the canvases in the Miro platform were useful to guide the conversations and to organise the notes taken from the conversation. This does not mean that they were not useful or that they did not achieve a process of collective intelligence, but that there were other elements at play, related to speech, body language and the possibility of longer interventions from participants, that made the face-to-face interaction different from the digital one.

At the time of writing in late 2021, digital workshops have become part of daily lives. Since the experience discussed in this chapter in May 2020, different variations of these canvases for action-research and knowledge exchange projects between universities and communities have been used by both tutors and alumni of the Civic Design CPD course with various purposes, demonstrating how this knowledge could be taken up in professional practice and action-research. The authors have used it for engaged teaching and learning, as well as for consultancy projects facilitating co-design processes, which might be considered an activity of 'embedding practices' (see Section III of this book, as well as Chapters 1 and 14). Some students have also used their own versions of the canvas in their professional experience. Since it is an open-source method, each year we build a stronger methodology of work that builds on the previous years' experience, where everyone contributes to knowledge.

Notes

1. The creation of this course was funded by the Bartlett Innovation Fund.
2. This initial collaboration with Granville Community Kitchen has led to various partnerships in teaching, research and knowledge exchange projects. In the most recent research project, funded by the Roddick Foundation, we involved an MPlan student (Lili Pandolfi) through the MPlan City Planning placement scheme, and a PhD student (Irene Manzini Ceinar) as research assistants.
3. The Civic Design Method explained in this section has been developed by Domenico Di Siena. More details on the *Civic Design Method Whitepaper* (Di Siena, 2019).
4. The latest version can be found at https://civicdesignmethod.com (last accessed 6 December 2022).

References

Adshead, S. D. 1910. 'An introduction to the study of civic design', *The Town Planning Review* 1(1): 3–17.
Bartlett 100, 2019. 'At the service of society', *Bartlett 100*, Day 70, https://www.bartlett100.com/article/at-the-service-of-society.html (last accessed 6 December 2022).
Civímetro, n.d. https://civimetro.org/about/ (last accessed 6 December 2022).
Di Siena, D. 2019. *Civic Design Method Whitepaper*, https://civicdesignmethod.com (last accessed 6 December 2022).
Fals Borda, O. 1987. 'The application of Participatory Action-Research in Latin America', *International Sociology* 2(4), 329–47.
Fals Borda, O. 1995. 'Research for social justice: some north-south convergences', Plenary Address at the Southern Sociological Society Meeting, Atlanta, http://comm-org.wisc.edu/si/falsborda.htm (last accessed 6 December 2022).

Gordon, E. C., D'Ignazio, G. Mugar and P. Mihailidis. 2017. 'Civic media art and practice: toward a pedagogy for civic design', *Interactions* 24(6): 66–9.

Haraway, D. 1988. 'Situated knowledges: the science question in feminism and the privilege of partial perspective', *Feminist Studies* 14(3): 575–99.

Lawless, P. 2006. 'Area-based urban interventions: rationale and outcomes: the New Deal for Communities programme in England', *Urban Studies* 43(11): 1991–2011.

Malone, T. W., and M. S. Bernstein (eds). 2015. *Handbook of Collective Intelligence*. Cambridge MA: MIT Press.

Miro. n.d. 'The online whiteboard for easy collaboration', https://miro.com/online-whiteboard/ (last accessed 6 December 2022).

Ravetz, J. (2020). *Deeper City*. London: Routledge, https://www.perlego.com/book/1563336/deeper-city-pdf (last accessed 6 December 2022).

Sendra, P., and CivicWise. 2017. 'The Westway: four decades of community activism', *Urban Transcripts* 1, http://journal.urbantranscripts.org/article/the-westway-four-decades-of-community-activism-civicwise/ (last accessed 6 December 2022).

Sendra, P. 2018. 'Civic Design UCL Summer School'. In C. Ciancio and M. Reig Alberola (eds), *Civic Design*. Valencia: Civic Innovation School, 298–9.

Sendra, P., and D. Fitzpatrick. 2020. *Community-Led Regeneration: A Toolkit for Residents and Planners*. London: UCL Press.

Sendra, P., and R. Sennett. 2020. *Designing Disorder: experiments and disruptions in the city*. London: Verso.

Sennett, R. 2019. 'State and civic society'. *Welfare after Beveridge, LSE*, https://welfareafterbeveridge.wordpress.com/civil-society/ (last accessed 6 December 2002).

Smith, J. B. 1994. *Collective Intelligences in Computer-Based Collaboration*. Chapel Hill NC: University of North Carolina at Chapel Hill.

Section III
Embedding practices

In this section we present four chapters about extra-mural spaces of learning and activities of embedding practices of education. They are written by academics and their collaborators and go beyond the teaching programmes of the university; the activities involve neighbouring communities living near university campuses, school-aged students, city research networks, and organisations working with marginalised urban groups. These are alternative spaces of critical pedagogy, where the diverse collaborations emerge from the search for wider participation in planning and place-making and built environment education. At the same time, they have great relevance as part of a wider ecosystem of active learning for the university with students who are urban stakeholders. They cross the normative boundaries of higher education practice for engaged urban pedagogy 'embedding'.

The first alternative space is that of community researchers, those local people not at or in university, but who live nearby and become active in research work with academic support. As discussed in Chapter 10, the University of Birmingham designed community researcher activities with the intention of giving greater 'visibility' to their neighbour communities within built environment higher education. Hassan and O'Farrell describe how perceptions of institutions as exclusive, including university education and top-down planning work, can have alienating effects on residents. This observation adds weight to the case (see Chapter 1) for reconnecting universities to surrounding urban processes.

The community researcher initiative presented by Hassan and O'Farrell involves training provided by university staff for local people in urban areas that are well-known to be socio-economically excluded. In responding to the poor local relations and providing educational services more widely, higher education offer is reworked for community researcher training. In addition, the university builds up its 'anchor institution' role within the region. As an immediate practical impact, this educational programme can directly generate work opportunities on university projects research for trained community researchers. More fundamentally, it is directed at embedding research capacities within the neighbourhood, such as can promote self-directed enquiry about major urban development processes. Across the activities there are moments for active learning in exchanges between academics and these new neighbour-students, not only in their community researcher training but in further co-productive research with academics.

The second space is that of school-aged children. As discussed in Chapter 1, wider participation in planning and place-making is a priority today, and how urban development will work for future generations is central to academic debates. However, while urban processes matter greatly in everyday quality of life, and urban development is a well-established field in practice, built-environment disciplines are complex and can appear arcane and jargonised to people of any age. This too creates a form of alienation. How then to connect children and explain its relevance and meaning in early years development? Strachan has provided an entertaining solution, where a team of staff and students from Newcastle University engage children in play around hot food amenities, which involves thinking about consumption and issues raised such as production of waste, as well as where responsibilities for managing the processes lie. The game starts to develop awareness among school-aged children of the importance of collective action, as well as skills of communication and knowledge of built environment forces.

In Chapter 11, Strachan explains the purpose and process of engaging these people in an imaginative playful extracurricular activity for university students. The communications are facilitated with a board game that helps stimulate critical thinking on topics of planning and place-making. Like the community research programme, these encounters offer opportunities for bridging social capital, that is to say that it can be used to build up the social networks that enable people to usefully tap into institutions. The game is introduced in schools by university staff and students. The actions foster links between people in the university and the school that can unlock future employment and learning opportunities for the groups of participants. Further, this activity brings university students' moments for active learning and teaching role experience within a wider educational system.

Students are gaining experience and practising communication skills in a way that challenges passive learning tendencies. This echoes lessons on the value of student podcasting assignments (Chapter 8), but also positions them as teachers nurturing critical thinking in a younger cohort of students (i.e., rather than stepping into a more professionalised field with people who are mainly older than they are). This embeds active learning within the education of two groups of younger people, with knowledge sharing between university students and school pupils.

In Chapter 12, the challenge at hand is the global challenge of sustainable urban agriculture, and how academics might connect with practitioners across the world. Importantly, this is not framed as knowledge dissemination of research output, but as a means of co-learning where all involved bring knowledge and different forms of expertise. The authors, Sedlitzky and Santomauro, discuss how local experiences are brought together with global scientific inquiries. Efforts are focused within the alternative learning space of international knowledge exchange, involving a wide landscape of actors, diverse academics and other international actors from three continents. Funders are diverse, and the institutions of higher education play a critical role in providing independent input and research support for the initiative.

In Chapter 13, the alternative space is one of 'learning and making' with marginalised ethnic groups and poorer communities in northern coastal France. Lancrenon *et al*. discuss how certain neighbourhoods have been treated with little consideration through top-down state interventions and, at least historically, have garnered less attention from built-environment experts. A new 'FabLab' education is provided by a collective of practitioners and academics, who also intervene in local urban space with works to upgrade estates and provide communal facilities. The work is a form of knowledge exchange and political activism, and the experience of witnessing abandonment of localities and destruction of common goods by other actors is fuel for critical thinking.

These last two chapters demonstrate particularly well the pressures on higher education to extend beyond institutional boundaries to include specific groups of people in the community of learning. In a learning form of activism, the academics and others from urban professions and civil society, volunteer their time outside their institutional roles to connect to the knowledge and activities of urban stakeholders. This is not to suggest any shortcut in producing knowledge, or some kind of diversion around critical intellectual development. It is certainly not an attempt to undercut full postgraduate degree training with professionally accredited, research-led, academic-designed higher learning programmes. On the contrary, the activities rely on academic teaching, qualified professionals and research expertise. Indeed, the new connections afforded in these alternative educational spaces are a means of further developing pedagogies beyond the university. They promote active learning for the long term, and encourage ongoing explorations of diverse ways of knowing the city, and as such they are part of the loops of engaged urban pedagogy. For this reason, the work is intellectually risky and its support mechanisms precarious. Nonetheless, these activities contain unique potential for developing critical thinking about the built environment.

Each embedding practices activity goes beyond university curricula, and in our view the scale of their ambition is well worth the risk. The target is learning *within* urban development processes; a critical pedagogy that means to change the world by making planning and place-making practice more inclusive and alive to the lived realities of stakeholders and people. It echoes Freire's metaphor of learners walking together, and is akin to activities of reviewing and teaching in universities, which also aim to promote skills and capacities for critical appreciation of urban development. Here though, the efforts are directed towards people who might be more involved in planning and place-making, rather than focusing on teaching programmes within the university. Self-evidently, the learning moments do not come with the standard obligations of teaching, or commitments to the longer term, more associated with university research. Further, and as in the other two sections, we hear concerns about the demands made on students' and teachers' time and energies.

10
Co-production and the pedagogy of exchange: lessons from community research training in Birmingham

Sara Hassan and Liam O'Farrell

Co-production is a term that is applied to a range of different forms of engagement with society to identify challenges and articulate solutions to these challenges. In the context of urban planning and development, co-production builds on debates in planning theory that stem from collaborative and communicative planning. Co-produced research is found within a number of disciplines, including (but not limited to) development, health, education, housing, public policy and social care. However, the term 'co-production' can be profoundly different in its application and implications across different fields and contexts. This chapter draws lessons from the use of co-production in 'left-behind places', which is a term that can refer to places with higher concentrations of poverty, unemployment or marginalised populations such as ethnic minorities. Findings from the process demonstrate the reality, applicability and challenges of co-producing knowledge with left-behind communities.

The Unlocking Social and Economic Innovation Together (USE-IT!) programme was an innovative intervention that developed a community research training model organised by the University of Birmingham. The programme sought to empower local communities and articulated a new active role for the university as an anchor institution with overarching social justice principles (O'Farrell *et al.*, 2022). The project was a three-year Urban Innovative Actions initiative that was part-funded by the European Regional Development Fund (ERDF) and ran from 2016 to 2019. USE-IT! involved a participatory action research approach with communities adjacent to large-scale urban transformation projects in a deprived transect of inner-city Birmingham. The core focus of USE-IT! was tackling urban poverty through testing and developing co-produced knowledge, and applying principles of collaborative governance as part of a partnership of anchor institutions.

The community researcher training project successfully achieved its target outputs, including training and mentoring more than 80 community researchers from a super-diverse area of Birmingham, a city undergoing a rapid urban transformation driven by inwards investment predicated on the High Speed Two (HS2) rail connection with London. The research presented in this chapter highlights that the project was able not only to empower local communities but also to influence inclusive growth, challenge assumptions of planning thought in urban regeneration, and involve communities in the co-production of knowledge as equal partners in the identification of problems and articulation of proposed solutions. The research planning and evaluation was not predetermined, but instead embraced the different voices of participants and diverse stakeholders. While initially used as a community engagement method, the community research methodology offered great insights into a wide range of processes, relationships and knowledge exchange at the community level.

This chapter begins by reviewing the context of current literature on universities and their civic role. It then introduces the case study of the USE-IT! programme in Birmingham, which is followed by detailed analysis of the delivery of the project's community research training model based on co-producing materials, collectively identifying challenges and partnering with relevant organisations to suggest community-led responses. While noting that USE-IT! was a successful case of empowerment and engagement, the lessons learnt from this programme and its implications on both the university and local communities are described so as to suggest future steps to embed this approach, whereby knowledge can be produced and continued as a legacy of the project. This research thus contributes to the literature on urban planning pedagogy, community engagement and co-production. The chapter closes by suggesting further research and the change required to enable and sustain these mutually beneficial pedagogies of exchange that disrupt established hierarchies of power and knowledge in both teaching and research. It also advocates the call for more qualitative and participatory research that tackles problems and issues identified by communities themselves.

Context

Universities in the United Kingdom are under increasing scrutiny to demonstrate the impacts of their activities. While many have strengthened their reputations as castles of research expertise, as teaching powerhouses and, in some cases, as international brands with campuses overseas, universities often overlook the importance of playing active civic and economic roles within their local communities. While some universities strive for global recognition, boasting of the internationally recognised excellence of their academic staff and resources, they have also become increasingly invisible to their local areas and surrounding populations. Many universities have, in essence, become gated knowledge hubs, perceived to be for those who do internationally orientated research without paying attention to how this directly benefits their local communities. Meanwhile, universities have built their prestige in teaching that caters to people aspiring to careers requiring higher education degrees. Our initial conversations with residents living around the University of Birmingham found that many local people perceive the university as a surreal place that is not for them or for their children, but instead is accessible only to those who can afford – or need – such education. Moreover, while academic literature discusses universities' role as anchor institutions and civic centres in their localities, the full extent and potential of this role is not currently activated (O'Farrell *et al.*, 2022).

The literature suggests that higher education institutions can affect change in growth and development through coordinating their supply chains towards local spending, local recruitment, and increasing the local level of human capital through auditing their training and development activities (Ehlenz, 2018). This frames universities as large examples of anchor institutions, which are rooted in place and have a significant impact on the economies of their local areas (McCauley-Smith *et al.*, 2020). Recent studies show that universities are prioritising their role in regional economic development with limited priority given to social or community-level initiatives (Goddard *et al.*, 2014; Lebeau and Cochrane, 2015). This can be attributed to the strong influence of national research agendas and funding priorities. Within the context of neoliberalism and an increasingly financialised higher education sector, there is a particular focus on knowledge exchange and creating partnerships with industry to commercialise research. Universities in the United Kingdom are thus compelled to demonstrate the return on investment of their research, teaching and knowledge transfer. Far less attention is paid to the role of universities in building connections with their local areas and empowering marginalised communities through active engagement strategies.

The USE-IT! partnership aimed to facilitate collaboration and the coordination of actions by public institutions and charities, building social resilience into communities challenged with urban poverty and the risk of displacement in an inner-city district undergoing a rapid transformation. The project partners held monthly board meetings to agree on the programme's scope, aims and progress. The partner board also got detailed updates on changes and agreed a common agenda for the USE-IT! programme. The programme included seven work packages or projects delivered by 15 partner institutions. These included the delivery of a community research training scheme, a skills matching programme to identify unrecognised overseas medical qualifications, a social enterprise support scheme, and a legacy projects plan that could continue after the end of ERDF funding for the programme. USE-IT! was thus both people-focused and place-focused in its intentions, designed to concentrate on a highly diverse transect area of Birmingham adjacent to the city core and under growing gentrification pressure. The area included Soho and Ladywood of inner-city Birmingham and neighbouring Smethwick, which is part of the Sandwell council area (see Figure 10.1).

After the Second World War, a significant section of this area was developed into a large social housing estate for Birmingham's industrial working class, which has since become a key destination for migrants and refugees moving to the city in recent decades (Zwicky, 2021). The many challenges facing this area characterise it as 'left behind', including high poverty rates, low employment and weak educational attainment when compared to national averages. Demographic data on the Ladywood ward within the transect show that only 36.9 per cent of residents are of white British ethnicity, with large numbers of South Asian, Chinese, Black African, Black Caribbean and non-British white residents (Birmingham City Council, 2020). As such, it is also an active site of superdiversity, with a highly diverse population from multiple countries of origin who are internally stratified by factors such as legal status, income and education level (Vertovec, 2007). Our experience on USE-IT! of finding 200 highly trained professionals in the transect, with medical qualifications gained overseas that had not been accredited for work in the United Kingdom, further demonstrates the diversity of the population of this area.

The catalyst for the programme was a series of major infrastructure projects planned to be built in and around the transect that pose a significant risk of gentrification. Ladywood already had some of the fastest

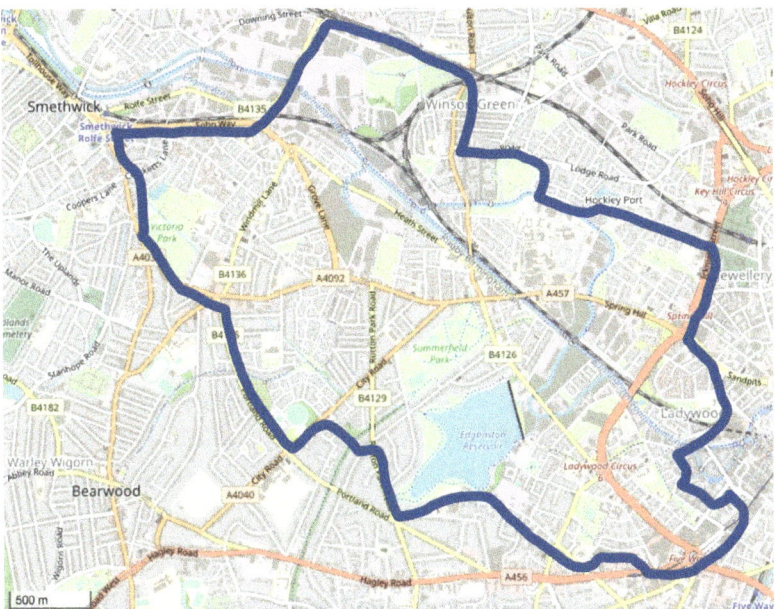

Figure 10.1   Area map of the USE-IT! transect.
Source: Author

growing house prices in the United Kingdom in 2017 (Jessel, 2019). USE-IT! was therefore designed to address these challenges through creating mechanisms to affect change. The community research training model sought to give residents a stake in this urban transformation through mitigating negative impacts and building on the positive impacts of development in their neighbourhoods. As part of the participatory action research agenda, the USE-IT! academic team developed and delivered an accredited training scheme for community researchers. The community research training model was used to empower and upskill residents and enable them to work with the University of Birmingham to define the problems that they face, gather data, and write policy recommendations and reports to inform decision-making processes among the USE-IT! partnership, which included Birmingham City Council, a range of local non-governmental organisations and a local hospital. The scheme thus sought to overcome the discrepancies between university and community priorities identified in literature on universities (Harris, 2019).

Qualified community researchers were commissioned to conduct research on behalf of the partnership. In total, 85 participants gained community research qualifications alongside work experience as a researcher. Two were awarded scholarships to subsequently study a master's degree at the University of Birmingham. Five received additional training enabling them to deliver the training to others, ensuring the capacity to replenish the skills transferred to the community in the years ahead. Although some of the training units were found to be challenging for several community researchers, the model was able to satisfy the demand among citizens in the local area to access the knowledge and skills a university can offer without the barrier of high fees, also providing participants with the lived experience of learning and working in an academic environment, which encouraged some to seek out further study on campus that they would not otherwise have considered. USE-IT! laid the foundations of a community research social enterprise that can be sustained beyond the end date of the programme and benefit both residents and institutions through its knowledge generation activities. Further legacy achievements include the establishment of the Birmingham Anchor Network to enable future collaboration and the coordination of anchor institutions' activities across the city.

Community research training model

The free accredited community research training model set up as part of USE-IT! focused on training local people in conducting social research and then developing further self-contained research projects in partnership with these 'experts of their neighbourhoods', as people that know about their area and are engaged with their own communities. The co-production this involved meant uniting technical and lived knowledge, overcoming the arbitrary dichotomy between the two noted in the literature (Negev and Teschner, 2013). Community researchers were commissioned to work on research projects for institutions within the USE-IT! anchor network and thus support the decision-making processes of organisations from across the West Midlands region.

Co-production models typically have a social empowerment mission at their core and the USE-IT! model is no exception. Operating in a superdiverse inner-city ward undergoing rapid urban transformation, the project team recognised the significant potential for population displacement from gentrification in Birmingham (Zwicky, 2021). As such, USE-IT! sought to give residents in the area a stake in the process of urban change and the ability to influence decisions made about them and their neighbourhoods, thus strengthening community assets and mitigating the risks of top-down planning and decisions that are not adapted to local needs and aspirations. This is particularly important given that the demographic characteristics of the area mean it can be characterised as marginalised or left-behind. Thus, the area is already at high risk of being the target of policy interventions that may be constructed on stereotyping and stigmatisation, both intentionally and unintentionally, be decision-makers far removed from the lived reality of the citizens in question (Møller and Harrits, 2013). The USE-IT! approach is also in line with other work carried out with marginalised groups – for instance, engagement with Roma migrants in Manchester – which has shown the benefits to service design of allowing service users to participate in identifying and tackling problems they face, redesigning service delivery in a way that learns from this insight (Cools *et al.*, 2017).

As the leading partner for the community research training, the University of Birmingham engaged with local partners to reach out and gain trust among the different communities with the aim of encouraging residents to apply for the training on offer. The university organised and delivered the community research training, while local USE-IT! partners and charities used their embeddedness and knowledge of the area to promote the training and support offered through other USE-IT! projects, such as the social enterprise support and skills matching schemes. Some local partners also further supported the community researchers as mentors and trainers. The community research training developed by the university comprises four practice-orientated modules. These modules covered social research skills, practising qualitative methods (e.g., conducting interviews and surveys), analysing data, and reporting and presenting results. The training modules were co-designed with the first cohort of community researchers and further developed based on different experiences and cohorts. The training was designed to support the participants towards carrying out their own research projects in their communities and neighbourhoods, with a view to subsequently working as professional researchers on commissioned projects from the USE-IT! partnership. In addition, community researchers had to conduct a research project as part of their training, with support from the academic team and mentors. These projects had to be beneficial or of relevance to the USE-IT! focus area and the communities living there. In order to gain further experience and increase the capabilities in doing research, more than 20 commissioned research projects were organised, with some including teams of accredited community researchers.

Pedagogies of exchange

The research findings and lessons learnt presented below build on three years' worth of data gathered by the USE-IT! team. In particular, the qualitative material in the next section is drawn from 36 semi-structured interviews and 10 focus groups. Interview participants were asked about their perceptions of the university and other partner institutions, as well as how they felt about their experiences on the USE-IT! programme. In addition, responses from surveys conducted in the first and third years of the programme have been incorporated to develop a fuller picture of change in perceptions over the course of the programme. Survey questions related to life experiences, economic challenges people faced and their aspirations for the future. Almost one-quarter of the interviews analysed for this research were carried out by community researchers as part of commissioned research, with discussion guides co-designed alongside the academic team in workshops on campus.

USE-IT! was based on methods that could respond flexibly to opportunities and challenges that arise in a context of rapid urban change. Thus, a bottom-up approach was decided on to identify needs and assets that USE-IT! could build on, incorporating the lived expertise of residents into the design of the programme. The project was based on past experience of community researcher training with various communities, with members of the academic team having previously worked on participatory action research projects and community research training among marginalised communities at Birmingham's Institute for Research into Superdiversity (IRiS). There is a rich heritage of community-engaged scholarship at the University of Birmingham. IRiS itself is engaged in many of the same issues that preoccupied the seminal work of the Birmingham Centre for Contemporary Cultural Studies founded by the cultural theorist Stuart Hall, which was closed by university management in 2002. USE-IT! was influenced by this academic milieu that has a strong interest in issues such as racial and gender inequality, noting the impact of class within intersectional studies, and seeking to actively empower citizens through research and teaching agendas, as well as the use of innovative methods such as co-production. The project was guided by the aim that community researcher training delivery should be as flexible as possible and led by community needs and constraints, such as time, rather than being determined by the academic team (Goodson and Phillimore, 2012).

There are several lessons learnt and challenges uncovered by our academic team and community researchers as knowledge was exchanged on USE-IT!. These are outlined below. External project evaluators at the Centre for Local Economic Strategies (CLES) wrote an impact report on USE-IT!'s effect on the area and among the participants in the project (CLES, 2019). These findings address many of the challenges facing universities and their local communities, particularly considering left-behind and marginalised groups.

Community researcher recruitment

The community research training project started with the challenge of recruiting residents onto the training programme. Initially, this was done solely through community organisations and charities embedded in the local area. However, this proved to be problematic. Many local organisations had a limited understanding of the aims of the project and understandably prioritised more pressing challenges with their users. The recruitment phase therefore lagged and took more time than planned. Thus, there is a need for an approach of building longer-term relationships to engage local, community-based organisations with university research, so as to be able to reach out to potential participants and inform them about projects and potential benefits for them. The academic team organised local 'recruitment events' and attended neighbourhood events to inform residents about the project. Word-of-mouth recommendations from community researchers already participating in the programme was very successful, as well as leaving leaflets at places where people must wait and have time to read, such as in medical practices. One of the community researchers spoke about recruitment for the project, saying 'you always find people with amazing skills, you simply have to look for them. There is no shortage of skills.'

Another challenge for recruitment was that some people had not been in touch with the world of academia before and were intimidated by doing research and work with the university, or they did not see the benefits of doing so. Many participants described consultation fatigue, with a sense that they were constantly asked for their views and were encouraged to participate but did not see any changes as a result. Having information sessions and meetings in neighbourhoods and not at the university allowed a low-threshold access to the programme on familiar ground for the community being recruited. The academic team quickly realised the importance of having a physical presence in the neighbourhood for more successful recruitment and ongoing management of community research training. Therefore, the team was co-located at a community centre in the area so that the project team was accessible and in a setting that was more accessible and less intimidating to the target group.

A solid communication strategy was key to reach out to the community. The strategy emphasised how community researchers and their communities could benefit from USE-IT!. Community researchers told us that the benefits of taking part in the community research training needed to be clearly stated in the strategy for future recruitment, which helped inform an iterative approach towards promoting the scheme. Community researchers described benefits they perceived, such as:

- doing their own research project for personal interest;
- developing professional skills;
- broadening their own personal perspectives and meeting new people;
- receiving an accreditation from the university for their CV;
- being engaged in work that is beneficial for their community and feeling that they were doing something useful;
- making the needs of their communities heard and better understood by local institutions (e.g. the city council);
- working with the university to increase the credibility of the work they were already doing in their local area; and
- being part of community research network and building up links to academics at the university.

As part of the communication strategy, feedback from participants to shape the approach was critical. Community researchers told us it was important for the academic team to mention what is important about the community researcher methodology itself, as a motivation to those being trained. Working together in co-production workshops, we identified benefits to the university and wider USE-IT! partnership of using this method, such as:

- receiving information and evidence from hard-to reach communities and gaining hyper-local knowledge;
- reaching communities that can be very difficult for an 'outside researcher' to understand and gain trust;
- bringing in different perspectives on the local situation;
- making the local communities heard and their needs better articulated; and
- bringing local projects forward by establishing connections between community researchers, local organisations, city-wide institutions and research projects of mutual interest.

Through the local knowledge and embeddedness of the community researchers, the academic team became more sensitive to the local situation and gained knowledge on residents' lived experiences, which gave a more holistic impression of challenges than would have been the case with solely accessing the technical knowledge held within the university. This process helped the project team to increase empathy, which helps to better understand communities' different challenges and needs, and to identify issues that may not have been considered had a 'classic' research project been conducted. For example, some of the research identified problems such as a high incidence of knife crime in specific pockets of the area or concerns with children being used as drug mules. Classic academic research projects often identify challenges at the outset based on an external perception of an area, such as perceived issues with relation to unemployment or the need for more investment. Instead, USE-IT!'s community research approach resulted in a research agenda co-produced with hard-to-reach groups and the very specific knowledge they had about neighbourhoods and local cultural and social perspectives, meaning a wide range of collaboration opportunities were available for researching sensitive topics.

The training modules

Interviews with participants of the community research training demonstrated benefits related to empowerment and building social connections, as well as the knowledge and skills gained. Most community researchers expressed positive thoughts about the training. For example, one reflected that 'it was practice-oriented, mostly jargon free language and the 'homework' helped to test the methods learnt'. The training not only helped to improve participants' research skills but also enhanced their confidence in applying those skills in practice. The CLES impact report (2019) evaluated the training scheme as follows:

> It was reported as a well-designed programme of learning, which was accessible for people with no formal education, or with limited language skills. The course was praised for being very practical, about learning by doing, and an exchange of ideas. Finally, it was also considered important that some elements of the training course were delivered at venues in the local community, which were locations where the community feel comfortable, and are easily accessible. It also created trust between staff from the University, and the community – a vital step in the development of the programme.

However, there was also criticism of the initial training that too much was expected of the participants in terms of learning outcomes. This highlights the importance of academics reflecting on the different kind of curricula that might be drawn up for community-orientated courses rather than courses embedded in degree programmes. One participant shared that many of their fellow community researchers felt that 'training was too academic, and experience of the programme depended on educational background'. In addition, the participants found themselves in different starting situations in terms of available time and interests. In this regard, some participants needed more support than others to be able to continue the training. While the training was free, it nevertheless required a time commitment that meant disproportionately recruiting from those who were not in full-time work, including retirees. There was also a general under-representation of male participants on the project.

The community researchers appreciated that the training allowed them to get to know each other, collaborate, exchange ideas and network across the area. These possibilities were consciously promoted throughout the training. In addition, participants were given access to other academics and the university staff. As one participant explained in an interview to evaluate the scheme, 'an important aspect of the community research programme was the approachability of the university team. This eases things and made everything more personal.'

Mentoring

Mentoring was a crucial part of the community research training. It was designed to support the community researchers as they worked on their projects, with personal mentors assigned to each participant. Mentors were either drawn from the academic team at the University of Birmingham or worked at one of the USE-IT! partners. The community researchers could contact their mentors through email and arrange face-to-face meetings to ask for advice and feedback. Throughout the training, community researchers were encouraged to go through the results of training interviews, discuss their experience of applying knowledge gained on the training modules, and raise issues such as how to engage the community in their projects. The academic team also organised regular drop-in sessions at a local community centre. Some were held on fixed dates and others were on-demand sessions. Mentors contacted participants regularly to discuss the progress of their research and ensure steady progress on the training.

Mentoring was an important part of the training project. This was in part because it was a means of providing technical guidance on matters such as how to structure a survey or conduct and analyse material from interviews. However, the mentors also provided the community researchers with confidence, reassuring them that they could make it, and that they were a contact they could build a relationship with, and ask questions about USE-IT! and the aims of the organisations represented on the programme.

Commissioned research projects

The commissioned research projects were an important complementary development to the training. Midway through the project it was observed that some community researchers did not have an individual research project and/or had lost interest in the training. The commissioned research projects allowed those researchers to continue working and complete their accreditation. In addition, those who worked on the projects were paid for their work. This was highly appreciated and gave a strong motivation to continue with their participation on USE-IT!.

Commissioned research projects were developed to meet a need for information from one of the institutional partners on USE-IT!. An additional benefit was that this meant the community researchers could see that they were working as real researchers to solve real-world problems for a commissioning organisation. It was important to pay the researchers so that they would not feel exploited but instead could see themselves as peers whose time was valuable to the partnership. In addition to gaining knowledge – including from hard-to-access communities – the costs to pay for researchers' time on the commissioned community research projects were lower than rates for an established consultancy company. The community researchers worked alongside academics from the university on these projects, thus enabling an exchange of knowledge, contacts and research practice.

USE-IT! funding for this research allowed the investigation an array of topics that could have been very hard to fund otherwise and can be viewed as seed funding for small projects with the potential to uncover issues for further research in the future. For example, based on encouraging findings from one project, a larger bid was made for funding to research childhood obesity strategies for the city, which won £150,000 in funding for the local council. This is not to claim that the value of research should be measured solely in monetary terms, but instead to highlight that community research can deliver a significant return on investment on these terms. In an interview with a member of the academic team, one participant explained, 'it was important for us to value the time commitment of community researchers and show the appreciation of their work', with paying the community researchers to conduct work as professional researchers being instrumental in this regard.

The commissioned research projects encouraged community researchers to bring in their own perceptions in addition to the perceptions of participants who were interviewed. Their personal perceptions provided new perspectives, given that some participants were users of services they were researching and thus able to identify problems in service design through their lived experience in a way that might be more challenging for someone removed from the situation who has not experienced using the service. Some projects proposed by the community researchers allowed them to conduct research on projects and topics that matter to them and their communities. However, many of the projects ran the risk of going nowhere, as sometimes community researchers did not have a target institution to take up the results and follow up with actions. The need to match a community researcher-in-training with a target institution early on is thus an important piece of learning for the academic team, which can be recommended to others working on similar training projects to factor into their own practice.

Personal skills development

The community research programme contributed not only to achieving research skills, but also to developing personal skills. Above all, the programme promoted the personal development of the community researchers. Many community researchers mentioned the increase of self-confidence that came with completing the training. They developed a network of other community researchers and academics, and contacts in their communities and in public institutions, which has subsequently led to a higher engagement with their neighbourhood. Working on commissioned research projects raised participants' self-esteem because 'someone wants your results', as one community researcher put it. This feedback suggests that the USE-IT! model of community empowerment through participatory action research can provide an important social benefit as a tool for overcoming the consultation fatigue that many residents described feeling at the outset.

Community researchers were optimistic about the potential of the collaborative efforts on the project. For example, one spoke about the links between loneliness, feeling disempowered and having poor mental health, commenting on the need for public services to collaborate on these issues. The community researchers felt that the link to the university gave them additional credibility as researchers and helped them make contacts and gain access in ways that were not possible for citizens working alone. This can help break down the idea of the university as an 'ivory tower' or place for privileged people, as such, democratising knowledge and knowledge production. On a personal level, one participant spoke about how presenting their work at Birmingham's central library was also a special moment in their life; such meaningful personal experiences are difficult to quantify but are an important output of a training scheme geared towards empowerment.

The USE-IT! programme has increased the university's presence in the area. Our conversations within the university and with those working in other public institutions across the city encourage us that USE-IT! was able to demonstrate to leaders a practical way of activating the economic and social roles that the university can play as an anchor in its community. The community research training scheme has created a pool of local experts that live locally and have research skills, technical and lived knowledge and a network of contacts. While the impacts that this might have on the city in the future cannot be controlled or predicted, there is hope that the 85 accredited community researchers from USE-IT! will continue their work of researching and advocating in the interest of their communities. In terms of legacy outputs, the Birmingham Anchor Network coordinates the activities of anchor institutions in the city with the aim of building community wealth. Skills transferred to the community can also be replenished by community researchers who have been trained to deliver the training, and there are ongoing discussions about creating a community research social enterprise that can continue the model of community researchers being commissioned to conduct social research in the area on behalf of external organisations.

Universities' visibility and communities' aspirations

USE-IT! was interested not only in economic impacts but also in transferring knowledge to the community, building resilience among marginalised groups and helping to mitigate the impacts of development that can displace these groups. As such, the project aimed to increase the visibility of local residents in knowledge production and decision-making about the future of their area. Considering the university as a space for visibility entails reflecting on the literature around space and power. The issues of seeing or being seen at the university, and who the university is for, were raised by participants who felt that campuses were for elites and were not places that those without degrees could or should access. Such perceptions of the university as a closed space were repeatedly expressed at the USE-IT! community meetings. For example, at the beginning of the project, an attendee at a community meeting commented that the 'university is for rich people, not for people like me'. Similarly, another local resident felt that access to the university was restricted to those who had something to offer in return: 'the doors are closed unless there is funding, volunteering, investment … there is an exclusive business perception when it comes to the university.' One participant on our training scheme said that they had never visited the university before, despite living in the area.

However, the training scheme helped alter these perceptions, with participants reporting that they felt the training bridged the gap between communities and the university. For instance, when community researchers in focus groups reflected on the training, one noted that beforehand they perceived research to be elitist, but that community research could overcome elitism and allow a wider range of people to take part. Another noted how USE-IT! had enabled them to visit the campus which made them feel empowered, saying that it proved universities were for everybody, not only for people with degrees.

The project therefore sought to overcome the barriers to marginalised groups accessing the university and seeing it as a space where they feel welcome and heard. Throughout the project, notions of how change can be visible in university operations were discussed by community researchers and academic staff, considering issues such as local recruitment, local procurement, and the university supplying products and services that are more ethnically and culturally diverse. We also noted different definitions and descriptions of what constitute 'communities'. Where researchers might refer to groups of people as 'communities', people living in a particular place or having one particular demographic trait might not feel or identify as such. For example, a participant on USE-IT! told us they felt that 'community is a middle-class construct. Nobody in this neighbourhood would understand themselves as being a community'. Moreover, many made comments that framed universities as big schools detached from the real world, rather than as diverse organisations with operations that go beyond research and teaching. Some local representatives reiterated that 'if you went into any school in the city and asked if they were thinking of working at the university, I don't think a single one would put their hands up'. Many of the participants believed that universities rarely make attempts to be visible and present in their areas. Universities were instead perceived as places where people had to pay for access, creating a significant perceptual barrier for those on lower incomes or those who live in deprived areas.

Many participants expressed their frustration at not being included in universities as public spaces, with multiple comments criticising academic projects that parachute into communities for a few years without long-term impact or legacy. As one participant commented, 'I'm sick of telling my story, it doesn't make any difference'. Another added that 'not a lot happens' after participating in research. Academics were accused of using their own language and narratives that further exacerbate the barriers between themselves and the very communities that they intend to work with. One participant explained this, saying that 'no one wants to live in a deprived area, so do not label us'. Another felt that, while there are attempts to include and empower local people, their representation in the research is only to be used as a source of data, a descriptive 'about us but not with us' approach. One local resident wanted the university to 'tell a better story about this place; we want to have pride in it!'. Another wanted the university to understand people's lived experiences, saying that 'the community could enable the university to learn about reality'. The community research training model helped shift these attitudes towards more positive perspectives, providing a practical demonstration of how universities can be visible within their local areas and break generational barriers of elitism in favour of empowering minorities and poor people, through acknowledging their lived experience as an equally valid and powerful form of knowledge.

Based on the success of the commissioned research projects, several community researchers have developed the idea of a community research social enterprise, which is currently in development. The idea of the social enterprise is to continue with community research and look to both help other communities develop their own team of researchers and to provide a long-term pathway for other agencies to unlock community expertise. This is a very important step to delivering a legacy for USE-IT! beyond the formal end of the project and providing a sustainable platform for the local community to articulate its needs as an equal partner, gathering knowledge that could support more holistic and sensitive interventions by organisations that seek to work in the area. In the impact report, the evaluators state:

> This is a significant opportunity for the researchers to continue to pursue their research interests and do so in a manner that rewards them financially. It also has the potential to influence the wider

West Midlands area in terms of the ways in which research is done, the types of projects that are developed, and in bringing in 'lost voices' to research. Finally, there is the potential to cement the legacy of USE-IT! by creating this asset within the neighbourhood. (CLES, 2019)

It has also demonstrated to the partner organisations that the community researchers are able to carry out research to the standard they require, with the added benefit that community researchers come with local knowledge and lived experience of marginalisation that many professional researchers working in universities and other organisations often lack. USE-IT! also provided an opportunity for the community researchers to be paid for their time and gain not only an accredited qualification but also professional experience as a researcher, which may shape their future careers or social and political activism in ways that cannot be predicted.

Universities have civic and social responsibilities in relation to supporting community development. This needs to be supported by having more meaningful interactions with communities, underpinned by universities demonstrating their long-term commitment to collaboration for building trust rather than 'parachuting in' each time a new project begins, as one participant put it. Linking to this is the need for universities to 'communicate better', using terms and language that people outside the university can understand, and spend more time 'working and learning in communities to break open the gates', as one resident at our community meeting stated. The USE-IT! programme demonstrated that there is a real appetite among citizens to access the knowledge and skills held at their universities, and that the process of doing so can be mutually beneficial for communities, universities and organisations commissioning research alike. Universities can empower citizens through active participation in research, while also supporting community capacity building at the local level, inviting left-behind groups onto campus or meeting them in their local area to learn in a two-way pedagogy of exchange. At the same time, this moves knowledge and its production outside the walls of the university and into the public realm, establishing a presence for the university in the community and helping shift perceptions of what a university is, does and can be.

Reflections and recommendations

With the results of the community research training scheme, embedded within a multi-year programme of projects that brought together institutions across a city collaborating on tackling urban poverty and social marginalisation, several lessons arise that can guide and inform future practice and attempts to activate the potential of universities to have a visible and active role in their local areas. These lessons relate to debates around the concepts of civic universities and anchor institutions, as well as the way in which the notions of visibility and empowerment are operationalised in planning, development and policy research in the United Kingdom.

Community research training is a powerful tool that can be used not only to empower local communities but also to deliver results that can inform decision-making and policy and service design. It has the potential to change the dynamics of the current policy arena and have a significant impact through enabling more democratic, co-produced agendas for left-behind places that are tailored to local needs and aspirations. The USE-IT! experience showed that partnerships with communities increase the chance of interventions that are inclusive and are more sensitive to local needs and outcomes. The project's bottom-up methodology in practice complements the academic theories of collaborative and participatory planning discourses. Enabling citizens and service users to take a meaningful role in shaping the design of policies and institutions fundamentally increases the democratic legitimacy of such decisions and the interventions that are developed as a result. This is not to present technical expertise of academics and policymakers as being oppositional to the lived expertise of citizens; instead, both can complement each other and can lead to more holistic outcomes. As such, universities – along with a wider array of institutions – should begin by reflecting critically on established modes of gathering data and conducting research, considering whether there is space for an approach that taps into the expertise by experience of the citizens who are most affected by decisions regarding the delivery of services.

Another advantage of the community research approach is enhancing access for both communities and universities. Citizens, particularly those from more deprived or marginalised groups, should be supported to engage with universities, on campuses or in their neighbourhoods. Through co-producing knowledge with academics, citizens gain access to training, knowledge and skills that are free at the point of access, rather than having to pay high fees that serve as a barrier. Academics and policymakers benefit in turn, gaining far greater access to hard-to-reach communities and rich data to inform decision-making that is gathered by researchers who are more trusted than academics who are perceived to be 'parachuting in' and are often not attuned to the everyday life of the community in question. While USE-IT! faced an array of challenges including time constraints, difficulty of encouraging buy-in from centralised institutions, and of course the perennial issue of budgetary constraints, the flexibility of the project design and committed engagement of the academic team helped to overcome these problems.

A number of challenges were encountered that prompted us to reflect on problems with the design of the project and the cultural change required to make a network of public institutions be more than just a cumbersome talking- shop. For example, on a practical level getting and maintaining the buy-in of senior leaders can be difficult, as can be the logistics of multiple organisations of varying scale seeking to co-ordinate their efforts and reduce duplication. Nevertheless, in our experience the USE-IT! model of co-production proved to be a flexible mechanism for transferring knowledge and skills between community and academic researchers, in turn delivering policy research projects that demonstrated benefit to the anchor institution network on the project, to the extent that they decided to continue their collaboration in the form of the Birmingham Anchor Network. The return on investment might be considered as the enhanced visibility and empowerment dimensions of the project, but in financial terms, data gathered by community researchers led to the awarding of a six-figure research grant orientated towards tackling childhood obesity in a community-led approach, representing significant potential cost savings for local government and the health service in the future.

Several recommendations can be made for future action research-based projects that use the community research methodology as a tool to facilitate community engagement and visibility. First, communication is key. Using trusted community organisations and making information available in places where people have time to stay and read is important. Putting effort into building longer-term relationships, rather than 'parachuting' in for projects, can help create mutually beneficial relationships of trust and, in doing so, can shift the perception that the university is present in its local community only when it wants something (be it research data, participants or funding). Once participants are recruited onto a training scheme, at the outset there is a need to assess their skill levels and deliver a tailored approach according to individuals' needs, recognising that some will have more qualifications, language proficiency or familiarity with research concepts than others. Therefore, some participants may need additional tutoring and training support. Other participants who already have more developed research skills could go through a fast-track process. The training modules need to be flexible, corresponding to different starting positions, interests and time capacities of the participants. Content should be iterative, responding to what does and does not work. In turn, sharing learning materials and best practice between universities could be beneficial to help reach common standards in delivering community research training.

While some community researchers praised the effectiveness and success of the training, some noted that the follow-up of research results was unclear or did not happen. Improvements that can be implemented in the future include focusing on particular topics of research ideas; identifying research interests of (local) institutions and organisations, and understanding at the outset in which areas they want to become active; linking these partner organisations with a community researcher early on to facilitate relationship building; and supporting community researchers to present their research findings at relevant institutions. Developing collaborative networks of anchor institutions, identifying where there are spaces for cooperation in work and gaps in knowledge that can be addressed with material gathered by community researchers, can help sustain the exchange of knowledge between communities, universities and institutions to create more holistic solutions to challenges. Transferring skills to the community, including training for five community researchers to train others, was one way of embedding the USE-IT! approach in the community and continuing this knowledge production beyond the university. Likewise, efforts to establish a community research social enterprise that can be commissioned by organisations interested in the communities and places represented by these researchers is another dimension of anchoring the aims of the project.

The USE-IT! community research model presents the opportunity to address three types of connection between higher education and the built environment. This ranges from reviewing the design and delivery of community research training and recruitment, to teaching that includes creating space for innovative and experimental ideas coming out of co-production, as well as collaborating as equal peers to design research that is in line with citizens' motivations and issues. Finally, through successive cohorts of community researchers, the model creates a space for embedding this approach to research and knowledge exchange, including through the training of trainers practice, whereby accredited researchers get the opportunity to further their knowledge and recruit and train others beyond the university.

Future research could dive deeper into the cultural and institutional change required to enable universities to achieve their potential for social empowerment, matching the growing interest in community wealth building that has resulted from the wider understanding of universities as local anchor institutions. More research also needs to investigate how institutional partnerships can be developed with a formal role for citizens to feed into knowledge gathering and decision-making processes. Supporting the emergence of a culture of civic engagement to build truly participatory practices, while also facilitating the inclusion of local communities, is an important ongoing challenge to academia, particularly in highly marketised contexts. Researchers might perhaps also consider the dynamics of virtual space and the challenges and opportunities of online community research, which was not a consideration of this project that took place in a pre-pandemic world. Moreover, future research must continue to explore issues around social and public spaces where local people can be seen, speak and be heard, and be present in the co-production of new knowledge and ways of understanding the world.

References

Birmingham City Council. 2020. *Ladywood Ward Factsheet*. Birmingham: Birmingham City Council.

Cools, P., D. V. Leggio, Y. Matras and S. Oosterlynck. 2017. '"Parity of participation" and the politics of needs interpretation: engagement with Roma migrants in Manchester', *Journal of Social Policy* 47(2): 359–76.

Ehlenz, M. M. 2018. 'Defining university anchor institution strategies: comparing theory to practice', *Planning Theory and Practice* 19(1): 74–92.

Goddard, J., M. Coombes, L. Kempton and P. Vallance. 2014. 'Universities as anchor institutions in cities in a turbulent funding environment: vulnerable institutions and vulnerable places in England', *Cambridge Journal of Regions, Economy and Society* 7(2): 307–25.

Harris, M. S. 2019. 'The soft underbelly of universities as anchor institutions: the disconnect between university and community research priorities', *Higher Education Policy* 34: 603–21.

Jessel, E. 2021. 'Birmingham focus: will Ladywood learn the lessons of the past?', *Architect's Journal*, https://www.architectsjournal.co.uk/news/birmingham-focus-will-ladywood-learn-the-lessons-of-the-past (last accessed 8 December 2022).

Lebeau, Y., and A. Cochrane. 2015. 'Rethinking the "third mission": UK universities and regional engagement in challenging times', *European Journal of Higher Education* 5(3): 250–63.

McCauley-Smith, C., S. Smith, L. Nantunda and X. Zhu. 2020. 'The role of anchor institutions in creating value for SMEs: insights from North East of England owner-managers', *Studies in Higher Education* 1121–33, https://doi.org/10.1080/03075079.2020.1861593 (last accessed 8 December 2022).

Møller, M. Ø., and G. S. Harrits. 2013. 'Constructing at-risk target groups', *Critical Policy Studies* 7(2): 155–76.

Negev, M., and N. Teschner. 2013. 'Rethinking the relationship between technical and local knowledge: toward a multi-type approach', *Environmental Science and Policy* 30: 50–9.

O'Farrell, L., S. Hassan and C. Hoole. 2022. 'The university as a just anchor: universities, anchor networks and participatory research', *Studies in Higher Education* 2405–16, https://doi.org/10.1080/03075079.2022.2072480 (last accessed 8 December 2022).

Vertovec, S. 2007. 'Super-diversity and its implications', *Ethnic and Racial Studies* 30(6): 1024–54.

Zwicky, R. 2021. *Housing Governance in a Time of Financialization: a comparative analysis of Zurich, Birmingham and Lyon*. Zurich: VDF Hochschulverlag.

Ethical Approval from University of Birmingham: Ethical Review ERN_16-1484.

11
Role play activities: a methodology for transformative participation

Teresa Strachan

This chapter examines a methodology used by Newcastle University urban planning students as part of their extracurricular activities, to promote their engagement with young people in the north-east of England. Established in 2013, the YES Planning project emerged from the author's wish to create a *pro bono*-type of programme, where students across the School of Architecture, Planning and Landscape might offer a few hours of their time per semester to share their learning about the planned environment with young people in the region. The workshops created under the YES Planning banner support topic-based learning in planning, creating unique cross cohort and cross degree collaboration, and were managed by the author as part of their recent teaching and scholarship contract with the university.

Student volunteers sign up for the projects that they are interested in and offer only the time they can afford to give, to fit alongside their studies and work commitments. While many of the student volunteers aspire to be planners, others may go into property, urban design, teaching, postgraduate study or other varied career routes. YES Planning presents the volunteer with an opportunity to enhance their own understanding of planning's impact on communities, to develop specific skills of engagement and to investigate and appreciate how local young people perceive their environment. The students can accrue their hours on the project towards a university-wide volunteer award, while developing key engagement and employability skills.

One of the workshops within this project – Canny Planners – focuses on the impact of hot-food takeaways on local high streets and their communities, investigating their effect on amenity and lifestyles and understanding the planning policies that relate to these outlets. The term 'canny' was chosen to emphasise the discerning and shrewd nature of the workshop participants as they take on the role of the planning experts and councillors as part of the mock planning committee. 'Canny' is also a colloquial term of endearment in the northeast of England, meaning 'good' or 'pleasant' (Cambridge English Dictionary: online). Canny Planners has been delivered to several schools and youth groups in the north-east since 2018. Comprising a suite of activities, the workshop places an emphasis on using the principles of role play to promote learning. This chapter evaluates the workshop's impact on its participants in relation to the barriers faced by young people and their engagement with a planning process. Looking specifically at the concept of transformative participation, the chapter considers if the Canny Planners workshop has the potential to inform how we engage young people in planning matters and deliver higher education to future town planners.

The Canny Planners workshop case study is explored from an academic as well as a planning and educational practice perspective. The views of those taking part in the workshop over the two-year period are organised in relation to the key literature on transformative learning through games and role play, illustrating the impact of the activities undertaken. One of the principal reflections emerging from the workshop is the pivotal role that student planners can take in its delivery. In sharing their planning knowledge and in facilitating the workshop themselves, the students develop their own skills of community engagement while better understanding the young people's perspectives around places and planning.

This chapter begins by presenting the case for involving young people in plan-making and planning decisions, the principle for which is endorsed in literature across a number of disciplines including geography, psychology, education and children's rights. It then goes onto highlight a range of reasons why engagement with young people has not advanced in England despite the multilateral benefits claimed, suggesting institutional, procedural and a potential absence of appropriate skills among planning professionals. The key theoretical concepts that underpin the case study around transformational learning and the use of board games and role play in learning are then discussed. Following an explanation of the Canny Planners workshop components, the chapter concludes with a reflection on the potential for transformative participation when university students and young people in the community share the same pedagogy.

The potential for youth participation in planning

The United Nations (UN) Convention for the Rights of the Child (1989) defines 'children' as being those up to the age of 18 years. The UN defines 'youth' as between the ages of 15 and 24. For the purposes of the Canny Planners workshop, this definition neatly includes the ages of the planning students who facilitate the workshops, and are 19–22 years old, being in their second year and above of their undergraduate degree courses. Master of Planning (MPlan) students returning from their work placement also bring their practice insights, growing confidence and engagement skills to the workshops. They may also be joined on the project by postgraduate students on the Urban Planning MSc course who can offer their undergraduate knowledge from a range of disciplines. To simplify how the chapter defines its participants, a distinction is drawn between the 'young people' as participants of the workshops (aged 8–18) and planning students who are the facilitators (aged 19–22).

Participation in the United Kingdom's planning system is often criticised as representing a 'bolt on' or a 'box ticking' exercise, perhaps seeking affirmation of predetermined options, at best, and which have little likelihood of really shaping planners' thinking, community understanding, effective policy creation or truly reflecting the diversity of identities presented by that community (Jenkins, 2005). In England, in particular, young people enjoy even less of a clear participatory role within the town planning process, despite them having a right to be heard on matters that affect them (UNCRC, 1989; Wood *et al.*, 2019). Translating those rights into a voice that influences planning at the local level continues to challenge champions for young people's rights and this agenda has been the focus of research across different disciplines over the past four decades (Chawla, 2007; Freeman and Cook, 2019; Hart, 1979; Percy-Smith, 2014; Prince, 2014; Skelton, 2007; Valentine, 2017). Through a young person's attachment to, and pride in, their local area (in play and everyday activities) they acquire a deep-rooted local knowledge and understanding regarding not only how places can change over time, but also in relation to how others (usually adults) hold the power to bring about that change (Hart, 1979; Prince, 2014). They can make their own assessment of places that they like or dislike, places that feel accessible or safe and form an attachment to places that reinforce their own sense of well-being. Research has shown that such fine-grained insights often focus on the positives rather than the shortfalls of the local area and on the needs of others in that locality (Nordström and Wales, 2019; Prince, 2014; Visser *et al.*, 2015). The power of this place attachment also has the capacity to transform the individual's and others' future role within that place, through a new sense of empowerment and agency (Blanchet-Cohen, 2008; Breakwell, 1992; Prince, 2014; Twigger-Ross and Uzzell, 1996). However, as a community of young people, the value of their local expert knowledge continues to be largely disregarded as a starting point in the pursuit of inclusive place-making, where such groups continue to remain marginalised and unengaged. Understanding and addressing this inequity was a key motivation behind the YES Planning outreach project.

The opportunity for young people to learn about the planned environment and the planning process within the English primary school system (ages 5–11), relies mostly on an alignment with individual teacher knowledge and interests, as it sits outside the formal requirements of the national curriculum. Matters relating to other young people's rights (e.g., healthcare and democratic processes) may be included within citizenship-type activities across the age range discussed here. Additionally, the potential for learning about planning at secondary school level (11–18 years) is determined by opportunities within the curriculum and the choices made by young people as they progress through their assessed work at GCSE (age 16) and A level (age 18). Premiums on teachers' time, school resources and in-house expertise often mean that local environmental projects may be delivered only by external bodies such as Newcastle University and the YES Planning venture, as free-standing one-off programmes or events.

In addition to the lack of opportunities to introduce discussions around local planning issues in an educational context and despite the academic evidence and the rhetoric from an international community relating to young people's rights, the English planning system has failed to engage with young people's local knowledge or to capture their potential to influence local place making (Wood *et al.*, 2019). Some of the blame for this lack of engagement can also be placed at the door of planners not having adequate skills to support that participation (Strachan, 2016). Using a checklist of potential skills for working with young people, informed by literature and a range of stakeholder interviews, planning students in their placement year considered the three key skills for youth engagement in planning should be the ability: 'to explain how the planning system works in words that young people understand'; 'to understand local issues'; and 'to lead fun activities to enable young people to learn'. In comparison, while the young people and teacher responses also recognised the value of understanding the planning system to some extent, they concluded that planners' key skills for youth engagement in planning should be the ability 'to listen' and 'develop a sense of trust'

(Strachan, 2016: 68). The prioritisation of the need for planners' skills that explain planning and local planning issues appears to be somewhat inconsistent across the two perspectives.

Furthermore, the impact of poor or absent participation can then perpetuate a cycle exacerbating poor future relationships between planning and communities (Percy-Smith, 2014). Therefore, the additional challenge for planners and planning is not only how to draw on the local expertise that currently exists among young people, but also to nurture their proactive citizenship into adulthood and enable them to feel empowered to take part in future participatory processes. As part of the Canny Planners workshop, the Healthy High Street board game offers the opportunity for young people to consider, reflect on and discuss their knowledge, opinions and aspirations for their local place in a supportive and informative environment.

Also, and of significance to this chapter regarding role play, Bigger and Webb (2010) recognise that while the lived experiences of young people are a critical element that can contribute to effective placemaking, they can also respond to fiction or fictitious places and scenarios where they can compare these to what might be happening in the real world. This ability to cross between a fictional and a real planning scenario informed the development of activities that comprise the Canny Planners workshop.

Barriers to young people's participation

Planning practitioners often understand the term 'young people' to mean a homogenous section of the community that is 'hard to reach'. In reality, the term conceals a range of ages, interests, cultures and capabilities, requiring a bespoke approach to involving them in what might be seen as adult decision-making processes. Piaget's exploration of children and young people's environmental perception across age groups suggests a young community characterised by a constantly evolving appreciation of and engagement with the world (Piaget, 1950). Such a variation in a young community's profile and capabilities in environmental perception demands appropriate engagement methodologies and skills that planners may not readily have at their disposal.

Critics also consider that the complex, shifting, relationships that determine the balance of power between young people, their gatekeepers, adults in the community (who may be more articulate in making their own voices heard) and those politicians and planning professionals who deliver place-making, can undermine the capacity for young people's agency to influence genuine changes in their environment (Tisdall, 2013; Percy-Smith, 2014; White, 1996).

While the case for seeking a young person's voice in place-making appears compelling, structural barriers remain that prevent effective participation from taking place. Tisdall's six barriers to effective participation with young people highlight the inherent difficulty with the formal process structures to which young people are expected to contribute, and the lack of longer-term continuity through changes in priorities, funding and staff responsible for its delivery (Tisdall, 2013). Shortcomings are also evident in the methods of participation themselves, where perhaps minimum consultation is sought, within limited time frames and without feedback to the young people themselves, therefore preventing any constructive longer-term dialogue or opportunity for a cumulative impact (Tisdall, 2013).

Transformative learning and participation

An examination of the pedagogical literature surrounding transformative learning affords us a better understanding of how young people learn as a result of their engagement with their local environment and its planning issues. Transformative learning draws on a simple principle, whereby, in experiencing new situations and absorbing new information, we adjust our thinking about ourselves, our values and what we believe (Mezirow, 2006). For transformative participation in planning, this means that young people can acquire knowledge from a planning scenario, allowing them to build on their prior knowledge of their local area (Barratt Hacking *et al.*, 2007 in Bigger and Webb, 2010; Fleming, 1995; Kolb, 1984). Their revised perspective then embeds itself into the individual's psyche, moulding understanding and attitudes and creating a 'vehicle for both personal and social change' (Hromek and Roffey, 2009: 629). In addition, the process 'empowers' the individual to seek the changes that may then be desired as a result of this new knowledge (Tisdall, 2013: 185).

Significant limitations with (and hence substantial barriers to) employing experiential learning with young people are the societal and ethical constraints that prevent that direct exchange with what might be regarded as an 'adult world' and with the planning process that might also be considered an adult domain. This case study illustrates that by using a hypothetical or 'mock' world scenario within a familiar local environment (and hosted within the school curriculum), experience of a planning process can be simulated, generating thinking, discussion and constructive responses among young people. This case study will demonstrate the potential for how planners can begin to think differently about how they approach the involvement of young people in a participatory process, by considering what they want the young people to learn and reflect on around a real-world planning issue.

Role play and board games as part of transformative participation

Through the suite of activities that comprise the Canny Planners workshop, the planning students were challenged to use and adapt their own knowledge for a younger audience, setting them tasks based on their own new learning, reviewing how it is received and 'internalised' by the young people and then making modifications for future versions of the activities where necessary (Bloom *et al.*, 2001; Brookfield, 1995; Kolb, 1984; Sotto, 1995).

Central to the process of transformative learning, is the concept that existing power relationships are disregarded, involving 'blocking out power relationships engendered in the structure of communication, including those traditionally existing between teachers and learners' (Taylor and Cranton, 2012: 93). Within a classroom setting, this approach allows young people not only to reconsider, through reflection, their own beliefs and stance on the matters under consideration, but also to think freely about the framework in which they might take action to address these concerns. Dismantling existing power relationships as part of an educational role play activity with young people can create an environment within which critical and free thinking takes place. It also offers a 'power platform' for young people, where formal teacher-learner relationships are removed, enabling the identification of suitable remedial action to the planning conundrum posed (Daniau, 2016). Used within a scenario for learning about planning issues, role play would therefore seem to hold considerable potential in enabling young people to become more socially and emotionally aware, more inclusive of others' views and to be focused on identifying a course of action to address the situation they have explored, through a strong reflective process (Hromek and Roffey, 2009). Others go further to suggest that role play can also help to build communities of interest as those identities are explored (Daniau, 2016).

The value of games as a method of promoting social and emotional learning have also been recognised for some time and is also relevant to this discussion where skills of identifying one's own emotions, developing a respect for others and improving in communication and negotiation all play a large part in their personal development (Hromek and Roffey, 2009). Finally, compared to a more traditional teaching method, Prince (2004) considers how students more effectively recall the learning undertaken in small groups on real-world issues, over those delivered through a more traditional teaching method that may also be likely to be removed from real world scenarios.

The Canny Planners workshop

The scope and potential for the YES Planning engagement approach with young people was explored during 2012–13 through a final year MPlan linked research project that offered teaching, learning and module outcomes to explore the possibilities for the project and the likely interest of the young people themselves for participation in planning. Following the development of a number of well-received workshops, the resultant Canny Planners workshop and its three elements were developed and delivered by the YES Planning volunteers over a two-year period from 2018 to 2019, working with a range of age groups within north-east schools and youth councils. Ethics approval was sought from the University's Ethics Committee to ensure that all aspects of the programme, with its potential as a research project, had been explored and considered to protect participants' and facilitators' interests and to promote best practice in working with vulnerable members of the community. This section explains the activities and the key outputs generated.

The planning topic under discussion in the Canny Planners workshop was hot-food takeaways. Presenting a contemporary planning issue that emerges at local level and is of daily interest to young people, the workshop allowed this high street topic to be considered in terms of its visual impacts such as litter, signage and illumination, and its impact on traffic, parking and delivery vehicles waiting at the premises. The purpose of the workshop was to explore a young person's attitude towards takeaway outlets, especially in light of increasing evidence that suggests that society's consumption of fast food is leading to increasingly unhealthy lifestyles (Townshend and Lake, 2017). In recent years, planning policy at the local level has responded to this growing evidence by restricting new outlets in certain locations. Canny Planners enables young people to consider questions of health and lifestyle alongside more environmental and aesthetic issues through a planning lens on their local area.

Through three main components, the Canny Planners workshop encourages its young participants to:

- progress from thinking about places that they value in their local area, to reflecting on what would be important in planning their future neighbourhood in a diamond-ranking exercise;
- consider the environmental, behavioural and health-related issues that relate to the location of hot-food takeaways in their local high street by participating in the Healthy High Street Board Game; and
- present, discuss, listen and propose the outcome of a fictitious planning application for a new hot-food takeaway, using role play within a mock planning committee scenario.

Diamond-ranking activity

During the first part of the Canny Planners workshop, the young people are asked to think about their local neighbourhood and to consider how they would plan it in the future. A PowerPoint presentation is used to introduce the workshop and the key features of the local area, with questions to explore how and when this change came about. This preparatory discussion also helps to situate the role of planning within the process of that change, the local council, ward councillors and the community. It enables the participants to think about what they like and dislike about their area and what they identify with as being important for their future neighbourhood.

The diamond-ranking activity requires the young people to work in groups to choose a shortlist of nine images from those supplied and then to rank these in order of importance, answering the question, 'what is most important when planning your future local neighbourhood?' (see Figure 11.1). The ranking task facilitates a discussion around the priority that the young people afford to each component of their future area and once decided on as a group, the image is inserted and pasted into the diamond at the appropriate level, with notes to explain the ranking suggested by the participants (Woolner *et al.*, 2010).

Student facilitators help the young people in their discussions, assisting them to make comparisons and judgements between different facilities and services, asking questions to challenge thinking and to help resolve conflicting priorities. The activity also has potential to develop

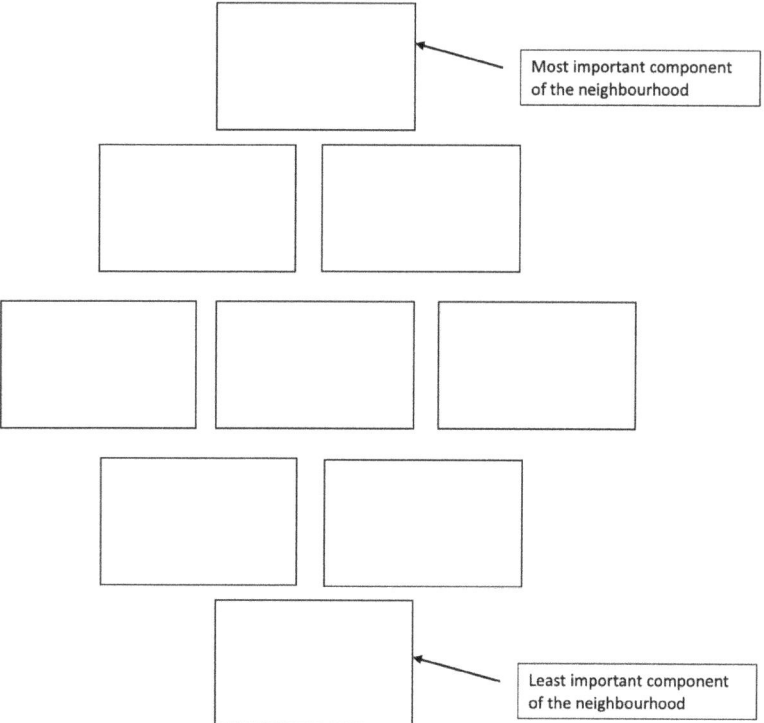

Figure 11.1 Diamond-ranking activity (based on Woolner *et al.*, 2010).
Source: Author

into a class discussion around the criteria that were used in this ranking process, and from there the young people could be challenged to use these same criteria to set out their overarching vision for their neighbourhood.

For the top of the diamond, many groups often chose pictures of hospitals and doctors' surgeries. Others selected houses or schools as being the most important (or within the top three places). For the explanations, the young people often reflected on the importance within their group of feeling 'safe and secure', of being able to have emergency care for them and their families, to access open space or to be able to live a sustainable lifestyle. The young people began to frame their thinking for the future of their area in terms of the values that they discussed as part of this first activity. It was also useful to revisit these values at the end of the overall workshop once decisions had been made in the mock planning committee and to test if these were still important to the young people in making their planning decision.

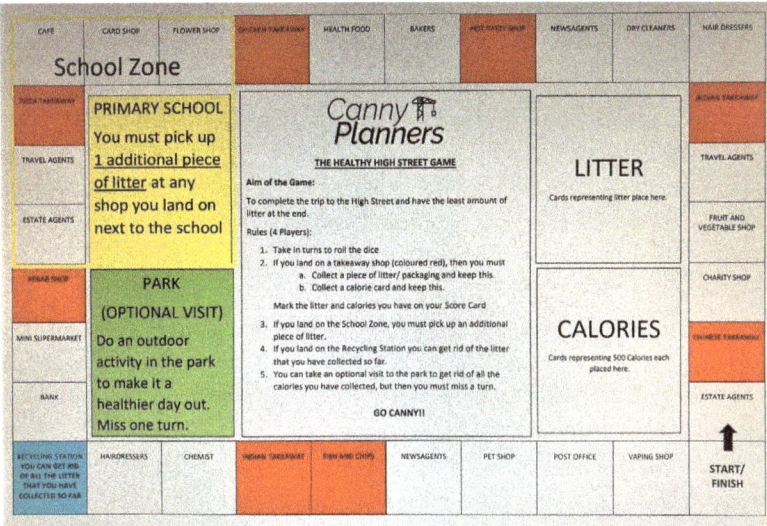

Figure 11.2 'Canny' planners; the Healthy High Street game.
Source: Author

The Healthy High Street board game

Also designed by the planning students, the second activity, the Healthy High Street board game, allows participants to imagine their own walk down a local high street (see Figure 11.2). Participants roll the dice to move around the board, collecting a 'litter' and a 'calorie' token if they land on a hot-food takeaway property. Having already discussed the local area and the issues connected with it, the board game gives the young people the opportunity to explore their own feelings about their fictitious journey through the high street and about how retail premises might differ from each other. They learn to interact and collaborate as game participants, to observe each other's choices on rolling the dice and to discuss outcomes of their decisions as they make their way around the board (Hromek and Roffey, 2009).

Several additional elements can be introduced to a basic circuit of the board, including picking up additional litter in the 'primary-school zone', eliminating all the calorie tokens collected by taking a turn-cancelling, quick-burst run in the park, or being able to remove all their individually accumulated litter by visiting the recycling centre. The young people often say they enjoy playing the game for its competitive elements. Other features on the board allow the student facilitators to lead exploratory discussions around the issues that the game raises, such as the number of hot-food takeaways on the high street; what constitutes a hot-food takeaway; the generation of litter and its impact; the generation of calories and their impact; whether there should be hot-food takeaways near to schools; why taking exercise is important; and the provision of recycling stations (see Figure 11.2).

The game guarantees keen competition and excited voices as the young people find that their attempts to make quick progress around the board can often lead them to having to pick up unexpected litter or a calorie token, which then requires them to quickly get rid of the tokens to stand a chance of winning the game. The winner is the person to finish with the fewest litter tokens, which may not necessarily be the person who finishes first. The planning students take more of an overseeing, listening and where necessary, a referee-type role, enabling the young people to enjoy the experience without formal teaching taking place. The students are also trained and encouraged to ask open and non-intrusive questions to encourage the young people to reflect on their own lifestyles and values (see Table 11.1).

The mock planning committee

Having introduced the issues relating to hot-food takeaways in both the diamond ranking and the board game, the young people are then introduced to a hypothetical scenario for their local high street, where a new takeaway is being proposed. Working in groups and supported by students using their newly acquired questioning techniques, they are encouraged to think about the 'good' and the 'bad' aspects of each proposal from their own youthful perspective, noting these down and giving as much explanation as possible to justify their thinking. These groups then take on a role as a different member of the community, a consultee or a member of the planning committee. The students challenge the young people to think beyond their own circumstances to those, say, of the business community, a residents' group, their parents or a local councillor representing the wider community and potentially the longer-term interest of the neighbourhood (see Table 11.1).

Working in their new roles, the young people develop their arguments 'for' and 'against' the proposal, ready for when they are invited to present to the committee meeting. These arguments are developed through careful use of their own supporting evidence based on their local knowledge. With the planning students' guidance, they formulate short scripts to summarise these opinions and evidence.

Table 11.1 Impact on young people's personal outlook (Hromek and Roffey, 2009)

Key to quotes: YP = young person; PS = planning student; T = teacher	
Interaction with peers and facilitator	'I liked working as a team, I like sharing my opinion and hearing others' opinions.' YP1, 'The group I was helping also learned to communicate between them, instead of shouting and arguing they were taking turns and listening to each other's idea's first.' PS1
Engagement and pride in place and identity development that imagines future self (Prince, 2014)	'I would have this job because it is interesting and enjoyable.' YP2 'The debate gave reality of what real life can be like.' YP3
Questioning of own and others' prior knowledge and understanding of processes and changes	'A real-life context was engaging for them, and they were able to draw on what they know in their community to help them make decisions.' T1 'It helped the young people understand more about their community and how planning decisions can have a huge impact on the health and well-being of residents.' T2
Developing relationships, observing/critiquing others' behaviour	'I liked being able to debate with our friends and being able to talk from the perspective of someone other than you.' YP3 'They were able to "form their own viewpoints"; "understood there were positive and negative points of view"; "able to prioritise different aspects of town planning".' PS2
Internalisation of values	'They learnt what "goes on behind the scenes" in the places they know of – the planning committee session I think got this message across best because they got to act it out themselves.' PS3
Developing emotional literacy	'You have to think about what other people need.' YP4 'I learnt today that you vote to see what the local residents have to say before it gets built.' YP5
Promoting life-long learning (Ruben, 1999)	'It helps them understand more about decision making and how much goes into that and its good for them to know what is available to study at university.' PS4

Using this basic script, members of the mock planning committee can adapt this to their own views to fit the specific location and their own interpretation of the role. The hypothetical example mirrors a recent, real-life planning application's journey through the planning committee, where the proposal is put forward, questions are asked by councillors and interested parties are invited to make their representations. On the invitation of the chair, a vote is then taken by the committee as to whether the application should be approved or refused. The decision then requires the chair to explain the committee's decision.

The young people often surprise themselves as they overcome personal conflict between their own views and those whose mantle they take on. After the final committee decision, the workshop facilitator explains that the proposal is fictional, comparing this and the issues that it raised to what actually happened in the real-life planning application. Planning issues such as the impact on the enjoyment of the area, the appearance of the unit, the premises' effect on litter, traffic and health are the key considerations normally covered in this comparison to the real-life scenario.

The three tables (11.1, 11.2, and 11.3) offer the participants' reflections on their learning during the engagement workshops. These reflections are articulated through three separate lenses: that of the young people (YP); the planning students (PS); and the teachers (T). The tables draw on the key findings of Hromek and Roffey (2009), unless otherwise stated.

Conclusion

This chapter showcased the Canny Planners workshop that was delivered by Newcastle University planning students to local young people in the north-east of England. The workshops focused on hot-food takeaways and comprises three activities that develop young people's learning from a discussion about their local neighbourhood, to taking part in a board game that represents their local high street, to a role-play mock planning committee where they make a decision on whether a fictitious new takeaway premises should be granted planning permission. Tables 11.1, 11.2 and 11.3 detail the perspectives of the young people, the planning students and the schoolteachers once the workshop had taken place. The perspectives confirm that the young people developed skills of working with each other and with the planning students through listening, discussing and negotiating. They had learnt about their local area, the issues relating to hot-food takeaways, and the range of views of community and

Table 11.2 Impact on young people's social and wider world outlook (Hromek and Roffey, 2009)

Key to quotes: YP = young person; PS = planning student; T = teacher	
Enhancing empowerment, own future lives and increasing citizenship (Blanchet-Cohen, 2008; Hart, 1979)	'I would need to think of reasons why I do agree, or I don't agree to make it a fair process.' YP6 'I would need to plan to make sure that it is right for everyone.' YP7 'The project has made me realise how little people, especially children, know about the built environment industry but more specifically that there are such things as town planners!' PS5 'My lifelong dream to be a councillor.' YP8 'I feel this was eye-opening and empowering for our students as this was based on their local area and gave them a sense of awareness of being able to understand the processes of planning of their local high street. I certainly feel it developed in many of them an increased perception of their local area and a sense of awareness of taking ownership of their own well-being.' T3

professional roles that are presented at a planning committee when new takeaways are proposed.

The workshop also promoted the young people's appreciation of their own sense of agency offering reflections on their own authority, the wider world and future place-making around the changes they felt necessary (see Table 11.3). The young people noted the lack of 'fairness' in relation to the location of takeaways, suggesting that there were 'too many' in the area under discussion. They were also keen to stress the need for fairness in decision-making, stating that they did not know how 'planners can please everyone'. The teachers commented that it was good to see the young people looking beyond what might be the more obvious answers in their discussions leading up to the mock committee, as they reflected on how they would improve the community and the local environment.

As facilitators of the workshop, the planning students were able to observe and reflect on the young people's experiences of their own neighbourhoods as they supported them in developing their arguments for and against the hypothetical proposal for a new takeaway outlet. It allowed the planning students to perceive the impact of change and planning

Table 11.3 Creating a young person's sense of agency and a desire to take action

Key to quotes: YP = young person; PS = planning student; T = teacher	
Creating agency/future policy/world position/ future action (Blanchet-Cohen, 2008; Doorn et al., 2013; Hart, 1979)	'Some places in Newcastle have an unfair amount of takeaways.' YP9 'It has to be fair for the environment and its residents.' YP10 'How do they (planners) weigh up all of these issues?' YP11 'How do planners please everyone?' YP12 'Young people obviously care about the future of their community.' PS6 'Fantastic afternoon that really got our children thinking about our local area. It was lovely to get past our initial thoughts and look at the wider picture.' T4 'As well as helping students develop an understanding of the theory and practice of town planning in general, these lessons were able to support and develop students' understanding of the issues around planning for healthy lifestyles, thus, supporting various social, moral, and cultural aspects of the curriculum.' T5
Visioning to bring about change in sustainability, more 'socially sensitive' (Chawla, 2007; Leavenworth et al., 2021; Middlemiss, 2014; Taylor et al., 2012)	'It is taking care of the world and making people's lives easier.' YP13 'I want to improve my local environment.' YP14
Transforming their sense of purpose, own values and thinking (Mezirow, 2006)	'They explored more than just the obvious solution or answer and created alternative viewpoints and thought processes that I did not even think of.' PS7

decisions on the community, rather than reading about it in textbooks, policy documents or through mere speculation. It also enabled them to develop skills in communication working alongside the young people and of explaining planning in as straightforward a manner as possible. The workshop instilled in the students the concept that not only can a very young audience learn about complex planning issues, but they can also make sophisticated arguments by thinking the proposal and its impact through to a future point in time. The workshop feedback demonstrated that the young people progressed through learning about a local planning issue to knowing that their opinion was valid, and also that the planning students could see that engagement with young people brings the significance of real planning issues to life, as they share their knowledge and enthusiasm for their subject.

The teachers' responses reflected on the workshop's benefits in terms of bringing understanding about planning and decisions made within this process; the impact of change on local communities; the development of young people's skills of collaboration; the sense of young people's views being valued; the young people being able to extend their thinking beyond what was immediately obvious to them; linking their learning across different parts of the curriculum; drawing on their local knowledge; and offering insights into further study and roles in the community. The teachers also said how much the young people had learnt about an aspect of their local neighbourhood and about their personal well-being through the lifestyle choices they make.

From a project lead perspective, preparation for the workshop had been key, having previously visited the schools and wider location and gaining an insight into the young people's level of interest in local planning issues. Local hot-food takeaways were already a popular subject of discussion for the young people and their teachers. The topic had also been highlighted as a matter of local concern for the local planning authority. Critically, by taking such a live topic, it immediately made the broader term of 'town planning' much more relevant to the young people. In developing the workshops, the planning students were able to use and extend their existing subject knowledge to set tasks and create questions that would facilitate the young people's own learning around the topic in a local context. Supported by the project lead, students also used their emerging knowledge of a planning process – in this case the planning committee – to promote role play and the benefits of experiential learning, which also proved to be an enjoyable interactive process for all concerned.

Canny Planners has demonstrated that young people's learning about the planned environment can take place at the most sophisticated level where their values and attitudes are explored and reflected on. This creates a firm foundation for personal empowerment for both the young people and for the planning students who facilitate the sessions. Canny Planners has transferred the focus for learning from a more traditional teacher-student relationship, to one where the participants are immersed within the 'live' planning topic under consideration. While many university planning schools deliver modules that take project-based learning as their starting point, Canny Planners promotes student-young person exchange of knowledge and views to generate empowerment on both sides, 'embedding' this knowledge for future use beyond university and reflecting a key theme of this book. Above all, it is the convergence of the two learning trajectories through the role play activities that promotes the transformative learning, where each 'side' gains a clearer appreciation of the other's knowledge and understanding, generating strong, long-lasting mutual benefits. Canny Planners has enabled the students to be immersed within a transformative pedagogy enabling them to develop their own community engagement skills whilst empowering young people for future planning participation.

References

Barratt Hacking, E., R. Barratt and W. Scott. 2007. 'Engaging children: research issues around participation and environmental learning', *Environmental Education Research* 13(4): 529–44.

Bigger, S., and J. Webb, J. 2010. 'Developing environmental agency and engagement through young people's fiction', *Environmental Education Research* 16(3–4): 401–14.

Blanchet-Cohen, N. 2008. 'Taking a stance: child agency across the dimensions of early adolescents' environmental involvement', *Environmental Education Research* 14(3): 257–72.

Bloom, B. S., L. W. Anderson and D. R. Krathwohl. 2001. *A Taxonomy for Learning, Teaching, and Assessing: a revision of Bloom's taxonomy of educational objectives*. New York: Longman.

Breakwell, G. M. 1992. 'Processes of self-evaluation: efficacy and estrangement'. In *Social Psychology of Identity and the Self*. London: Surrey University Press, in association with Academic Press, 35–55.

Brookfield, S. D. 1995. *Becoming a Critically Reflective Teacher*. San Francisco: Jossey Bass.

Cahill, C., and R. A. Hart. 2006. 'Pushing the boundaries: critical international perspectives on child and youth participation – series introduction', *Children, Youth and Environments* 16(2): viii–ix.

Cambridge English Dictionary online, https://dictionary.cambridge.org/dictionary/english/canny (last accessed 8 December 2022).

Chawla, L. 2007. 'Childhood experiences associated with care for the natural world: a theoretical framework for empirical results', *Children Youth and Environments*, 17(4): 144–70.

Daniau, S. 2016. 'The transformative potential of role-playing games: from play skills to human skills', *Simulation & Gaming* 47(4): 423–44.

Doorn, N., and J. O. Kroesen. 2013. 'Using and developing role plays in teaching aimed at preparing for social responsibility', *Science and Engineering Ethics* 19(4): 1513–27.

Fleming, D. 1995. *I'm Different not Dumb: modes of presentation (V.A.R.K.) in the tertiary classroom*. Lincoln, New Zealand: Lincoln University, https://vark-learn.com/wp-content/uploads/2014/08/different_not_dumb.pdf (last accessed 8 December 2022).

Freeman, C., and A. J. Cook. 2019. *Children and Planning*. London: Lund Humphries.

Jenkins, P. 2005. 'Space, place and territory: an analytical framework'. In A. C. Hague and P. Jenkins (eds), *Place Identity, Participation and Planning*. London: Taylor & Francis, 19–37.

Hart, R. A. 1979. *Children's Experience of Place*. New York: Irvington.

Hromek, R., and S. Roffey. 2009. 'Promoting social and emotional learning with games: "it's fun and we learn things"', *Simulation & Gaming* 40(5): 626–44.

Kolb D. A. 1984. *Experiential Learning: experience as the source of learning and development*. Englewood Cliffs NJ: Prentice Hall.

Leavenworth, L. M., and A. Manni. 2021. 'Climate fiction and young learners' thoughts – a dialogue between literature and education', *Environmental Education Research* 27(5): 727–42.

Mezirow, J. 2006. 'An overview on transformative learning'. In J. Crowther and P. Sutherland (eds), *Lifelong Learning: concepts and contexts*. New York: Routledge, 40–54.

Middlemiss, L. 2014. 'Individualised or participatory? Exploring late-modern identity and sustainable development', *Environmental Politics* 23: 929–46.

Nordström, M., and M. Wales. 2019. 'Enhancing urban transformative capacity through children's participation in planning', *Ambio* 48(5): 507–14.

Percy-Smith, B. 2014. 'Reclaiming children's participation as an empowering social process'. In C. Burke and K. Jones (eds), *Education, Childhood and Anarchism*. London: Routledge, 235–46.

Piaget, J. 1950. *The Psychology of Intelligence*, trans. by M. Piercy and D. E. Berlyne. London: Routledge.

Prince, D. 2014. 'What about place? Considering the role of physical environment on youth imagining of future possible selves', *Journal of Youth Studies* 17(6): 697–716.

Prince, M. 2004. 'Does active learning work? A review of the research', *Journal of Engineering Education* 93(3): 223–31.

Ruben, B. D. 1999. 'Simulation, games, and experience-based learning: the quest for a new paradigm for teaching and learning', *Simulation & Gaming* 30: 498–505.

Skelton, T. 2007. 'Children, young people, UNICEF and participation', *Children's Geographies* 5(1–2): 165–81.

Sotto, E. 1995. *When Teaching Becomes Learning: a theory and practice of teaching*. London: Cassell.

Strachan, T. 2016. *Engaging Young People in the Local Development Framework Process*, https://issuu.com/schoolofaplnewcastleuniversity/docs/engaging_young_people_in_the_local_/36 (last accessed 8 December 2022).

Taylor, E. W., and P. Cranton. 2012. *The Handbook of Transformative Learning: theory, research, and practice*. Hoboken NJ: John Wiley & Sons.

Tisdall, E. K. M. 2013. 'The transformation of participation? Exploring the potential of 'transformative participation' for theory and practice around children and young people's participation', *Global Studies of Childhood* 3(2): 183–93.

Townshend, T., and A. Lake. 2017. 'Obesogenic environments: current evidence of the built and food environments', *Perspectives in Public Health* 137(1): 38–44.

Twigger-Ross, C. L., and D. L. Uzzell. 1996. 'Place and identity processes', *Journal of Environmental Psychology* 16(3): 205–20.

UNCRC. 1989. *UNICEF Summary of the UN Convention of the Rights of the Child*, https://www.unicef.org.uk/wp-content/uploads/2010/05/UNCRC_summary-1.pdf (last accessed 8 December 2022).

United Nations. 1981. *General Assembly Resolution 36/28*, http://www.worldlii.org/int/other/UNGA/1981/ (last accessed 8 December 2022).

Valentine, G. 2017. *Public Space and the Culture of Childhood*. London: Routledge.

Visser, K., G. Bolt and R. van Kempen. 2015. '"Come and live here and you'll experience it": youths talk about their deprived neighbourhood', *Journal of Youth Studies* 18(1): 36–52.

White, S. 1996). 'Depoliticising development: the uses and abuses of participation', *Development in Practice* 6(1): 6 15.

Wood, J., D. Bornat and A. Bicquelet-Lock. 2019. *Child Friendly Planning in the UK: a review*, https://www.rtpi.org.uk/media/1633/childfriendlyplanningintheukareview2019.pdf (last accessed 8 December 2022).

Woolner, P., J. Clark, E. Hall, L. Tiplady, U. Thomas and K. Wall. 2010. 'Pictures are necessary but not sufficient: using a range of visual methods to engage users about school design', *Learning Environments Research* 13(1): 1–22.

12
City-to-city learning as impulse for engaged urban pedagogy

Raphael Sedlitzky and Fernando Santomauro

The internationalisation of cities as an enabler for learning and co-operation

Cities have emerged to be epicentres of globalisation, expressed through their concurrently increasing internationalisation and manifested in growing diversity but also inequality (Bassens and van Meeteren, 2014; Harvey, 2006; Sassen, 2001). This increasing internationalisation of cities facilitates growing co-operation of local governments across national borders. Cities from different countries and contexts increasingly join forces to tackle contemporary urban challenges. This knowledge exchange between cities regarding all aspects of sustainable urban development is also referred to as city-to-city learning (Bontenbal, 2010). Even though the financial volume of development assistance that is provided through city-to-city learning is relatively low compared to bilateral aid agreements, city-to-city learning has proven to be very effective in the mobilisation of local governments for global development objectives such as the sustainable development goals or the Paris Agreement (Latek, 2017). Furthermore, it is a chance to establish a learning process that draws from different urban realities while overcoming simple unilateral knowledge export. In this contribution, the authors will be drawing from their own experience with city-to-city learning that they gained as practitioners in this field. Both authors share the common experience to work for the world secretariat of a major city network. In this role, they have been involved in the organisation of a series of city-to-city learnings. They can each draw on additional individual experiences regarding international co-operation and sustainable urban development that include academia and direct engagements with cities in Latin America.

The authors build in this contribution on the lessons that they learned while working with different cities on the continent and reflect on city-to-city learning and its implications for sustainable urban development. The central aim of this contribution is to present city-to-city learning as an instrument that exemplifies the strengths of cross-cultural knowledge exchange of urban actors and as a form of engaged urban pedagogy. Furthermore, it tries to demonstrate how such mutual exchange can be an accelerator for sustainable urban development. Last, it will be argued that successful instruments from international co-operation and urban planning practice, such as city-to-city learning, can provide fruitful inspiration for the higher education system and especially for the training of future urban practitioners.

Urban learning as comparative and collaborative exercise

Learning in the context of urbanism has always been conceived comparatively as the study of urban forms and organisation that happens mostly through comparison to other places (McFarlane, 2011: 28). City-to-city learning as an instrument that confronts urban practitioners with different urban realities builds on this assumption and creates a setting where participants are enabled to learn from elsewhere (Robinson, 2016a). Historically, comparative approaches have a long tradition in social science, including disciplines working on urban studies. This includes major schools of thought like the Marxist and Weberian tradition, and other modernist concepts that have stronger roots in urban studies, such as the social ecology of the Chicago school (Robinson, 2011). Nevertheless, all these approaches have in common that theory-making was inspired by the observation of major northern cities. Consequently, urban theories with the aspiration to be globally valid were deducted without the consideration of cities at the global periphery. This entails not just the exclusion of most cities in the Global South, but also the neglect of smaller and more peripheral cities in the Global North. The increasing critique regarding such a modernist comparative urbanism in the 1970s and 1980s, together with a general turn towards post-structural approaches in social science, led to a decline of comparative approaches in the last decades of the twentieth century (Nijman, 2007). However, since the turn of the century, comparative approaches in urban studies are experiencing a renaissance (Robinson, 2016b, 2011, 2006; McFarlane, 2012,

2011, 2010; Peck, 2015; Lees, 2012; Nijman, 2007). This new generation of scholars can be characterised by the ambition to overcome the imperfections of modernist comparative urbanism, such as the categorisation of cities in cultural hemispheres or in developed and underdeveloped cities. The avoidance of such *a priori* categorisation allows the proposition of a postcolonial perspective in comparative urbanism (Robinson, 2006: 41–2). The central recognition that underlies this change of thought is that learning through differences is at least equally revealing than learning through the comparison of similarities (McFarlane, 2010; Robinson, 2006: 62). This presents a rupture with the widespread practice in urban development to use established good practices that are mainly western cities such as Copenhagen, Barcelona or New York and to intent to rebuild it elsewhere. This rupture also paves the way for mutual urban learning across geographical and cultural boundaries. In this way, contemporary comparative approaches provide a solid theoretical foundation to assess city-to-city learning.

Another important aspect is the acknowledgement that the historical concept of teaching as a 'one-way channel' is becoming obsolete. Interactive learning with different levels of equality and mutuality among students and teachers has proven to be more effective (Topping *et al.*, 2017: 8–10). This applies especially to city-to-city learning as it enables two important characteristics of the instruments. First, a postcolonial learning process between cities of the Global South and cities of the Global North (Topping, 2005). Second, a participative approach to learning that goes beyond the engagement of established stakeholders and addresses the whole and diverse landscape of urban actors. More concrete, it brings together local actors such as planners and experts, politicians and other officials, non-governmental organisations (NGOs), local initiatives and civil society representatives. Moreover, it can involve universities and other educational institutions or even international experts and agencies. Ideally, a setting is created where all participants are equally considered students and teachers and reciprocal learning processes are encouraged. The engagement of citizens and civil society groups in such learning experiences is at least equally important as the representation of city officials and experts. The participation of local NGOs and civil society associations such as neighbourhood groups, religious communities or other civil society members enriches the knowledge exchange by representing the diversity of urban societies. This enables a multi-actor knowledge exchange that draws from different urban realities and can inspire and reinforce collaborative approaches in all participating cities. In other words, it is a chance to combine collaborative urban planning with an international learning experience. This is important as collective learning is a requirement for urban innovation and for progressive urbanism in general (McFarlane, 2011: 1–2). A declared result of such exchange is the establishment of long-term relations between the participating cities and actors that facilitate continuing mutual learning. Once established, these communities of urban actors can continue operating quite autonomously. In this regard, the role of city networks or other forms of associations that reunite subnational governments must be mentioned. These platforms have not just become established actors in international relations, they are also leading facilitators of city-to-city learning (Lee and Jung, 2018; Moodley, 2009). Together with more established actors in international co-operation such as development agencies, development banks or UN-agencies, they promote city-to-city learning as an effective form of partnership-based development co-operation (Ilgen et al., 2019).

City-to-city learning in practice – empirical examples from Latin America

After embedding city-to-city learning in an adequate theoretical and contextual framework, two case studies will be used to illustrate the mechanism and potential of this instrument. To begin, a characterisation will be provided to present the different actors engaged in city-to-city learning. This refers to the different stakeholders from the participating cities, including local planners, city officials, private sector, universities or civil society organisations, but also to the facilitator for such exchanges. The facilitator plays a passive role regarding the knowledge exchange and creation, but an active and essential role in the organisation of this process. This role is frequently taken by development agencies or banks, city networks and local government associations or NGOs. The facilitator is also responsible for the creation of a setting that ensures that the cultural, geographic or economic backgrounds of the participants are put aside to avoid *a priori* categorisations. Given this precondition, extremely diverse groups of urban actors from different urban realities can learn from each other in a mutual way.

Another important premise for a successful knowledge exchange is the definition of a common urban challenge that all participants share. Figure 12.1 illustrates how this provides the entry point for the different actors of each city and builds the bridge to exchange experiences between participants. Once this common challenge can be identified, the problem-based learning and co-operation between the different actors can begin. Additionally, international experts sometimes support the knowledge

Figure 12.1 Common challenge as entry point for actors in city-to-city learning (Sedlitzky and Santomauro, 2022).

exchange but remain in a rather passive role and just support local participants in the development of their ideas and solutions. The concrete form of exchange can differ and may include joined workshops, site visits, staff-exchange and secondments or all other forms of co-operation. The long-term goal of city-to-city learning is the establishment of relations between the participating cities that bridge the different urban realities and allow a knowledge transfer that goes beyond the initial exchange. Such a permanent knowledge transfer requires a solid relation between the actors and the fundament therefore is normally laid during the first encounters. Therefore, in person meetings are preferred over virtual formats. The interpersonal relations that may sometimes evolve into friendships are the best guarantee for long-term knowledge transfer. It is regular exchange on current topics or challenges or sometimes just a chat that keeps such relations alive. More formal co-operation, such as delegation visits or joined conference participation, are of course the culmination of a permanent exchange, but the maintenance of these relations requires primarily social bonding between actors. The next two examples from Latin America will illustrate different ways that this can be translated into practice.

Urban agriculture as an enabler for co-operation between Guarulhos, Belo Horizonte and Rosario

The urban agriculture project 'Guarulhos seeding the future',[1] which took place from 2009 to 2013, brought together cities from Brazil and

Argentina. It emerged from the Mercociudades city network that reunites and facilitates exchange between Latin American cities from the whole continent. The project gathered municipal experts in urban agriculture from the Brazilian cities of Guarulhos and Belo Horizonte, and the Argentinian city of Rosario. The starting idea was to jointly improve Guarulhos local policy on urban agriculture. Further, it involved a series of other stakeholders such as local schools, neighbourhood associations or businesses and was directly supported by local politicians. The basis for this knowledge exchange was the recognised expertise of Belo Horizonte and Rosario regarding community-based urban agriculture. The city of Belo Horizonte had successfully developed a programme where school gardens were managed by students as part of the curriculum. The gardens provided food for the school kitchens and even for local communities in the neighbourhood. This initiative addressed thereby several local challenges such as sustainable local food production, community building, dietary education and urban greening.

In turn, the city of Rosario had extensive experience in urban agriculture projects that were driven by local communities and used agro-ecological management techniques. Guarulhos could also draw on some experience regarding urban agriculture. The city had just finished a project where unemployed women, registered at Guarulhos's social programme, occupied empty public land to grow fruits and vegetables. These organic products were then sold at local markets and generated an additional income for the participating woman. Thereby the involved citizens addressed similar challenges like the project in Belo Horizonte and could contribute to a greener urban environment and healthy and sustainable local food production. Furthermore, the initiative integrated different international and local stakeholders, receiving support by the Food and Agriculture Organization of the United Nations (UN-FAO) and the Federal University of Sao Carlos (Brazil). These two organisations supported the local actors with their international and scientific experience in urban agriculture. This included technical advice regarding the used technology but also recommendations based on the experience that these two institutions had with similar projects. Therefore, the knowledge exchange could successfully facilitate the transfer of best-practice solutions but also provided the opportunity that the participants could exchange their practical experiences regarding relevant technologies and techniques. All involved actors could draw on their pre-existing experiences, but local citizens benefited especially from the expertise of the UN-FAO and the University of Sao Carlos regarding state-of-the-art technologies. These two institutions in return, learned valuable lessons on how to implement urban agriculture projects in different urban settings. The involvement of public schools together with the financial support of the participating cities which covered all costs, could reduce possible barriers and ensure the inclusivity of the project. Furthermore, the project[2] generated learning methodologies[3] for the continuous training of local residents as successful urban farmers.[4] These methodologies were based on the experience of the participating cities and pedagogically supervised by the UN-FAO[5] and the University of Sao Carlos. Finally, the political support from officials of both cities led to an institutionalisation of the gathered knowledge in the form of improved urban policies on urban agriculture. The lessons learned from this exchange inspired similar projects that followed.[6] Furthermore, the project could reinforce the contacts between the involved cities and built the basis for an increased exchange and co-operation that lasted many years beyond the initial project.

The Mercocidudades network in which these cities are reunited facilitated this close relation, but the example also shows that a joined co-operation project such as 'Guarulhos seeding the future' can create even stronger ties than just the common participation in a city network.[7] In this way, the exchange achieved the same objective as most north-south development co-operation projects, but without major financial support and without unilateral knowledge export. The example shows that south-south city co-operation can provide the necessary expertise regarding technologies and techniques to enable cities to address pending urban issues. While classical development co-operation is centred on financial aid, this example demonstrates that local and often tacit knowledge is an equally valuable resource. This refers to the fact that municipal experts in the global south have commonly long experience in the management of local challenges with limited resources. Furthermore, they are well aware of the specific needs and priorities of southern cities. This knowledge is also difficult to impart and must be gained while working on the ground and in the exchange with more experienced colleagues. Another strength of south-south city co-operation is its ability to perceive all participants as equal partners and to generate a long-term co-operation culture among the involved actors. This applies of course to inter-city co-operation. However, an exchange such as this example can, due to its participatory character, also improve co-operation within the same city. Finally, the example shows that this form of co-operation might have even a higher impact than short-term financial aid and ensures that local priorities are addressed.

Waste management as catalyser for triangular city-to-city co-operation

City-to-city learning is not just limited to cities from two countries, it can be extended to triangular co-operation that includes cities from several countries. A good example is the extension of the Latin American co-operation to African and European cities that illustrates the potential of horizontal and multifaceted south-north co-operation. In this example, the facilitator behind the exchange was not a city network but national governments. In 2012, the Brazilian and French national government launched a call for city-to-city co-operation between Brazilian, French and African local governments. A joined proposal from the Mozambican cities Maputo and Matola, the French municipality Seine-Saint-Denis and the Brazilian city of Guarulhos was the first to be selected from this call and received substantial funding from the national governments of France and Brazil. The joined proposal of the cities was to facilitate a knowledge exchange on urban waste management and to establish a culture of co-operation that could provide long-term support regarding technologies and capacity building to the cities of Maputo and Matola. A central objective of this co-operation was to support the cities of Maputo and Matola in the development of a regional solid waste management plan. Compared to more traditional approaches in development co-operation, the support of the Mozambican cities was not led by international consultants or other experts. Instead, it was jointly organised by municipal experts and the international relation departments from the Brazilian and French cities. The city of Guarulhos could draw on its recent experience of integrating informal waste collector co-operatives in the urban waste management. Seine-Saint-Denis could draw on the experience of developing a regional and inter-municipal approach to waste management.[8] However, the cities from Mozambique were seen as equal partners and closely involved in the conceptualisation of the learning exchange. Additional expertise was contributed by Mozambican civil society organisations, local government associations and universities of the respective countries. Within the project, several on-site workshops and training were organised and could enable the cities of Maputo and Matola to develop a regional solid-waste management concept. Especial importance was paid to the inclusiveness, efficiency and alignment of the concept to the local conditions and priorities. To guarantee these characteristics, the participation of diverse local stakeholders was essential. For that, the same local actors who had already been successfully part of the development of Guarulhos solid-waste master plan[9] in 2011 were included in the learning process in Mozambique. These actors were waste-collector co-operatives, local businesses, neighbourhood associations and municipal agencies. In this way, the waste management concept could be developed in a collaborative manner that reflected the needs and interests of all local stakeholders, including, for example, informal waste collectors or women collectives. However, the beneficiaries of this exchange were not just the Mozambican cities but also the municipality of Seine-Saint-Denis and the city of Guarulhos. The French and Brazilian partners gained valuable experience in international co-operation. The successful transfer of their waste management policies confirmed the functionality of these approaches in other urban settings. Moreover, this engagement proved the capacity of Seine-Saint-Denis and Guarulhos to become a recognised actor in international relations. Even after the exchange on site, the involved cities, including the individual participants, remained widely in contact. In fact, even new learning initiatives have since then arisen from this initial co-operation. One example for such a spin-off activity is the city-to-city learning on cemetery waste and management which involved the city of Guarulhos and the Mozambican cities Maputo, Matola and Nampula. This activity was even financed with own resources[10] from participating cities and did not receive external funding. Moreover, these cities continued to engage in city-to-city learning in other settings and on other topics such as participatory budget or collaborative urban planning. This series of co-operation between and cities from Brazil and Mozambique was very active for many years and inspired several other spin-off activities involving new actors.[11] It can therefore be summarised that this first exchange in 2012 functioned as a catalyst for co-operation and learning between local governments.

City-to-city co-operation as an instrument to foster inclusion, learning and empowerment

The two case studies show that city-to-city learning is a solid tool to facilitate knowledge and policy transfer between local governments. Moreover, it enables the establishment of long-term relations between cities that pave the way for continuing co-operation and exchange. When looking at the mechanism of this form of knowledge exchange, the two examples demonstrate that it is not about the exchange or co-operation between cities as abstract entities, but about the interaction of urban actors from different cities. If cities are understood as an assemblage of urban actors that jointly shape and develop urban realities, city-to-city learning is about facilitating heuristic exchange between these urban actors. 'Heuristic', in this regard, refers to the condition that the involved actors learn in this exchange from each other and thereby increase their capacity to deal with urban challenges. Therefore, the establishment of certain structures that facilitate and institutionalise long-term co-operation is beneficial. Many cities from the two earlier examples established municipal learning and co-operation departments for this reason. These departments are dedicated to the facilitation of knowledge exchange and co-operation between cities. Cities that have such departments are more likely to maintain permanent relations with other local governments and are also less dependent on the support of third parties regarding co-operation projects. Another way to consolidate co-operation and exchange between cities is through organisation in associations and networks. The increasing number of such entities stresses the growing interest of local governments in international co-operation. Major city networks such as ICLEI, Global Covenant of Mayors, C40 or the United Cities and Local Governments confirm that this is a global phenomenon. This alliance of cities and their international engagement also strengthens the role of local governments within the multi-level governance system. In this sense, city-to-city learning is a form to empower cities in two directions. First, it fosters solidarity and inclusion by renegotiating the horizontal relations between cities. Second, it strengthens the role of cities by renegotiating the vertical integration of local governments in the national and international multi-level governance system.

Furthermore, the two case studies confirm the central assumptions of comparative urbanism that were presented at the beginning of this chapter. The productive learning between urban actors from the Global South demonstrates this through two important aspects. First, that it is possible to learn from elsewhere; and second, that this elsewhere does not have to be a northern city. The example of the co-operation between Brazilian and Argentinian cities on urban agriculture demonstrates that innovative urban policies can emerge equally in southern cities and can successfully inspire repetition in other cities. Moreover, the direct knowledge transfer between southern cities frequently better reflects local demands. In addition, the examples of triangular co-operation highlight the value of mutual learning experiences between northern and southern cities. However, this is still a radical counterproposal to one-sided knowledge transfer from the north to the south. The case of triangular co-operation between cities from Brazil, Mozambique and France shows that a French municipality can also benefit from the knowledge of Brazilian cities while improving its international profile through the assistance provided to cities in Mozambique. The Brazilian cities in this case could share their knowledge on solid-waste management with the cities in Mozambique while counting on the support of a French municipality regarding regional and inter-administrative co-ordination. Moreover, these two examples represent an inclusive and participative form of urban development. The approach is characterised by high accessibility, as it requires few resources from the participating cities. Furthermore, it brings together diverse urban actors and enables them to collaboratively address urban challenges. This refers not just to the integration of school communities, vulnerable citizens such as informal workers, NGOs or other civil society groups in the planning process, but also to their empowerment through exchange with similar urban actors from other cities. In this sense, urban challenges are jointly approached, and solutions are developed according to local needs and priorities.

Implications for engaged urban pedagogy

What the reflection on city-to-city learning tried to demonstrate is that urban learning beyond northern archetype cities is possible and valuable. The intention behind the presentation of these examples from Latin America is to bridge impressions from urban practice with current academic theory. With this contribution, the authors are aiming to underpin the arguments of comparative urbanism represented by scholars such as Robinson or McFarlane. More concrete, the presented examples confirm the central claim that southern and peripheral cities can equally enrich the understanding of urban development. This contribution intends to demonstrate that such a comparative perspective is not just heuristically valuable for academic assessments, but also provides an excellent basis for knowledge exchange in the form of city-to-city learning. The examples stress that city-to-city learning is receiving increasing attention and has become an established instrument in international co-operation. It is an instrument that allows a collaborative approach to urban challenges as it involves diverse urban actors including more marginalised groups. It has the objective to address urban challenges through exchange and to provide concrete solutions through collective problem-solving process. Moreover, it empowers cities to internationalise their agenda and to accelerate sustainable urban development. In a rapidly urbanising world, such approaches that foster solidarity, co-operation and empowerment between cities are much needed.

In view of these findings, the question arises of what urban planners and other professionals involved in urban development can learn from these examples. How can higher education acknowledge the increasing internationalisation and networking of cities in the training of new generations of urban professionals? And maybe even more importantly, how can the principles of inclusion, learning and empowerment that distinguish city-to-city learning, be more strongly anchored in higher education curricula?

First, it is important to further mainstream a postcolonial understanding of urban learning in academic teaching. The first sensibilisation for urban topics happens mostly in the environment where students grow up. This can be their hometowns or the university towns that they moved to for their studies. It is in these places where they consolidate their interest in the functioning and development of cities, and where perhaps the first excursions and small research projects during their undergraduate degree take place. Later, they will be confronted with internationally established good practices regarding urban development and might even visit a few of them. It is important to note that most of these examples are either northern metropolises or southern cities that, in good practice, are perceived by northern standards. This comparison of cities is an essential part of the urban learning process and should have no negative connotations *per se* (McFarlane, 201: 28). On the contrary, it can be argued that urban role models or archetypes are an important part of socialisation as an urban planner. It is therefore critical that academic teachers steer their students carefully and make them aware of colonial traps that this learning process can entail. What is meant by this is the uncritical use of northern cities and planning approaches as models and guidelines. Even though Copenhagen, New York and Barcelona are, without any doubt, inspiring examples of urbanisation, these cities are not always valid models for the (one-sided) comparison with more peripheral cities. What this highlights is that academic teachers must be careful when creating archetypes that will influence the education and even socialisation of future urban planners.

Second, it is not just the academic teachers at university that set the norms and standards for young urban planners. This also applies to many other urban practitioners that influence the discourse in urban studies. It can even be argued that every actor involved in urban development shares the responsibility to show younger colleagues that the diversity of cities is one of the most fascinating aspects of urbanisation. In this sense, the responsibility of teaching goes beyond classrooms and involves not just academic professors.

Third, in a globalised world, urban planners should not just appreciate different forms of urbanisation but be able to read diverse urban morphologies. Therefore, a high level of awareness regarding different planning cultures is required. This allows urban planners to learn from places with different cultural settings and facilitates exchange with colleagues from other places. Furthermore, it helps to avoid a certain blindness that oversees the needs but also the good practices from less familiar places that are typically identical with more peripheral cities in the Global North and South.

Fourth, academic education must strongly reflect the increasing internationalisation of cities and the rapidly changing working environment of urban planners. The presented examples of city-to-city learning show that the probability of being confronted with transcultural projects is certainly increasing. This is not just valid for those who might be working in an international co-operation context. It is equally valid for many planners that will be joining big consultancies that operate international projects or even for planners that will work on projects in super diverse cities in their home countries. In this regard, transcultural competences and foreign languages are becoming increasingly demanded skills. Academic education should reflect these demands through the integration of respective activities in the curriculums. A concrete proposal for that could be the enhanced support of student mobility in the form of exchange semesters and short-term research stays abroad. Additionally, increased mobility of university lecturers could further diversify academic teaching.

Fifth, the increasing internationalisation of cities and urban development is leading to a diversification of stakeholders and regulatory guidelines. Global sustainability frameworks (e.g., the sustainable development goals and the Paris Agreement) have become guiding principles in urban development and illustrate the relevance of global frameworks at the local level. However, they co-exist with local and national regulations. This leads to a diversification of regulatory guidelines through an increasing and direct incorporation of global guiding principles in urban development. The same blurring of the scales can be observed for the stakeholders in contemporary urban development. International bodies such as UN agencies have not just become notable actors regarding the regulative setting of urban development but are also increasingly relevant actors in the implementation of projects. This applies particularly to projects in the field of international co-operation, although it is not limited exclusively to this area. Moreover, the diversification of stakeholders further includes a growing number of philanthropies, different city networks, development agencies and all forms of private public partnership that address sustainable urban development. This is another dynamic that must be mainstreamed in the curricula to provide young urban planners with sufficient orientation regarding the increasingly diverse and rapidly changing landscape of urban actors.

The last conclusion that can be drawn concerns the empowerment of peripheral cities and more vulnerable urban citizens. The examples illustrate that innovative forms of urban development such as city-to-city learning can mobilise and engage cities and citizens that are too often overlooked. Moreover, it exemplifies that urban planning can make an important contribution to the creation of inclusive urban societies that are a precondition for truly sustainable cities. All actors in academic teaching must be therefore encouraged to further anchor this challenge as an immanent responsibility of urban planners.

Notes

1. 'Guarulhos semeando o future' in Portuguese.
2. Summarised by Mercociudades, participants and partners: https://sursurmercociudades.org/sursur/?q=es/node/95; https://1ffdc373-e964-439c-9855-d18e7471d78f.filesusr.com/ugd/1d9679_60a324012f7f414ca2a9181471467cdf.pdf; and https://balancocri.wixsite.com/balanco/in-mercocidades.
3. Within the project, a training tool was developed to support the training of new urban farmers in the city, https://1ffdc373-e964-439c-9855-d18e7471d78f.filesusr.com/ugd/1d9679_97480e6f93de41b380736eab1dfe5a6e.pdf.
4. More can be found here, https://sursurmercociudades.org/sursur/?q=es/node/97.
5. As a consequence of the project, the city of Guarulhos signed the Milan Pact on urban food policy, https://blogfonari.wordpress.com/2016/12/05/guarulhos-integra-pacto-de-milao-sobre-politica-de-alimentacao-urbana/.
6. Since then, the project is one of the references for local universities, https://integri.com.br/wp-content/uploads/2020/06/GALLO-Rodrigo-MATTIOLI-Thiago-A-atuac%CC%A7a%CC%83o-das-cidades-nas-Relac%CC%A7o%CC%83es-Intenacionais.pdf.
7. The project triggered spin-off activities on urban agriculture and local economic development within the Mercociudades network: https://sursurmercociudades.org/pt-br/guarulhos-semeando-o-futuro-en-el-congreso-regional-de-agricultura-urbana-de-sao-paulo/. Furthermore, the project led to the creation of a specific platform to facilitate south-south co-operation with cities, universities and other partners: https://sursurmercociudades.org/sursur/.
8. A project report was produced by the city of Guarulhos: https://1ffdc373-e964-439c-9855-d18e7471d78f.filesusr.com/ugd/1d9679_16e578c57b8d4be5ab045c54c521fe38.pdf. A website was also created to report other south-south and triangular city-to-city learnings that involved the city of Guarulhos: https://balancocri.wixsite.com/balanco/trilateral.
9. For more about the collective process of Guarulhos solid-waste master plan (2011) see http://arquivo.ambiente.sp.gov.br/cpla/2017/05/guarulhos.pdf.
10. More about the technical visits of African cities to Guarulhos that emerged from the project can be seen here: https://www.youtube.com/watch?v=dAGNfsUkS6U.
11. More about co-operation and learning activities between Brazilian and Mozambican cities that followed the project can be found here: https://balancocri.wixsite.com/balanco/anamm-fnp; https://www.uclg.org/en/media/news/learning-city-city-cooperation; and https://youtu.be/lWPRwjw30N8.

References

Bassens, D., and M. van Meeteren. 2014. 'World cities under conditions of financialized globalization: towards an augmented world city hypothesis', *Progress in Human Geography* 39(6): 752–75.

Bontenbal, M. 2009. 'Strengthening urban governance in the south through city-to-city cooperation: towards an analytical framework', *Habitat International* 33: 181–9.

Harvey, D. 2006. *Spaces of Capitalism: towards a theory of uneven geographical development*. London: Verso.

Ilgen, S., F. Sengers and A. Wardekke. 2019. 'City-to-city learning for urban resilience: the case of water squares in Rotterdam and Mexico City'. *Water* 11(5): 983.

Latek, M. 2017. *Decentralised Cooperation in the Context of the 2030 Agenda*. Brussels: European Parliamentary Research Service.

Lees, L. 2012. 'The geography of gentrification: thinking through comparative urbanism', *Progress in Human Geography* 36(2): 155–71.

Lee, T., and H. Jung. 2018. 'Mapping city-to-city networks for climate change action: geographic bases, link modalities, functions, and activity', *Journal of Cleaner Production* 182: 96–104.

McFarlane, C. 2010. 'The comparative city: knowledge, learning, urbanism', *International Journal of Urban and Regional Research* 34(4): 725–42.

McFarlane, C. 2011. *Learning the City: knowledge and translocal assemblage*. Oxford: Blackwell.

McFarlane, C., and J. Robinson. 2012. 'Introduction: experiments in comparative urbanism', *Urban Geography* 33(6): 765–73.

Moodley, S. 2019. 'Defining city-to-city learning in southern Africa: exploring practitioner sensitivities in the knowledge transfer process', *Habitat International* 85: 34–40.

Nijman, J. 2007. 'Introduction: comparative urbanism', *Urban Geography* 28(1): 1–6.

Peck, J. 2015. 'Cities beyond compare?', *Regional Studies* 49(1): 160–82.

Robinson, J. 2006. *Ordinary Cities: between modernity and development*. London: Routledge.

Robinson, J. 2011. 'Cities in a world of cities: the comparative gesture', *International Journal of Urban and Regional Research* 35(1): 1–23.

Robinson, J. 2016a. 'Thinking cities through elsewhere: comparative tactics for a more global urban studies', *Progress in Human Geography* 40(1): 3–29.

Robinson, J. 2016b. 'Comparative urbanism: new geographies and cultures of theorizing the urban', *International Journal of Urban and Regional Research* 40(1): 187–99.

Santomauro, F. 2010. 'The best place in the world is here and now/El mejor lugar del mundo es acá y ahora'. In *Revista Diálogo: construyendo integración regional desde las ciudades*. Rosario: Mercociudades.

Santomauro, F. 2017. 'Local governments and a new possible world/Os governos locais e um novo mundo possível/'. In *Paradiplomacia do Estado do Rio de Janeiro (2007–2017)*. Niterói: Imprensa Oficial do Estado do Rio de Janeiro.

Sassen, S. 2001. *The Global City: New York, London, Tokyo*. Princeton NJ: Princeton University Press.

Topping, K. 2005. 'Trends in peer learning', *Educational Psychology* 25(6): 631–45.

Topping, K., C. Buchs, D. Duran and H. van Kee. 2017. *Effective Peer Learning: from principles to practical implementation*. London: Routledge.

United Cities and Local Governments (UCLG). 2017. *Local and Regional Governments Report to the 2017 HLPF: national and sub-national governments on the way towards the localization of the SDGs*. Barcelona: UCLG.

13
Building together and co-building the city: do it yourself!

Dominique Lancrenon, Stephan Hauser, Patrick Le Bellec and Melia Delplanque

Contextualisation of the actions

This chapter concerns initiatives that seek to encourage participation of local inhabitants in the development of their city, the metropolitan area of Dunkirk, in the north of France. It focuses on two 'real world' engagement projects (to borrow the term from Chapter 1), En Rue (meaning 'on the street') and Fab Lab Effet Papillon (meaning 'butterfly effect'), and offers reflections on some of the key moments that were decisive in their development. This gives insights into work that is live and ongoing, and collaborations involving people from across higher education institutions, public authorities, civil society, non-governmental organisations and local businesses. While the piece cannot possibly represent the participatory initiatives in Dunkirk in all their fullness or the perspectives of the many and diverse actors involved, it aims to express concerns around participatory democracy for planning practice in Europe and to explore associated challenges for building together and co-building the city.

As envisioned in the 'Charter of Participatory Democracy: a call for action towards a balanced democratic system' (ECTP-CEU, 2016), the nature and goals of participatory democracy are tightly bound with urban development and place-making. The basic principles of participatory democracy via spatial planning make clear the importance of the governance context in Europe where national and local authorities are expected to engage, and indeed lead, in promoting participation. Bouche-Florin (2019) set them out thus:

- We are convinced that the quality of living requires access to essential services and mobility or particular needs of specific social groups. These must be considered human rights.
- Authorities from local to national level have, and must assume, a shared leading role in spearheading the promotion of community participation. The success of any democratic participation process depends on the commitment of these authorities.
- We consider as essential the recognition and enhancement of the role played by civil society, through associations and groups of individuals, as key player and driving force in developing and sustaining a true participatory democracy.
- We are convinced that real-time information systems need to be managed, interpreted and properly checked with respect to lay knowledge.

At the same time, and equally as important, they also highlight the fundamental value of citizen inclusion in the city and the need for commitment to engagement by others. This echoes long-standing arguments for the value of lay knowledge in cities to drive socially just urban development and spatial planning (e.g., Fuller and Moore, 2017; Natarajan, 2019). It relates to built environment professionals and scholars' interest in understanding citizens' lived experience of diverse social needs (Altomonte *et al.*, 2020). It also points to the live nature of urban processes and the challenges raised in respect of knowledge and learning.

The live nature of information and lay knowledges described suggests that participatory democracy city-making arises from a specific skill set, comprising abilities to 'make' the city *materially as well as politically*. The endeavour is one of inclusion and co-production. Collectively, those involved have the various capacities needed for building the city together.

In reflections on Dewey's writings on democracy and education (e.g., Englund, 2000), the case has been well made that pedagogy needs to unlock skills for deliberation and analysis of structural powers, which can underpin full citizenship. As Bouche-Florin puts it, 'democracy assumes a level of critical questioning of decision-making from all who engage with the system, thus socially constructed knowledge and social studies were prerequisites for the realisation of democracy' (Bouche-Florin, 2019: 125). This argument is prominent within works on citizenship, including 'critical literacy' of youth activists (Bishop, 2015) and global consciousness (e.g., Alviar-Martin and Baildon, 2016), which recognise the importance of a more critical pedagogy to sense-making and communication via textual works (Lankshear and McLaren, 1993).

The material dimensions of constructing and performing city-making are needed for co-production. This means that the democratic work centres on processes of building (collaboratively constructing), which include processes of deliberation (participating in communications). The physical presence of actors is crucial in building together and co-building the city, they are needed for the activities of 'do it yourself' urbanism. As discussed in the rest of the chapter, the En Rue and Fab Lab Effet Papillon initiatives in Dunkirk involved both material and deliberative participatory processes, with social interactions for the production of shared or 'common' goods, such as works of art, urban spaces, local amenities, and more.

Reflecting on En Rue and Fab Lab Effet Papillon

The authors of this chapter are involved directly in two Dunkirk projects – En Rue and Fab Lab Effet Papillon – and the work involved in setting up active processes to develop participatory democracy in spatial planning within communities. They share their insights and reflections on the steps of the project and experiences, giving their perspective as built environment practitioners. They are also all members of Territoire Europe, an association that aims to create concrete experiences with groups of residents and actors involved in the transformation of neighbourhoods. Territoire Europe was established in 2019 by spatial planners from different European countries and diverse fields of work who wished to share their experiences and conduct experiments on participatory democracy. The overall approach of Territoire Europe is based on the charter of participatory democracy, which has been adopted by the European Council of Spatial Planners – Conseil Européen des Urbanistes (ECTP-CEU, 2016). In the rest of the chapter, the diverse issues, challenges and problems are explained based on grounded experiences from En Rue and Fab Lab Effet Papillon. Discussion surrounding these projects centres on three main challenges of participatory democracy, which were seen at the outset of the projects. Challenge 1: while developing common spaces and common goods with a collective, how can the risk of appropriation and exclusion from one group to another be managed?

There is a real risk that must be recognised, and the inevitable imperfection of commons is powerfully expressed as the 'tragedy of the commons' (Hardin, 1961). However, this has not prevented the search for solutions, nor did Hardin suggest that it should (Battersby, 2017).

Indeed, the diverse place-based collectives in Dunkirk set out to find ways to resolve this dilemma in their localities. Drawing on the principles of participatory democracy, recognition and enhancement of the role of civil society is necessary. This would require respectful behaviour, mutual willingness by all members to adjust and adapt to each other and healthy communication between the various stakeholders.

Challenge 2: how can participatory processes be organised in view of administrative constraints and potentially limiting viewpoints of public authorities? Article 6 of the ECPT-CEU Charter states that, 'Everyone who feels concerned and affected by a planning project or policy must have access to a choice in the means of expression, giving them the opportunity to voice their needs and concerns' (ECTP-CEU, 2016:4). This is particularly important in considering how the processes of participation connect to the everyday life of inhabitants. These processes ought to improve relationships, knowledge, local economy and cultural exchanges, for everyone in a neighbourhood – and local government is a key actor. However, in the projects, the associations experienced difficulty in engaging local public authorities. There may be political reasons for authorities not wishing people to speak out, and their position may not present an obvious or strict opposition to public debate. Importantly though, the lack of encouragement sets the tone and may dampen enthusiasm for wider discussion. This is unhelpful, as the feeling of complete freedom of speech is an important requirement in co-production. For this reason, it was considered that external mediation from artistic groups could be valuable as a stage in the processes.

Challenge 3: how can the progress of public spaces be ensured with both public and private partners? There is a particular interest in the involvement of public and private actors for the processes within public spaces. On the one hand, the public consists of individual citizens, and municipal authorities work in public forums. On the other hand, the involvement of other actors, including businesses and enterprises, as well as professional and educational organisations, is also important. When private interests connect with the participatory process as a whole, the process unlocks more possibilities for developing joint actions for diverse objectives, with all the various stakeholders of the area. This provides additional security for the interests of public actors and private actors over the long-term.

The inclusion of educational organisations is an equally important process to consider when discussing progress in public spaces, as well as in planning governance. Academics have long considered the sharing of knowledge as linear, where scientific outputs are presumed to be conveyed to and assimilated by decision-makers in policy processes (Cook and Overpeck, 2019). This behaviour and its assumptions are no longer fit for purpose. Knowledge is also produced beyond universities, and for progress to be achieved and scientific results to be used by policymakers, there is a need to shift the way that knowledge flows. This requires further and better interactions between academics, citizens, associations and decision-makers. The extensive network of professionals, scholars, citizens and representatives of public authorities within Territoire Europe serves this objective through each project in which it participates.

Sharing experiences from Dunkirk

The study shared in this chapter comes directly from experiences within a specific context. The projects took place in Dunkirk, a port city in the north of France with about 200,000 inhabitants. It contains a historic industrial harbour, as well as multiple social housing areas and a strongly interventionist approach to redevelopment. In addition, there are several scales of governance involved in shaping development in Dunkirk.

After the total demolition of the city during the Second World War, the French state managed to create an industrial place with a maritime steel industry. Although the state had been the authority for the harbour since the end of the war, this changed in 2008. Since then, port authorities are the owners of the land, but they also include far more local stakeholders in the decision-making process (Hauser, 2019). More than 30 per cent of local housing is public provision, with around 25,000 homes that are social housing. The neighbourhoods of public housing, or 'quartier sociaux', have suffered impoverishment in their local populations as a result of past industrial decline. The original populations are linked with the historical industrial activity, with workers from former coal mines and migrants from former French colonies in North Africa.

Local authorities play a significant role in the organisation of cultural and social life of the population. Typical examples of public policy include reliance on heavy demolition and reconstruction, as well as a willingness to introduce 'mixité sociale' or social diversity into neighbourhoods that are considered 'social ghettos'. The renewal of the 'quartier sociaux' is determined by national policy that supports financing for intensive and heavy-duty processes of demolition and reconstruction.

To understand these projects, it is important to grasp how the process of participatory democracy is directly under the influence of institutions of national and local authorities. The national institution that provides finances, both to local authorities and social housing developers, is Agence Nationale de la Rénovation Urbaine (ANRU – the National Agency for Urban Renovation). Its aim is to support the transformation of neighbourhoods in cities across the country. It typically demolishes and/or renovates buildings in order to reshape entire areas. Broadly speaking, its aim is to reconnect their socio-economic and other urban functions to the rest of the city, and to facilitate growth in social diversity. However, the procedural rules governing the processes for such transformations, including the use of removals and rehousing of families, demolition and reconstruction, are extremely constraining. This rigid framework provides no space for public participation and sociocultural expression; yet these are often places with a low socio-economic context, where the memories and feelings of inhabitants must be considered in a participatory manner and within the strategy of transformation to soften the transition for people.

An inclusive co-building association: En Rue

The association En Rue was set up in Dunkirk by local actors and is developing participatory processes to support collective action. The name is a take on 'ANRU', the national institution for urban renewal. Beyond the pun, the name asserts the freedom and independence of the collective, from all the institutions that steer urban renewal, as a situated and social neighbourhood association. Since 2017, En Rue has taken over public spaces in several parts of the metropolitan area of Dunkirk to carry out joint redevelopment actions in an open and inclusive manner. Videos and fanzines testify the actions of the association to promote public participation during renewal operations (Makery, 2018). This independence of the group is one of the key points for the success of the projects that it supports.

The self-management of this independent group, as well as its lack of hierarchy, is a representation of its ideals. It is an association of inhabitants, which represent the neighbourhoods, the concrete grounds or actual local 'terrains' of the projects. A municipal employee in charge of culture is making the link between various types of professional and stakeholder, who is also responsible for an association promoting wooden construction. Artists are also associated with projects in the neighbourhoods while living in seasonal residences. Architects chose to get involved to help co-construct the buildings and plan spaces, while sociologists investigate the self-management strategies and its efficiency. In the longer term, social workers step in to support the endeavours of residents in softening the transition. The diversity of this informal group creates a real dynamic by crossing cultures and practices of people from different backgrounds and fields of work.

The approach of En Rue is straightforward: participating together in the realisation of concrete projects through the creation of joint initiatives carried out in the public domain. The aim is to develop a variety of tools based on values shared between all stakeholders. The resources of the project come from the city and the synergies between the different partners. Funding comes variously from both public and private sources who are involved in cultural developments and supporting local initiatives.

The ambition of this association and gathering of stakeholders is to create third places, such as those based on the Fab Lab idea of doing things 'in common' (Fab Lab, 2014). This constellation of actors allows for the crossing of different interests and sharing in three key areas:

1. Sharing spaces of conviviality in the public space, by creating pieces of urban furniture and games, among other things;
2. Sharing tools to use in manufacture (e.g., in carpentry or woodwork); and
3. Sharing knowledge about the environment of the neighbourhood by reporting on its inhabitants, history, culture and environment.

The role of artists and their creations is crucial in allowing the cross-expression of the diversity of actors present.

Developing local actions beyond the original locality: Fab Lab Effet Papillon

When the collective En Rue met the Fab Lab social project in 2019, the proposal initiated by Territoire Europe was to develop an integrated approach to planning that could spread throughout the city and beyond. This project is underway today under the name of Fab Lab Effet Papillon, which translates as 'butterfly effect', making direct reference to the ambition of this project to grow beyond its local grounds (Territoire Europe, 2022).

A key objective of the project Fab Lab Effet Papillon is to develop tools that enable the circular economy. In response to problems of

Figure 13.1 Example activities of the Dunkerquois participatory circular project.

Source: Author

production and consumption of resources and the global challenge of sustainable development, the proposition of a more 'circular' approach is to have better management of materials, energy, water and land involved in the built environment. Williams suggests there might be three fundamental types of action: 'Looping, regenerating and adapting underpin the resource cycling processes (natural and synthetic) within the city' (Williams, 2019). The circular activities for the Dunkirk project include (but are not limited to) work on land reclamation, water systems, agriculture, biodiversity knowledge, construction materials and cultural heritage of active communities (see Figure 13.1).

There exists a partnership between the informal dimension of the associations involved and public institutions, such as the metropolitan association Communauté Urbaine de Dunkerque (CUD, 2022) and the local municipal authorities. This is built through several associative interfaces: Eco Chalet (an association working in low-income neighbourhoods on the appropriation of public spaces), Territoire Europe, TILT (an association of experts in transforming volunteers' activities into jobs) and Collective Aman Iwan (another association dealing with socio-spatial issues). It is also articulated around universities (Université du Littoral Côte d'Opale, Paris 8, the Art School of Dunkirk) and architectural firms committed to the participatory approach, such as the Saprophytes.

Expériences Dunkerquoises: lessons from Dunkirk

Reflecting on the ambitions, activities and experiences in the Dunkirk projects described above, several lessons emerge. The *expériences Dunkerquoises* are set out below, then we draw wider conclusions about the 'do it yourself' idea, before returning to the three original challenge areas (see Figure 13.2).

Figure 13.2 Example of furniture created by En Rue.
Source: Author

Breaking the commons

The use of institutional lands to create 'commons' or 'third places' may risk appropriation, privatisation by a social group and exclusion of other groups. In Dunkirk, a third place had been created in a vacant building owned by the city. During the experiences of the collective En Rue, there were two notable events that happened simultaneously and effectively broke the commons.

The building in question was initially used as official venue housing for teachers working in the school in the district. Inhabitants called this three-storey building 'the Cube' because of its distinctive form. The building, which also serves as a kindergarten (Kindergarten Denis Papin), had been abandoned and selected for demolition in the mid-term as part of an urban renewal project – in response, En Rue seized it. Along with local residents, En Rue carried out reconstruction works, fitting a kitchen, a workshop, some temporary accommodation and meeting rooms. The group's self-management approach made it possible for inhabitants to create projects together in order to share the knowledge and skills of all the participants, in parallel with the process of the demolition of the housing that had been initiated by the public authorities. It allowed for the creation of urban furniture such as terraces, gardens and benches (see Figure 13.3). However, two events broke the space:

1. Local elections and political change to a far-right party, which asked for the third place to be shut down.
2. A moment of contestation between the key actors in the project about the uses of the third place, with the accommodation and the kitchen being taken over by two individuals of the group.

Both events created a tense situation, with conflicts between local people, which overshadowed the collective and reduced the work done thus far – and the common experiences as a whole – to *almost* nothing.

What remains is a series of learning points in respect of those actors involved in the creation of participatory process. First, where public and private authorities neglected the neighbourhood and its population, a group of residents and other local stakeholders emerged to tackle the situation. To achieve its objectives, the group supported the empowerment of local residents, sharing the skills of its network of actors and enabling a space for co-creation of resources. Second, the hybrid group of actors demonstrated a horizontal form of governance and gave itself the right to act in the public space for the common good. Its aim was not to replace public power and authorities but to pinpoint and support a neighbourhood in dire need of intervention. Third, the institutional abandonment of the district resulted in a new dynamic. The project fostered conflict between the actors of the project that crystallised thinking on the third place. This situation was the result of the many and sometimes conflicting interests of the various actors involved. Yet, this was also fuelled by political change in the area, whereby the democratic processes around the transformation of certain neighbourhoods stalled and left the community 'abandoned'. However, this did not extinguish the work on the commons.

Re-making the commons

The failures just described did not prevent En Rue from continuing its work and live support for the district through other projects. It continues to draw from the experiences. In moving forward, associations should keep in mind the importance of the specificities of each place and the wider context, as it is vital that both be considered.

The remoteness of the community and the pace at which the public administration led urban renewal projects, prevented any sharing on a cultural or social level. It was also incompatible with the principle of 'doing it together', which determines the success of urban transformations.

The process of the urban renovation of social housing districts has existed in France for 40 years. These neighbourhoods play a crucial role in welcoming people that are in dire situations. Urban renewal is above all a financing tool for landlord owners to upgrade their properties. Yet it does not protect vulnerable inhabitants, but instead places them in a more exposed and difficult position. The transformation of neighbourhoods along with the relocation of populations can also be a political weapon for local public authorities 'choosing' their population.

The disconnection between inhabitants and urban projects transpires through the framework that facilitates public self-expression. The compulsory consultation of local inhabitants in the early stage of transformations, although detailed in the contracts of rehabilitations, demolitions and re-constructions, is extremely time constrained. It is one of the reasons why En Rue proposes returning to the original purposes of a common, and creating shared cultural spaces where social and ethnoracial class issues are recognised. The involvement of the young generation in these issues is an important part of the long-term success of the strategy. En Rue recognises the importance of working with and including the young inhabitants (aged 15 to 20 years) over time and throughout the project. It creates opposition to the dominant system that ignores and underestimates input from local communities.

Urban renewal strategies from public authorities often give rise to opposition groups that end up powerless in the face of great public and private interests. The Fab Lab project offers the opportunity to maintain the memory of the district's history, its population and struggles, and to incorporate it in the strategy of urban renewal, softening the difficult transition for inhabitants and authorities. To protect and value this memory, there is a need for places where collaborative things can happen to allow inhabitants to express their attachment to the place.

From this perspective, there are two projects of particular interest as the work in Dunkirk continues. First, the artistic interventions that are particularly meaningful and constitutive in the process. Second, the public-private partnerships that can secure a longer-term future for initiatives around the commons. What follows describes the Durkirk experiences involving work with 'unhabitants' and 'White Butterflies'.

Artistic facilitation of 'unhabitant's' self-expression

The group fostered creative workshops to help the inhabitants express their feelings. Thanks to the participation of an artist in residence, Oonagh Haines,[1] in collaboration with Hugo Bricout,[2] a show was organised with the inhabitants En Rue invited people to experience, through parody, the participatory process, best described as 'in a neglected garden-city we try to find our way in a changing landscape'.

En Rue organised several events in the city during June 2020. Participants were seated in a circle around a drawn map of the city of the Railwaymen with strings stretched over the grass in the garden. Each participant wore a photo of one of the houses of the garden city on their head. They had previously written their identity on a sign that hung around their neck. Scenarios were written on slips of paper passed from one hand to another.

The scenarios caricatured what public authorities often propose to be 'choices' in a project mode. The first project, Ville Fleurie 4 Fleurs, promotes the idea of a city giving more space to green areas and environment protection in its planning policies, and is based on the national label *Villes et Villages Fleuris* ('flowery towns and villages').[3] The second scenario, Where Life Rolls Out, refers to a slow way of living in the city, a classic vision of the family-oriented town. The third project, similar to the first one, is a reference to another initiative, the more security orientated *Voisins Vigilants et Solidaires* ('vigilant and supportive neighbours'),[4] where inhabitants of the same neighbourhood get in touch to tackle burglaries. The final scenario is the City of All Ambitions, which relates to the idea of a city where public authorities and inhabitants take the initiative to elaborate innovative planning strategies. The participants voted

Figure 13.3 The abandoned garden city where the event took place.
Source: Author

by a show of hands for each scenario and used fake 'big arms' cut out from cardboard boxes. Each participant was accompanied in a pretence at 'gaining height', whereby they would pretend to look beyond the horizon and through binoculars see their picture appear at the window of an abandoned house. This was to provide a feeling of being an 'unhabitant' of the garden city.

Next, each person-house was invited to position themselves on the map of the garden city, and the neighbourhood created was invited to chat to each other, from one street to the next, about the perspective of each participant. This process came as a relief to people, who felt that they could get closer to each other because of how they related to the solemnity of being in the large circle around the garden district.

The artists' performance ended with conviviality and the traditional drink, which seemed quite surreal in the context. With about 30 people gathered in the heart of a garden city you could feel the irony of the event – the creation of a dialogue in a place abandoned for almost 30 years by its institutional owners.

Through the event, En Rue, with the help of Oonagh Haines, exposed the emptiness of the proposals to transform the garden city of railway workers. Ultimately, this was an attempt to demonstrate the necessity of promoting collective action and improved political support, as well as improving the supply of information to local people and a form of critical education encouraging reflection by the inhabitants about the structures of power.

The collaboration between public and private actors was another excellent way to foster innovative actions. The 'White Butterflies' is an example built on a dynamic between the private charity for the disabled known as *Papillons Blancs* ('white butterflies') and the local community.

The Degroote district, which is undergoing urban renewal with 300 social houses and facilities, adjoins the Fab Lab Papillons Blancs land in Teteghem (a municipality that is part of the metropolitan area of Dunkirk, see Figures 13.4 and 13.5). This private charity has agreed to develop third places available to all, and thus to support residents in the process of renovating the district.

This collaborative project touches on many different themes. It aims at improving the quality of the environment and awareness around its vulnerability through the creation of a laboratory greenhouse and the development of phyto-management techniques around the site. Building on this first theme, the people involved in the project attempt to develop permaculture and increase the biodiversity using experimental gardens, observatories and herbal teas or medicinal plants. The objective is also

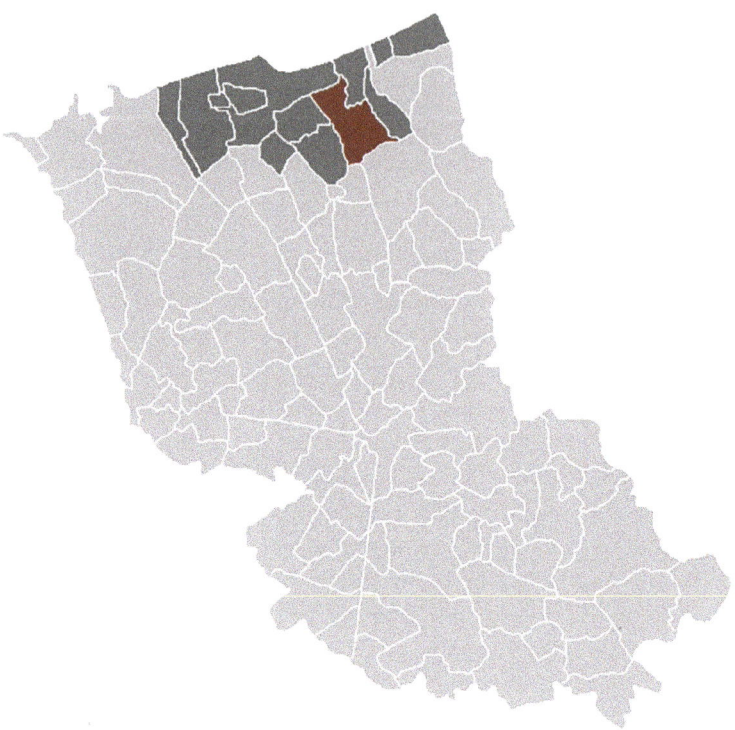

Figure 13.4 Map of the north region of France, with the metropolitan area of Dunkirk in dark grey, and the city of Teteghem in red.
Source: Author

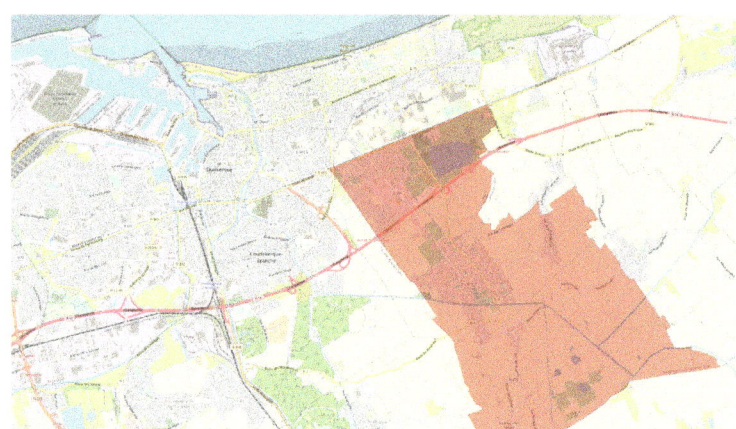

Figure 13.5 Map of the metropolitan area of Dunkirk, with the city of Teteghem highlighted in red. Made by S. Hauser on QGIS and based on OpenStreetMap.

to raise the awareness of inhabitants on the importance and availability of their local natural networks through the creation of paths connecting the natural corridors (the green and blue network) of the metropolitan area of Dunkirk. This approach to sustainability includes educational activities around circularity with the re-use of materials from demolished buildings, the use of organic materials and the creation of an open-access library on these different elements. To better connect these themes and the activities around them, the project relied on artistic interventions in collaboration with local art schools.

The organisation of this inclusive project brings together citizens, professionals and disabled people. The project takes place on the land owned by the Papillons Blancs and gives visibility to otherwise invisible land and people of the neighbourhood. The plan proposes to build a place called La Halle, which runs along a part of the green network of paths of Dunkirk. This project is made possible thanks to a multi-partner convention that defines the roles and involvement of each partner:

- The association of White Butterflies is the promoter of the project. It administers and communicates about the project with its staff and people with disabilities.
- Territoire Europe supports the project through the drafting of fundraising files, the production of maps to pool resources and the development of exchanges with other approaches and projects in Europe.
- The Saprophytes pilots the co-design of architectural operations and their implementation.
- TILT develops the conditions for creating jobs and businesses from its activities.
- The Université du Littoral Côte d'Opale carries out research based on soil analysis and the phyto-management of possible pollutants, as well as the establishment of an educational observatory for the phyto-management of the site.
- The Citizen Council of Teteghem leads and develops citizen participation in the project.
- The city of Teteghem supports the financing of the project.

Dunkirk Urban Community intervenes within the framework of its ecological transition policies of the territory, culture and citizenship, inclusion of all public and habitat.

The common interest between the private association of disabled people and the project of action on the renewal of a social neighbourhood coalesce. The partnership between associations, inhabitants, universities, artists, art schools and private firms was built with a long-term perspective. This inclusive process aims at demonstrating the benefits of public participation in projects of urban transformations, as empowered people feel understood and heard from public authorities.

Participation efficiency and the art of compromise

The authors of this chapter believe that it is important to place the experiences shared in this chapter into context before extracting a lesson. These participatory experiments took place in an industrial port city where public authorities, at both national and local level, have held the prominent role in the planning and development of the city for more than 60 years. Since the development of these participatory initiatives by associations, researchers, civil servants and inhabitants four years ago, many issues have appeared. The appropriation of a common space by individuals and the political abandonment that followed led to the end of some projects. But rather than seeing this as a failure, the various actors gathered again to recreate the process in other parts of the city, learning from their previous mistakes and sharing them.

The different if not conflicting viewpoints and interests of inhabitants and of public authorities are major obstacles. Yet, the early involvement of all parties in a common project advertised and connected by artistic interventions proved efficient in bringing stakeholders to a compromise for the longevity of such participatory projects. The principle of 'doing it together' must not be limited to local inhabitants and associations, it involves as many stakeholders as possible, from both the public and private sphere, in transforming common public spaces. The success of this wide and early inclusion was demonstrated through the collaboration of the White Butterflies and the creation of a common space on private grounds.

The success of this kind of project relies greatly on ground-based actions with diverse participants. This type of interaction goes beyond complex words and written contestation to focus on local resources, people and the built environment; it provides new moments of learning together. In doing so, 'doing it together' gathers people together that would not otherwise meet. By providing a crossing point for artistic, political, local and scientific knowledge and actors, these short-term and research-action projects are important tools that can also help to efficiently co-produce imaginaries and inspire spatial strategies.

Notes

1. See https://oonaghhaines.hotglue.me.
2. See https://www.compagniedestrebuches.com/qui-sommes-nous.
3. See https://www.villes-et-villages-fleuris.com.
4. See https://www.voisinsvigilants.org.

References

Altomonte, S., J. Allen, P. M. Bluyssen, G. Brager, L. Heschong, A. Loder, S. Schiavon, J. A. Veitch, L. Wang and P. Wargocki. 2020. 'Ten questions concerning well-being in the built environment', *Building and Environment* 180: 106949.
Alviar-Martin, T., and M. C. Baildon. 2016. 'Context and curriculum in two global cities: a study of discourses of citizenship in Hong Kong and Singapore', *Education Policy Analysis Archives* 24(58).
ANRU (n.d.) *ANRU c'est quoi?: Missions et chiffres clés*, https://www.anru.fr/presentation-de-lanru (last accessed 9 Decdember 2022).
Battersby, S. 2017. 'News feature: can humankind escape the tragedy of the commons?', *Proceedings of the National Academy of Sciences* 114(1): 7–10.
Bishop, E. 2015. *Becoming Activist: critical literacy and youth organizing*. New York: Peter Lang.
Bouche-Florin, L.-E. 2019. 'Charter of participatory democracy: a call for action towards a balanced democratic system', *Built Environment* 45(1): 112–29.
Cook, B. R., and J. T. Overpeck. 2019. 'Relationship-building between climate scientists and publics as an alternative to information transfer', *Wiley Interdisciplinary Reviews: Climate Change*, 10(2): e570.
CUD. 2022. *Communauté urbaine: L'institution*, https://www.communaute-urbaine-dunkerque.fr/communaute-urbaine/linstitution (last accessed 9 December 2022).
ECTP-CEU. 2016. *European Charter on Participatory Democracy in Spatial Planning Processes*. Brussels: ECTP-CEU. https://archive.ectp-ceu.eu/ectp-ceu.eu/index.php/en/publications-8/charter-of-participatory.html (last accessed 9 December 2022).
Englund, T. 2000. 'Rethinking democracy and education: towards an education of deliberative citizens', *Journal of Curriculum Studies* 32(2): 305–13.
Fab Lab. 2014. *About Fab Labs: What, Why, Who*, https://www.fablabs.io/about (last accessed 9 Decdember 2022).
Fuller, M., and R. Moore. 2017. *An Analysis of Jane Jacobs's: the death and life of great American cities* (1st edn). London: Macat Library. https://doi.org/10.4324/9781912282661 (last accessed 9 December 2022).
Hardin, G. 1968. 'The tragedy of the commons: the population problem has no technical solution; it requires a fundamental extension in morality', *Science* 162: 1243–8.
Hauser, S. 2019. 'The interplay of economic development and environmental protection: Dunkirk and the search for balance', *PORTUSplus* 8 (special issue).
Lankshear, C., and P. McLaren. 1993. *Critical Literacy: politics, praxis and the postmodern*. Albany NY: State University of New York Press.
Makery. 2018. *Collectif En Rue Fabrique avec les Habitants*, https://www.makery.info/2018/10/09/dunkerque-le-collectif-en-rue-fabrique-avec-les-habitants/ (last accessed 9 Decdember 2022).
Natarajan, L. 2017. 'Socio-spatial learning: a case study of community knowledge in participatory spatial planning', *Progress in Planning*, 111: 1–23.
Territoire Europe. 2022. *Le Projet Fab Lab Effet Papillon Se Construit Avec Les 'Mitoyens Commanditaires' Du Site Des Papillons Blancs Et Du Quartier Degroote À Teteghem-Coudekerque-Village*, https://www.territoire-europe.eu/nos-projets/fab-lab-effet-papillon/ (last accessed 9 December 2022).
Williams, J. 2019. 'Circular cities', *Urban Studies* 56(13): 2746–62.

14
Critical pedagogy with urban participation

Lucy Natarajan and Michael Short

Learning with the city

In 1892, an 'Outlook Tower' was refurbished for exhibition and live viewpoints over the city of Edinburgh, as an engaging form of urban learning for local residents (Geddes Institute, no date; Amati *et al.*, 2017). The building still inspires debate on 'creating consciousness and mobilisation toward a society premised on the successful evolution of humanity and the rest of nature' (Cera *et al.*, 2017: 96). Throughout this book, we have seen how participatory practices of planning and place-making have significant implications for critical pedagogy. The connections between urban development and built environment higher education have been conceptualised as activities of reviewing, providing teaching and embedding. We argue that engaged urban pedagogy is a distinct praxis that embraces the diversity of knowledges and forms of learning that exist in the city, and that it acknowledges the importance of urban stakeholders to students' active learning and skills development. It is inherently connected to non-academics who are directly involved in live urban processes and activities within and beyond the university campus. Students are developing knowledge alongside others in the city, as well as learning from their interactions with stakeholders and their experiences of urban processes. In this chapter, we reflect on the value, as well as the challenges, of learning with the city in higher education contexts.

The approach to education that we envisage – that of engaged urban pedagogy – is rooted in awareness of the constructed nature of urban development and the potential of students and teachers as actors within urban processes. It facilitates learning about urban environments

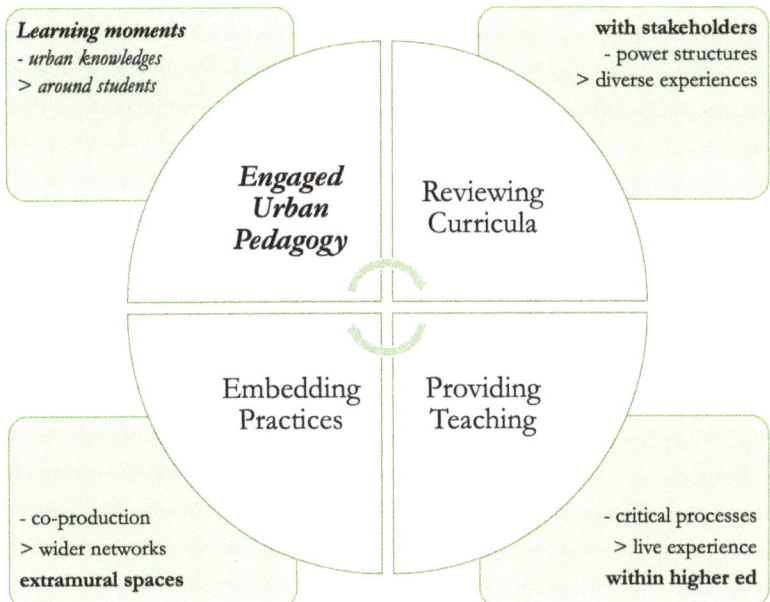

Figure 14.1 Model for engaged urban pedagogy.

and the sociopolitical complexities associated with them. We draw on activities in planning and place-making, which is a world of complex problems and responses that are unique and have effects that are not scientifically predictable (Rittel and Weber, 1973) – the fundamental dilemma is that the processes of problem definition and solution identification are intertwined. The challenge for educators is to facilitate learning around evolving socio-spatial truths, which include students' own subjectivities within ever-changing built environments. As such, engaged urban pedagogy focuses on the development of students' knowledge and intellectual capacities to empower active learning, which is both self-directed and meaningfully engaged with ongoing wider processes, including the knowledges and powers of diverse urban stakeholders. Such a pedagogy must be accountable to those involved and reckon with a context of higher education, where university teachers and the international cohorts of students find themselves deeply implicated within the structural powers of urban development.

The curricula of interest for an engaged urban pedagogy covers subjects of the environment, including human-made and natural spaces, and the sociopolitical and learning processes associated with their production. It takes a constructivist view of urban realities, which is a key tenet of participatory form of planning and place-making. Hence, there is a need for critical thinking on symbolic value as well as substantial effects on human and environmental flourishing. This is important in light of ethical questions about the roles of urban professionals, including educators and those working in public or private practice, such as advocacy on behalf of those facing discrimination, environmental crises and health emergencies, and particularly so in contexts of monetary poverty. Capacities for understanding urban development therefore involve a critical evaluation of the regional diversity of development impacts, considering racial minority groups in education as well as within society. In this regard, the affective dimension of learning (hooks, 1994) is particularly important given the international student body and how teaching may affect the chances for learning. The representation of multiple subjectivities of meaning-making evolving around development not only gives increased visibility to marginalised actors but also opens up powerful moments of reflexivity. Chances for active learning are boosted as students develop the means to self-evaluation of learning and are encouraged towards continued questioning of positionalities of urban stakeholders. This demonstrates how curricula re-orientation may provide opportunities for new 'intersubjectively formed moral frameworks' (Lennon, 2016).

Higher education is based in continuing academic research, and developing capacity for deeper ways of knowing the built environment is therefore central to engaged urban pedagogy. Research pushes the boundaries of knowledge and provides new areas for exploration of the built environment; for instance, recent work takes this enquiry into questions around the agency of non-human actors (Rydin *et al.*, 2021) and the force of natural environments (Castellanos and Queiruga-Dios, 2021). Engaged urban pedagogy builds on present participatory lines of research around collective responses to complex urban problematics and the voices of diverse actors (Beebeejaun, 2020), with a deeper focus on the co-shaping dynamics inherent in processes of participatory review, provision and embedding of built environment higher education.

Guided by the principles of inclusion, learning and empowerment, participatory activities and thinking can be used to facilitate students' learning. They help students grapple with their own agency as they develop new skills, particularly useful for decision-making in respect of knowledges of diverse others involved. Those include lived experiences in plan-making and civic co-creations in urban design processes. They can explore in depth the value rationalities of key actors and the force of new communication modes. This helps to become sensitised to the sociopolitical power of knowledge building, for example, around investor calculations and industrial expertise (see Chapter 6), such as open access media channels.

Learning in engaged urban pedagogy has the potential to direct learning towards action, which might be mistaken as a turn towards the lost virtue of *phronesis* (Flyvbjerg, 2001), that is, the least well known of Aristotle's three intellectual virtues together with *episteme* and *techne*, also known as 'value-rationality'. That would suggest a purely application-driven type of research or practical wisdom. Indeed, the immediacy of environmental problems has rightly driven an interest in higher education *for* sustainable development over the past three decades (Barth and Rieckmann, 2016). In addition, the notion of *phronesis* or practical wisdom also has long roots within planning theory (Flyvbjerg, 1992, 1998; Upton 2002; Rydin 2007) and, while the full debate is beyond the scope of this book, *phronesis* appears as 'mediator' in the search for new epistemological approaches that forces a choice between the ideal and the real. However, the engaged urban pedagogy approach draws more on the meta-cognitive function of *phronesis* that does not seek to reduce the power of any particular form of wisdom. This is perhaps most clearly stated in Hoch's work on planning imagination, where he argues that people who are 'studying and doing spatial planning need not choose [between theory from competing scholars]. They may adapt the insights of these scholars to inform their own practice. This happens less by analytic argument and more by reflective practical judgement' (2022: 2).

An engaged urban pedagogy approach does not seek to direct learners between pragmatic, effective, essential or any other type of truth. Instead, it embraces tension between understandings as productive space for learning about the built environment where matters are socio-spatial (Soja, 2017), deeply political (While and Short, 2011) and literally grounded in current experience of space (Natarajan, 2017; 2019). Importantly, it does this by providing a bridge for engagement between spaces of the mind and shifting urban development realities. Whatever the mental models within planning imaginations, or socio-spatial creations of civic design, they are brought into focus through moments of exchange with the 'real world'. Current concerns and ways of thinking can be embodied by non-academics from lay communities or people representing professionals, and this also offers students the chance to engage with subjectivities beyond that of any single educator.

The one constant for universities in engaged urban pedagogy is in seeking to promote wariness of urbanism and doctrine, as well as critical thinking on rationalities, their powers and what might shape those.

An overly structured approach to argument is known to introduce bias into what counts as valid or sound. Where the insistence on falsification undermines the search for knowledge, the list of fallacies is limiting/limitless or at least inevitably incomplete (Massey, 1981). There can be other considerations of intentionality in argument, such as current importance of the mistaken logic and of existing strength of conviction, and consequent strength of evidence needed to change minds, since communicative rationalities will be at play where learning is seen 'as an inherently motivational, cognitive, affective motional and social process' (O'Donnell, 1999). Certainly, teaching on structured argument is needed (Bellaera *et al.*, 2021), and for engaged urban pedagogy this is useful in understanding techniques of (de)constructing and falsification. Skills of critical thinking reinforce students' agency in learning, but at the same time diverse insights arise from beyond the realms of structured logic and there is express reliance on affect and ethics.

Engaged urban pedagogy suggests students should not rest on logical argument alone but seek to engage their own critical capacities in response to affect. Explanations from neuroscience (e.g., Linker, 2014) concur with the experiential insights of bell hooks (see discussion in Chapter 1), that cognitive processes happen in response to affect, and humans are productively triggered into thinking through emotions, and this opens opportunities to expand reflexive capacities. This is recognised in recent planning research: 'we acquire objectivity not by abstracting from emotional attachments, but by understanding the landscapes of emotional attachments that shape how we think about the future' (Hoch, 2022: 2). There is an affective component of learning, where freedom, choice and purpose are paramount. Students need time and space to explore emotions, and be aware of fear, joy, beauty and anger. This can develop a sense of relevance to their own lives, and hence motivation, as well as ethical literacy for expressing experience of living together and thriving (or otherwise).

A key goal for engaged urban pedagogy is to expand students' own intellectual capacities for future judgements and critical assessments of the value assumptions of cultural hierarchies. This echoes Deweyan ideals for leaning in democratic societies to continue to have value beyond the classroom (Garrison *et al.*, 2022). The educational prospects of engaged urban pedagogy thus depend on opportunities for students to experience urban development diversity within spaces of learning, and to intellectually connect to the lifeworld of urban stakeholders without othering people or being themselves othered. The participation of diverse non-academic actors provides students with opportunities to engage.

There are opportunities in participatory reviewing activities for connecting the voices of researchers to instructors as a means to critical thinking praxis, these are a form of 'research-action' within teaching (Bellaera *et al.*, 2021). There are opportunities in provision of teaching for tearing down the 'self-other' by connecting to urban actors' imaginations (Hoch, 2022). There are opportunities in embedding practices of higher learning within a wider system of research, learning and action, on the built environment. Therefore, the built environment higher education nexus links the university to urban development through its ways towards learning: through reflexive moments on its place within wicked urban problem-solutions; through making its processes legible for those in foundational education; and through its contribution to alternative spaces where 'research-action' is fomented, both internationally and locally.

Some aspects of engaged urban pedagogy are particularly challenging, and central to those is asking students to learn how to critique the world from within higher education. This is an established institutional space, with structural inequities (Lock, 2018; Leathwood and Read, 2020) that may be moving towards global knowledge governance (Mittelman, 2017). This dilemma has been discussed in regards a general education (see, e.g., Neufeld, 2013), where citizens are assumed to belong in a political system or social organisation (i.e., with cultural and material powers), yet are also somehow able to critique the same regime 'from within' its structures. Contesting the qualities of a regime is difficult enough from the outside, but importantly for education an institution may *tacitly encode* its own values. This is thought to be more common within vocational training or pre-professional fields (Neufeld, 2013), and when there is little diversity of voice on standards of excellence (Wood and Su, 2022). This relates to a further concern around the level of diversity that might be introduced through spaces of public engagement with higher education (Gabriel and Harding, 2021). We are also very conscious of the need for better distribution of opportunities *per se*, among both students (Jungblut, 2020) and educators (Lock, 2018; Leathwood and Read, 2020). This begs the question about alternative spaces of learning and their connection to universities.

Reflexive moments of education are pivotal to engaged urban pedagogy, and we argue that they have transgressive potential (hooks, 1994). Further, the continual introduction of other actors creates outwards connections to diverse subjectivities from beyond the institutions. These have significant potential as transformative opportunities in the three types of activity around the 'built environment higher education' nexus. They highlight areas of tension and, by making them visible, can act as a check or break against the reproduction of systems of belief. This continues more radical research forms, where diverse actors' inclusion in urban development and higher education may (not incidentally) boost accountability of universities. The potential for new groups of students in international higher education is particularly deserving of attention (Jungblut *et al.*, 2020). More transformatively, to borrow from Horton and Freire (1990), academics and associated communities may make the road of learning together.

The generative instability (Lumb and Roberts, 2017) in engaged urban pedagogy moments is directed towards urban development rather than educational purposes alone. This is because of the particular type of situatedness of subjects of the built environment, which have a materiality not found in pure political and social studies. Albeit primarily fear driven (Mobbs *et al.*, 2015), recent response to the narrative of climate change (Perkins *et al.*, 2021) demonstrates the interest in human survival and possibility of a holistic public interest in sustainable urban development. At the same time, the shared interest so constructed was only temporary, and the direction for future weather and development patterns continue to be uneven. What matters for urban development then, even in the most extreme states of nature, are the choices in response to environmental context. The assumption of pre-existing cultural power is unhelpful in as much as it reduces agency, but material land use constraints are undeniable.

The questions about choices in the built environment are already constrained and collective, but we would emphasise that this does not negate the importance of social morality within these bounds. Consideration of changing materiality is essential. Recent digital participatory experiences have disrupted face-to-face expert group norms and changes to digital canvasses also provided for decoding design structures. This demonstrates the power to boost reflexivity for students connecting to the uncertain, already noted for avenues of communication that are emergent, hybrid or have 'not-yet-ness' for higher education (Collier and Ross, 2017), or in dialogue with non-academics that contains 'practitioner-author unfinishedness' (Lumb and Roberts, 2017).

For engaged urban pedagogy there is critical hope (Horton, 2017) in a framing of 'student engagement' that speaks to the situatedness of the built environment and the agency of the student in respect of this. As Kahu (2013) nicely summarises, higher education studies tend to approach 'engagement' as a matter of psychology (e.g., student motivation and personality), socio-cultural understandings (teacher-student relations) and humanity (holistic personhood). Natural language and familial concepts thus dominate analyses of agency (see, e.g., Symonds, 2021) rather than via the particularities of the subject matter, as in this chapter. These appear within the studies as those powers within interpersonal relations. Nonetheless, a higher education student who has chosen to step into this space of learning, where the built environment is given dominant standing among all other concerns, is expressing a desire to extend their own agency within that bounded world of choices. There is a tacit commitment to engage, in the broadest sense, in the institutions of higher education, which for engaged urban pedagogy involves the development of skills and capabilities such as can set up an individual: to be wary of systems of control in the built environment; and to pro-actively learn ongoing. As such, the hope is to engage with ongoing questioning of institutional cultures, including invisible and embedded systems of belief (Fairclough, 2015).

Connecting to actually existing experiences

In this chapter, we have touched on critical pedagogy and education in urban disciplines; we now return to reflect on actually existing experience. Built environment research and urban contexts are in constant flux, and live connections to education are therefore a means to directly observe or experience the constantly changing processes and thinking. The particularities of any moment may be striking, and in studies of planning and urban design there is certainly room for learning about conflict and change. But what is the implication of pedagogic real world connections? As set out here, universities promote critical thinking about the issues and epistemologies of urban actors and hence also build inclusion via students' educational empowerment.

For engaged urban pedagogy, knowledge building is not the search for truth, but engagement with sociopolitical rationalities in urban development and associated governance processes. As a general education in democracy would have it, education is a space for the enactment of citizenship, and for planning and place-making there are multiple actors, wicked problems and multiple conflicting values to grapple with. This means looking at rationalities and testing logic of associated practices; for instance, by identifying tensions in the particular set of values, meanings and uses involved. This may revolve around internal conflicts of systems or externalities of practices that are inconsistent with the values that a student claims to hold. Take for example, the movement to create safer and more inclusive streets where cars no longer had priority over pedestrians. By installing shared surfaces and drop kerbs, this movement introduced new hazards for blind and partially sighted people as it obscured boundary markers at crossing points.

If engaged urban pedagogy is instruction then is it training in the practice of seeking alternatives, testing ways of thinking and navigating complexity where the observer is also a participant. Students have opportunities to develop capacities for identifying where evidence is occluded, by means of biases, fallacies or inconsistencies in values. This approach has its roots in a social-constructivist approach to education, which seeks to avoid reductive thinking. In any given moment, a phenomenon of interest will matter socially in multiple ways, including to the students and educators. Educators take into account emotions, affect, and matters of belief, as well as rationalities around environmental materiality. Students learn how to grapple with epistemological choices pertaining to built environments.

But ultimately engaged urban pedagogy is facilitation for the development of critical capacities, which happen within the minds of the students. It is not a means to control the growth of these intellectual skills. Just as architects benefit from practice with materials before they are ready to put their skills into action, so students of planning and placemaking subjects gain from encounters with living urbanism. They can be exposed to the urban through documented accounts, reading books and articles and watching or listening to media. They experience the built environment, mediated via direct engagement with diverse thinking and reasoning, but in spaces where different dimensions are made visible. Educators and collaborators can offer guidance and stimuli, and they too are learning. This feeds diverse experiences back into ongoing pedagogic development activities, which themselves may be collaborative.

Direct experience of the urban as a form of pedagogy should be treated with conspicuous care, as it involves the student in a series of power dynamics. In direct experience with the actually existing world, students are not just expanding their knowledge and testing their ability to appeal to reason, they are encountering the structures of power and have influence in the moment (no matter how small the effects of this may appear). The positionality of the student is a focus of attention, but the actually existing world is brought to the centre for the student in respect of knowledge claims (Rydin, 2007). Engaged urban pedagogy frames the value of real-world engagement as learning about hierarchies of social values and beliefs, with the purpose of identifying and moving away from oppressive structures. The educational effects of moments are important, but educators should also ensure that they are carefully negotiated with external parties.

Given the commitment to facilitating students' learning, the processes for engaged urban pedagogy need to be steered by educators, even if co-managed by students. While students may feel moved to action, they should not divert from the educational path of developing the student's intellectual capacities. As we engage with others in outreach initiatives, teaching collaborations and curricula projects, the focus of education must remain on critical thinking. Learning is expected to call on affect and foment empathic moral responses; however, these encounters are not primarily for formation of social bonds or political allegiances. Indeed, part of the justification for connection to spaces beyond the institution is a backstop against the reproduction of systems of belief. For the moment of education, they provide opportunities for developing capacities of reasoning about systemic problems in the built environment.

It is the engaged urban pedagogy contention that, since feelings of injustice may precede social change, deeper reflection is important as it can lead to powerful future efforts, and that higher education is one dedicated space for this purpose. While future efforts can invest in research and developing learning resources, this is certainly not the telos, and is very unlikely to be the only outcome, if an outcome at all.

Throughout this book, we have heard about potential barriers to questioning the norms of institutions. The activities presented aim to pro-actively open up norms to scrutiny, and the authors acknowledge factors that limit this. Some of these activities are anticipated in higher education, particularly those arising from the embodied experience of interaction (Mandler, 1989) and planning scholarship that appreciates the relevance of realities (e.g., Rydin, 2021). This indicates great potential in an urban pedagogy that makes space for students' subjectivities, urban materialities and the ongoing evolution of knowledge practices.

References

Bellaera, L., Y. Weinstein-Jones, S. Ilie and S. T. Baker. 2021. 'Critical thinking in practice: the priorities and practices of instructors teaching in higher education', *Thinking Skills and Creativity* 41; 100856.
Barth M., and M. Rieckmann. 2016. 'State of the art in research on higher education for sustainable development'. In Matthias Barth, Gerd Michelsen, Marco Rieckmann and Ian Thomas (eds), *Routledge Handbook of Higher Education for Sustainable Development*. London: Routledge, 100–13.
Castellanos, P. M. A., and A. Queiruga-Dios. 2021. 'From environmental education to education for sustainable development in higher education: a systematic review', *International Journal of Sustainability in Higher Education* 23(3): 622–44.

Collier, A., and J. Ross. 2017. 'For whom, and for what? Not-yetness and thinking beyond open content', *Open Praxis* 9(1): 7–16.
Fairclough, N. 2015. *Language and Power* (3rd edn). Abingdon: Routledge.
Flyvbjerg, B. 1992. 'Aristotle, Foucault and progressive *phronesis*: outline of an applied ethics for sustainable development, *Planning Theory* 7(8): 65–84.
Flyvbjerg, B. 1998. *Rationality and Power: democracy in practice*. Chicago IL: University of Chicago.
Flyvbjerg, B. 2001. *Making Social Science Matter: why social inquiry fails and how it can succeed again*. Cambridge: Cambridge University Press.
Gabriel, J., and J. Harding. 2021. 'Questioning "the public": exploring the meanings of public engagement in higher education', *Teaching in Higher Education*, https://doi.org/10.1080/13562517.2021.1952564 (last accessed 10 December 2022).
Garrison, J., J. Öhman and L. Östman (eds). 2022. *Deweyan Transactionalism in Education: beyond self-action and inter-action*. London: Bloomsbury Publishing.
Hoch, C. 2022. 'Planning imagination and the future', *Journal of Planning Education and Research*, https://doi.org/10.1177/0739456X221084997 (last accessed 10 December 2022).
hooks, b. 1994. *Teaching to Transgress: engaged pedagogy as two-way learning*. New York: Routledge.
Horton, J. 2014. 'Hope: an emancipatory resource across the ages'. In J. Horton (ed.), *Discerning Critical Hope in Educational Practices*. London: Routledge, 165–78.
Jungblut, J., M. Vukasovic and I. Steinhardt. 2020. 'Higher education policy dynamics in turbulent times – access to higher education for refugees in Europe', *Studies in Higher Education* 45(2): 327–38.
Horton, M., and P. Freire. 1990. *We Make the Road by Walking: conversations on education and social change*. Philadelphia PA: Temple University Press.
Kahu E. R. 2013. 'Framing student engagement in higher education', *Studies in Higher Education* 38(5): 758–73.
Leathwood, C., and B. Read. 2020. 'Short-term, short-changed? A temporal perspective on the implications of academic casualisation for teaching in higher education', *Teaching in Higher Education* 1–16.
Lennon, M. 2017. 'On "the subject" of planning's public interest', *Planning Theory* 16(2): 150–68.
Linker, M. 2014. *Intellectual Empathy: critical thinking for social justice*. Ann Arbor MI: University of Michigan Press.
Loke, G. 2018. 'So what next? A policy response'. In J. Arday and H. Mirza (eds), *Dismantling Race in Higher Education*. Cham: Palgrave Macmillan.
Lumb, M., and S. Roberts. 2017. 'The *inedito viavel* (untested feasibility) of practitioner imaginations: reflections on the challenges and possibilities of dialogic praxis for equity and widening participation', *International Studies in Widening Participation* 4(1): 18–33.
Mandler, G. 1989. 'Affect and learning: causes and consequences of emotional interactions'. In D. B. McLeod and V. M. Adams (eds), *Affect and Mathematical Problem Solving*. New York: Springer.
Massey, G. J. 1981. 'The fallacy behind fallacies', *Midwest Studies in Philosophy* 6: 489–500.
Mittelman, J. H. 2017. *Implausible Dream: the world-class university and repurposing higher education*. Princeton NJ: Princeton University Press.
Mobbs, D., C. C. Hagan, T. Dalgleish, B. Silston and C. Prévost. 2015. 'The ecology of human fear: survival optimization and the nervous system', *Frontiers in Neuroscience* 9: 55.
Natarajan, L. 2017. 'Socio-spatial learning: a case study of community knowledge in participatory spatial planning', *Progress in Planning* 111: 1–23.
Neufeld, B. 2013. 'Political liberalism and citizenship education', *Philosophy Compass* 8(9): 781–97.
O'Donnell, D. 1999. 'Habermas, critical theory and selves-directed learning', *Journal of European Industrial Training* 23: 251–61.
Perkins, K. M., N. Munguia, M. Ellenbecker, R. Moure-Eraso and L. Velazquez. 2021. 'COVID-19 pandemic lessons to facilitate future engagement in the global climate crisis', *Journal of Cleaner Production*, 290: 125178.
Rittel, H. W., and M. M. Webber. 1973. 'Dilemmas in a general theory of planning', *Policy Sciences* 4(2): 155–69.
Rydin, Y. 2007. 'Re-Examining the role of knowledge within planning theory', *Planning Theory* 6(1): 52–68.
Rydin, Y. 2021. *Theory in Planning Research*. Singapore: Palgrave MacMillan.
Rydin, Y., R. Beauregard, M. Cremaschi and L. Lieto (eds). 2021. *Regulation and Planning: practices, institutions, agency*. London: Routledge.

Soja, E. W. 2013. 'Spatializing *phronesis*: a critical evaluation of real social science', *British Journal of Sociology* 64: 752–8.

Symonds, Eloise. 2021. 'An "unavoidable" dynamic? Understanding the "traditional" learner–teacher power relationship within a higher education context', *British Journal of Sociology of Education*, https://doi.org/10.1080/01425692.2021.1962246 (last accessed 10 December 2022).

Upton, R. 2002. 'Planning praxis: ethics, values and theory', *The Town Planning Review* 73(3): 253–69.

While, A., and M. Short. 2011. 'Place narratives and heritage management: the modernist legacy in Manchester', *Area* 43(1): 4–13.

Wood, M., and S. Feng. 2022. 'Discourses of teaching excellence in higher education'. In *Pursuing Teaching Excellence in Higher Education: towards an inclusive perspective*. London: Bloomsbury Academic, 1–18.

Wood, M., and S. Feng. 2022. 'Towards an inclusive perspective on teaching excellence'. In *Pursuing Teaching Excellence in Higher Education: towards an inclusive perspective*. London: Bloomsbury Academic, 113–29.

Index

Page numbers in italic refer to illustrations

abandonment 183, 249, 250, 252, 253 256
ableism 57
academia: participants' contact with 193
accessibility 105, 147, 150, 151, 154, 159, 173, 187, 193–95, 209, 236
action-research process *78*
asynchronous learning 146, 153, 157, 160

bakla 59
Barcelona 228, 237, 240
Bartlett School of Planning 27, 41, 43–46, 58, 60, 63, 73, 109, 131, 134, 135, 137–39, 147, 160, 162, 165, 179
binary-gendered bathrooms 50
biodiversity 248, 253
Birmingham 144, 181, 185–92, 196, 199, 204, 206
boundaries 5, 7, 41, 77, 80, 181, 183, 224, 228, 260
Brazil 230, 231, 233–35
Britain 27, 31, 32, 42, 50
Brixton (London) 31
buildings 51, 63, 160, 168, 172–74, 176, 178, 246, 255
businesses 52, 53, 136, 147, 231, 234, 241, 244, 255

Camden (London) 69, 74, 79
campus developments 14, 133, 140, 181, 187, 190, 203, 258
canvases to facilitate collective thinking 164, 170–76, *173*, *175*, *177*
capitalism 14, 28, 240
Caribbean 188
ChangeMakers scheme 46, 58
childhood obesity 197, 204
citizenship 111, 211, 221, 242, 255, 265
city-to-city learning: defining common challenge 229–30, *230*
classroom practices/discussions 11, 12, 28, 30, 35, 36, 57, 96, 104, 110, 120, 122
co-design 61, 66–68, 70, 73, 81, 172, 176–78
colonialism 27, 45, 88
conformity with plans/standards 127
consciousness (global/collective) 4, 242, 258
conviviality 247
Copenhagen 228, 237
councils 67, 127, 208, 214, 215
coursework 72–79, 139, 167

COVID-19 pandemic 1, 105, 106, 147, 149–51, 164, 165, 167, 168, 177; *see also* lockdown
Crystal Palace (London) 135
curation 45, 104, 109–12, 115, 116, 122, 124
curriculum 120, 121, 131, 133, 142, 210, 222, 223, 231, 238
 inclusive design 53, 64, 66, 68
 queering 25, 44–60
 Race and Space 29–41

DCLG (Department for Communities and Local Government) 126, 130, 140
deal-making processes 118
decision-making processes 8–10, 77, 90, 95, 97, 112, 189, 190, 199, 203, 206, 211, 221, 242, 245, 260
decolonisation 29, 32, 36, 42, 43, 48, 66
democracy 7, 36, 62–64, 66, 69, 82, 83, 87, 100, 163, 175, 241–45, 257, 265, 268
Dewey, John 4, 64, 262
diamond-ranking exercise 215, 216, *216*
discrimination 34, 52, 59, 260
displacement of populations 19, 188, 190
diversity 8–9, 24, 32–35, 37, 44, 49–50, 96, 228, 237, 247, 262, 263
domination 36, 47, 51, 53
Dunkirk 245–56, *249*, *252*, *254*; *see also* Teteghem (Dunkirk)
dwellings (traditional/backyard) 89

ecosystem 106, 171, 181
Edinburgh 258
Effet Papillon 241, 243, 247
elitism 120, 200, 201
Emerson College (Boston) 163
empathy 71, 96, 195
engaged learning/pedagogy *passim*; *75*, *259*
entrepreneurial skills 70, 71, 77
equality 31–35, 36, 38, 39, 44
essentialism 50, 58
ethnicity 27, 30, 31, 34, 188
ethnography 8, 24, 38
evaluation 4, 15, 21, 46, 113, 186, 269
experiential learning 5, 6, 12, 13, 20, 21, 62, 66, 67, 74, 76, 79, 84, 160, 212, 223, 224, 262
extracurricular activities 182, 207

270

FabLab 183
family-oriented town 252
feminism 43, 52, 55, 59, 100, 180
financial crisis 117, 119
financialisation 110, 119, 121, 187, 206
fluidity, dealing with 80
Foucault, Michel 64
France 183, 233–36, 241, 245, 251, 254

games 113, 123, 208, 213, 214, 224, 225, 247
garden city 252
gender 6, 11, 21, 23, 24, 33, 36, 37, 44–46, 48–51, 53, 56, 58–60, 64, 192
gentrification 120, 188, 190
Global South 227, 228, 235, 236–8
globalisation 119, 226
government 18, 20, 21, 31, 33, 88, 90, 91, 93, 95, 99–101, 110, 114, 117, 123, 127–30, 133, 138, 140, 141, 204, 229, 233, 244
Guarulhos 230–34, 239

harassment 57
Haraway, Donna 169, 180
Headington 138
health 17, 52, 63, 73–77, 79, 84, 135, 153, 161, 185, 199, 204, 210, 215, 219, 220, 225, 260
Healthy High Street 217–18, *217*
healthy lifestyles 214–15
hegemony 20, 45, 47, 49, 52–54, 56, 57
heteronormativity/heterosexism 48, 49, 52, 56, 57
homosexuality 59, 60
hooks, bell 6, 11, 13, 25, 36, 40, 96
housing 17, 52, 73, 89, 94, 99, 116–18, 123, 129, 137, 165, 167, 168, 185, 188, 206, 245, 246, 249–51

identity 6, 14, 21, 28, 29, 32, 46–48, 53, 56–59, 83, 139, 140, 219, 224, 225, 252
imagination 40, 54, 109–11, 113, 115, 116, 119, 121, 122, 169, 261, 263, 268
immigration 42
imperialism 39
inclusiveness 11, 23, 34, 100, 145, 232, 233
industry 56, 57, 59, 74, 95, 160, 187, 221, 245
injustice 23, 267
innovation 9, 65, 71, 82, 150, 152, 164, 166, 169, 229
instrumentalism 14
intelligence 160, 164, 169–71, 174, 176–80, 225
intentionality 15, 262
interdisciplinary 19, 21, 24, 45, 116, 123, 144, 150, 257
internationalisation 42, 226, 237, 238
internet 147, 159
intersectionality 30, 49, 50, 52, 59, 100, 116, 163, 164, 171, 192
IRiS (Institute for Research into Superdiversity) 192
isolation/loneliness 76

justice 10, 11, 17–19, 24, 31–33, 35, 36, 38, 83, 119, 124, 179, 185, 268

Kilburn (London) 167, 172, 176
knowledges 6–12, 23, 36, 49, 54, 61, 69, 80, 82, 180, 242, 258–60

Labour governments (UK) 117
land 7, 41, 88, 90, 95, 96, 123, 126, 138, 166, 217, 231, 245, 248, 253, 255, 264
Latinx people 35, 42
learners 2, 4, 6, 7, 16, 18, 23, 25, 62, 147, 148, 153, 161, 184, 213, 224, 261
legislation 86, 88, 96, 97, 128–30, 133
LGBTQ+ people 25, 44, 47, 50, 52, 56, 60
liberation pedagogies 10–16
lifeworld 262
localism 126–29, 131, 138, 141, 143
Locality (NGO) 127, 130
lockdown (COVID-19) 144, 158, 164, 167, 168
low-income households/communities 87, 92, 98, 99, 248

MacPherson Inquiry 32, 33
Manchester 191
Manila 54, 55, 59
Maputo 233, 234
marginalisation 31, 202, 203
masculinity 56, 57, 59
Matola 233, 234
media 2, 42, 49, 72, 106, 113, 160, 161, 163, 170, 180, 225, 239, 261, 266
mediation 73, 81, 143, 244
mentoring 89, 98, 167, 186, 191, 196, 197
Mercociudades 231, 239, 240
Merhi 153, 161
Merton, London Borough of 166
methodologies 20, 47, 48, 50, 82, 129, 167, 211, 232
Miro (online platform) 105, 106, 164, 165, 168, 172, 178, 180
misogyny 58
'mixité sociale' 245
modernity 54, 55, 124, 240
motivation 66, 83, 148, 153, 161, 194, 197, 210, 262, 264
Mozambique 233–36, 239
MPlan (Master of Planning) 179, 209, 214

narratives (curatorial) 111–12
Negev 190, 206
neighbourhoods 37, 38, 52, 74, 104, 135, 136, 183, 189–91, 193, 195, 203, 243, 245, 246, 250, 251
neoliberalism 54, 59, 187
Netherlands 49
neuroscience 262, 268
Newcastle 182, 207, 210, 220, 222
NGOs 228, 229, 236
nightlife (LGBTQ+ venues) 52, 54
Nijman 227, 228, 240
normativities 45, 49

obesity 197, 204
objectivity 262
Olympic Games 113
online learning 144, 147, 163, 164, 166, 168, 178
open-mindedness 12

open-source methods 128, 163, 164, 177, 179
ortiz 24, 27, 28, 34, 37, 38, 42, 43, 60

Papillons Blancs 253, 255
pandemic *see* COVID-19 pandemic; lockdown
'parachuting in' 202–4
parking/traffic issues 93, 214
participatory urban development *passim*
 and pedagogy 1–18, 258–67
 and role play 207–24
permaculture 253
Philippines *see* Manila
phronesis 261, 268, 269
phyto-management 253, 255
Piaget, Jean 211
place-making 1–3, 5–10, 12, 14–16, 36, 79, 103, 105, 106, 144, 146, 151, 154, 181, 182, 184, 210, 212, 221, 241, 258–60, 265
planning schools 34, 86, 99, 113, 130–33, 223–4; *see also* Bartlett School of Planning
pluralism 95, 100
podcasting 17, 103, 105, 144–61, 182
politicians/policymakers 19, 92, 95, 120, 147, 203, 211, 228, 231
postcolonial perspectives 28, 54, 228, 237
postmodern pedagogies 61, 62, 66, 82, 84, 257
privatisation 249
privilege 9, 34, 40, 118, 180
problem-solving skills/processes 70, 71, 236
prototyping 170, 171, 176

'quartiers sociaux' 245, 257
queerness 44–60

race 6, 11, 23–25, 27–35, 38–43, 45, 56, 57, 60, 64, 100, 268
racism 24, 27, 29, 31–35, 45, 59
recycling 217, 218
'research-action' projects 263
research-led teaching cultures 104, 109, 111, 115, 183
research–teaching nexus 105, 145
retail (high-street premises) 217
'Rhodes must fall' 14
Roma migrants 191
Rosario (Argentina) 230, 231, 240
Royal Town Planning Institute 31, 33, 132

SACPLAN (South African Council for Planners) 85, 86, 88, 95, 101
school education 10, 15, 17, 182–3, 210, 231–2
Seine-Saint-Denis 233, 234
settlement 91, 93, 100, 129
sexism 34
sexuality 6, 23, 45, 46, 47, 49, 53, 55, 60, 64
Siena 105, 106, 162, 163, 165, 166, 169, 172, 179
site reconnaissance 9
situatedness 49, 106, 264
solidarity 25, 40, 42, 53, 235, 236

South Africa 85–99
South Kilburn (London) 167, 172
spatial experience and inequality 44–58, 88, 90, 93
spatial planning and participatory democracy 242, 243, 256
stereotyping 28, 58, 191
stigmatisation 191
Stonewall 54, 60
streets 9, 50, 51, 59, 137, 141, 211, 214, 215, 217, 218, 220, 221, 241, 253
'studio culture' 48
suburbs 89
superdiversity 190
sustainability 7, 9, 19–21, 25, 26, 84, 85, 105, 123, 133, 136, 222, 238, 255, 267

takeaway outlets 207–8, 214, 215, 217, 218, 220, 221
teamwork skills 149, 157
technology and pedagogy 17, 103, 105, 144, 146, 150, 153, 231; *see also* podcasting
Territoire Europe 243, 245, 247, 248, 255
Teteghem (Dunkirk) 253–55
tower blocks 167
towns 31, 33, 42, 45, 91, 92, 94, 100, 101, 123, 127, 128, 132, 139, 143, 179, 208, 209, 219, 221–23, 252, 269
traffic 93, 135, 214, 220
trans people 50–52, 56, 58–60, 225
transcultural competences 238

unemployment 185, 195
upskilling 189
urban renewal 37, 82, 117, 245, 246, 249, 251, 253, 255
urbanisation 25, 101, 237, 238
urbanism 55, 75, 227–29, 235, 236, 243, 261, 266

value-capture 111, 118, 119
Vauxhall (London) 135
viability-led planning 111, 118
violence 50, 51, 54, 55, 56
 racial 38, 40

waste 182, 233, 234
waste-collector 234
weather events 9, 264
welfare/wellbeing 63, 73, 74, 77, 79, 118, 121, 163, 180
West Hollywood 50–51
Westway (London) 166, 180
'White Butterflies' 251, 253, 255, 256
wildfires 94
Wimbledon (London) 166
workplaces 57
workshops as pedagogical tool 63, 68–79, 146, 151, 152, 154–56, 159, 163, 164, 167, 168, 172–79, 192, 194, 207–11, 214–24, 233

youth 53, 208–10, 214, 224, 225, 242, 257

Ingram Content Group UK Ltd.
Milton Keynes UK
UKHW051330270623
424116UK00002B/2